QUICK ESCAPES

from
San Francisco
30 Weekend Trips from the Bay Area

by

Karen Misuraca

A Voyager Book

The Globe Pequot Press

Old Saybrook, Connecticut

Photo Credits
Pp. 1, 3, 10, 19, 50, 56, 61: courtesy Sonoma County Visitors Bureau; p. 27: courtesy Napa Chamber of Commerce; p. 34: courtesy The Fetzer Winery; p. 41: courtesy The Gingerbread Mansion; pp. 76, 163, 214: courtesy National Park Service; p. 82: courtesy Marin County Visitors Bureau; pp. 87, 101: courtesy Santa Cruz Visitors Bureau; pp. 89, 150: courtesy California Office of Tourism; p. 95: courtesy Roaring Camp and Big Trees; pp. 110, 119: courtesy Carmel Visitors Bureau; pp. 127, 129: courtesy Sacramento Visitors Bureau; p. 136: courtesy Nevada City Chamber of Commerce; p. 143: courtesy Good Ideas; p. 157: courtesy The Union Hotel; pp. 165, 183: courtesy Lake Tahoe Visitors Authority; p. 174: courtesy Sorenson's Resort; p. 191: courtesy Trinity County Chamber of Commerce; pp. 198, 205: courtesy Shasta Cascade Wonderland Assocation; p. 220: courtesy Yosemite Park and Curry Company. All other photos by the author.

Copyright © 1993 by Karen Misuraca

All rights reserved. No part of this book may be reproduced or transmitted in any form by any means, electronic or mechanical, including photocopying and recording, or by any information storage and retrieval system, except as may be expressly permitted by the 1976 Copyright Act or by the publisher. Requests for permission should be made in writing to The Globe Pequot Press, P.O. Box 833, Old Saybrook, Connecticut 06475.

Library of Congress Cataloging-in-Publication Data

Misuraca, Karen.
    Quick escapes from San Francisco : 30 weekend trips from the Bay area / by Karen Misuraca. — 1st ed.
        p. cm.
    "A Voyager book."
    ISBN 1-56440-222-3
    1. San Francisco Bay Area (Calif.)—Tours. I. Title.
F868. S156M63 1993
917.94'610453—dc20
                                        93-2744
                                        CIP

Manufactured in the United States of America
First Edition/Fourth Printing

Acknowledgments

Thanks to the generous innkeepers of Northern California and to Michael and my girls for sailing steadfastly along with me.

About the Author

A native Northern Californian, Karen Misuraca makes her home in California's wine country, the Napa Valley. The author of *Selling Books in the Bay Area* and a specialist in golf and environmental travel writing, she is a frequent contributor to magazines, newspapers, and directories, including *Global Golfer, Women's Sports and Fitness,* the *New York Daily News,* and the *Christian Science Monitor.*

Misuraca escapes into California's great outdoors nearly every weekend unless she is on assignment abroad. Her dog-eared passport is matched by those of her three daughters, three granddaughters, and her companion, Michael Capp, world travelers, all.

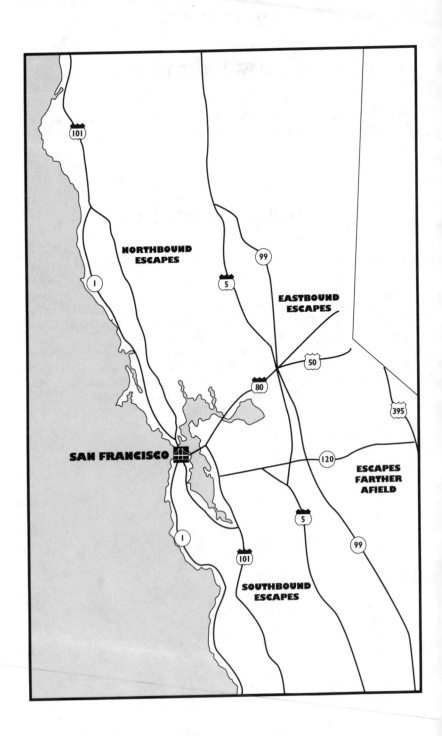

Contents

Contents

Introduction

When Horace Greeley traveled overland from New York to San Francisco in 1859, he mused, "As we neared the California trail, the white coverings of many emigrant wagons dotted the landscape, giving the trail the appearance of a river running between great meadows, with many ships sailing on its bosom."

Today's travelers still sail along Northern California highways, their hearts set on enjoying the natural beauty and historic richness waiting to be discovered in this part of the state.

Those of us who live in or visit the Bay Area are within easy distance of wine country, gold country, redwood country—villages by the sea, cabins in the mountains, houseboats on the delta. It's hard to avoid clichés when describing the wide variety of destinations accessible within a few hours. From the missions of the Salinas Valley to the historic mansions of Lake Tahoe, honky-tonk beach towns, country roads, hiking trails under the pines, seafood cafes beside a bay—you can escape every weekend for a year and still have a hundred places to see.

At a loss for what to do this weekend? These detailed itineraries provide everything you need to know for a getaway from the city. Every escape is a driving tour, with sightseeing, recreation, restaurants, and lodgings located and described. To give you a variety of activities from which to choose, days are lively, packed with sights and sidetrips. Annual **Special Events** are listed, as are **Other Recommended Restaurants and Lodgings. There's More** gives you a reason to return another time. And for advance planning, maps, and local visitor's bureaus, there's **More Information**.

If you favor weekends tucked away in one peaceful spot, use the chapters to book your hotels, choose restaurants, and read about what all the other tourists are doing.

For maximum enjoyment of your short, sweet sojurns, take care to avoid heavy traffic times—Friday and Sunday afternoons and commute hours. Keeping California's microclimates in mind, be prepared for weather changes throughout the year, particularly in the coastal and mountain regions. Fog and rain, or even snow, may not be what you expected, but discoveries made on a wintry weekend could turn you into a California lover, in more ways than one.

If you're looking forward to a particular bed-and-breakfast inn or a restaurant, be sure to call well in advance. And remember that in some resort communities, businesses may not be open every month of the year.

Most restaurants and lodgings listed are in the midrange pricewise;

a few special places are expensive. Rates and prices are not noted, because they can be counted on to change.

When you come across a memorable place that would be an appropriate addition to this book, or if you have comments on how the escapes worked out for you, please drop me a note. The next edition will be an update.

It's a good idea to include the following items in your getaway bag:

Jacket, long pants, and walking shoes for trail hiking and beachcombing in any weather

Binoculars (so as not to miss bald eagles circling and whales spouting)

Corkscrew, a California necessity

Daypack or basket with picnic gear

Maps: The directions and maps provided herein are meant for general information—you'll want to obtain your own maps.

California State Park Pass: Most state parks charge a day fee of several dollars. Annual passes are $75 for cars (discounts for seniors and those with a limited income) and $125 for boat launching. Information: (916) 653–6995.

For more information on Northern and Central California destinations, write or call the California Office of Tourism, P.O. Box 9278, Van Nuys, CA 91409; (800) 862–2543.

The information in this guidebook was confirmed at press time. We recommend, however, that you call establishments before traveling to obtain current information.

Northbound Escapes

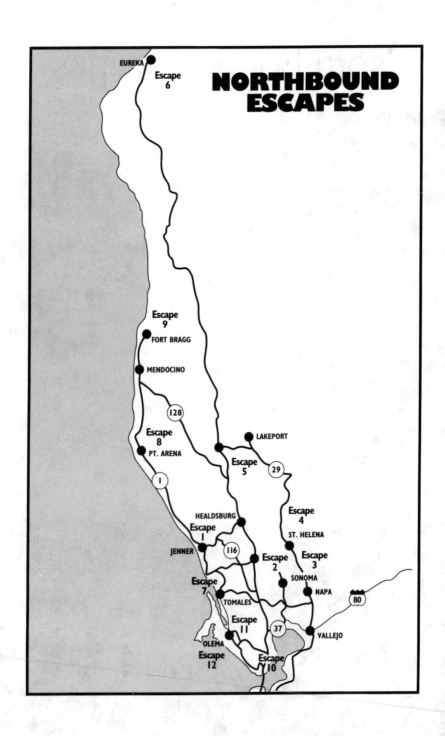

Wine Road to the Sea

A bridge spans over the beautiful Russian River.

The Russian River Route

————————————— 1 NIGHT —————————————

Wineries · Farm trails · Antiques shopping
Redwoods · River rambling · A night by the sea

In the mid-1800s tourists from San Francisco rode ferries across the bay and hopped onto a narrow-gauge railroad to reach summer resorts on the Russian River. The arrival of the motorcar and the decline of lumbering, followed by a disastrous fire that raged through the entire river valley in 1923, caused the towns along the river to fall into a

deep sleep for a few decades. The town of Guerneville never missed
a beat, however, thriving through the Big Band era when Benny
Goodman and Harry James kept the weekenders coming. In the 1970s
the tremendous growth of wineries began a new era of tourism. Now
more than fifty wineries can be discovered on the backroads of the
Russian River and Dry Creek valleys.

Winding through forested canyons, past sandy beaches, orchardlands, and vineyards, the Russian slides calmly all the way to the sea.
Rustic inns, casual cafes, leafy walking trails, great fishing holes, and
magnificent redwood groves are reason to spend several weekends
following its path.

At the end of a long day exploring the Russian River Wine Road,
your destination is the tiny town of Jenner-by-the-Sea, on a high bluff
overlooking a marshy bird sanctuary at the mouth of the river.

Day 1

Morning

Head north from the Golden Gate Bridge on Highway 101 to
Healdsburg, about one and a quarter hours, taking the central Healdsburg exit into the center of town, parking on the **Healdsburg Plaza**.

Breakfast: **Samba Java**, 109A Plaza Street. (707) 433–5282. Espresso,
lox and bagels, world-class scones and pastries, exotic juices.

Between the Alexander Valley (see Northbound Escape Nine) and
the Dry Creek Valley, the small town of Healdsburg is prime Sonoma
County wine country. Grown here are some of California's finest Zinfandels, a hearty red of Italian heritage. The Dry Creek Valley also
produces excellent Sauvignon Blanc, a dry but fruity white wine. Several winetasting rooms are within a block or so of the plaza, including
Windsor Vineyards (707–433–2822), **White Oak** (707–433–8429),
Clos du Bois (707–433–5576), and **William Wheeler** (707–433–8786).
Also nearby are the **Sonoma County Wine Library**, Piper and Center
streets (707–433–3773), and the **Healdsburg Historical Museum**, 221
Matheson (707–431–3325). Get a walking-tour map at the **Chamber
of Commerce**, 217 Healdsburg Avenue (707–433–6935).

Evans Designs ceramics, the world's largest producer of Raku pot-
tery, has a factory outlet and gallery worth visiting at 355 Healdsburg
Avenue (707–433–2502).

Proceed southwest out of town on Westside Road, stopping at the
sharp left turn and driving through the arch to see **Madrona Manor**,
1001 Westside Road (707–433–4231), one of California's largest and
finest Victorian masterpieces. Built in 1881, the huge manor is now an
inn and restaurant surrounded by magnificent gardens. Walk in and

ask for a tour of the museumlike rooms and outbuildings; depending on their bookings, it may or may not be possible but is definitely worth a try.

Mill Creek Wineyards, at 1401 Westside Road (707–433–5098), is a small, family-owned winery on a knoll overlooking the valley; it's fun to see their wooden mill wheel turning beside the creek.

You'll be following the **Russian River** now, all the way to the ocean. Valley foothills become mountains, oaks give way to dark redwood and fir forests, and the roadsides become ferny and damp. Along the riverbank in freshwater marshes grow silvery gray-green willows and cottonwoods.

Take a left on Wohler Road, passing more than a half-dozen wineries on your way to River Road, then turn west. Stop at **Korbel Champagne Cellars,** 13250 River Road (707–887–2294), for a tour of the winery and the gardens. Founded in 1886 by Czech immigrants, the ivy-covered stone winery is a piece of Old Europe tucked into the rolling, vineyard-carpeted hills of the Russian River Valley. The guided winery tour, including museum, film, garden walk, and champagne tasting, is one of the most complete and enjoyable of all California wineries.

Russian River Valley grapes thrive in warm days and cool, fog-blanketed nights, maturing slowly and with a high degree of acidity. Early ripening varieties—Chardonnay, Pinot Noir, and Gewurztraminer—ripen and are harvested before the threat of fall rains and lowering temperatures.

You'll follow the river and the redwoods a few minutes farther down the road to the summer-vacation town of **Guerneville,** chock-full of souvenir shops, cafes, and art galleries.

Lunch: **Little Bavaria and Beer Garden,** 15025 River Road, Guerneville. (707) 869–0121. One mile east of town. Indoors or on the patio overlooking the river; pasta, seafood, German specialties, sandwiches, salads; Sunday brunch.

Afternoon

In the middle of town, turn north on Armstrong Woods Road a mile or so to **Armstrong Grove Redwoods State Reserve** (707–869–2015), 750 acres of glorious redwood groves along Fife Creek. Easy paths lead to sunny picnic areas and old growth trees up to 300 feet tall. For a half-day horseback ride into the wilderness bordering Austin Creek State Recreation Area, call the **Armstrong Woods Pack Station** (707–887–2939).

The **Austin Creek Recreation Area** (707–869–2015) is 4,200 acres of hills, canyons, and river glens that campers, hikers, and horseback riders love to explore.

Ten minutes west of Guerneville, bear left across the bridge on Moscow Road, through the tiny burg of **Monte Rio** to **Villa Grande,** a small riverbend village that's changed little since the 1920s, when it was built as a summer encampment for vacationers from San Francisco. There is a beach here, a delightful array of early Craftsman-style cottages, and not much else.

Back on the main road, it's not far to **Duncan's Mills**, where a dozen or so shops nestle in a Victorian-era village, another 1880s railroad stop. Take a look at the only remaining North Pacific Coast Railroad station.

The **Duncan's Mills General Store** (707–865–1240) stocks fishing gear, groceries, and antiques. At the **Gold Coast Oyster and Espresso Bar,** Steelhead Boulevard (707–865–1441), oysters are barbecued in a garden courtyard in the summertime, and you can smell fresh-roasted coffee beans all the time.

As you head farther west, the river widens and sheep graze on open, windswept hillsides. The Russian River meets the sea at **Bridgehaven,** the junction of Highways 116 and 1, where you'll turn north toward **Jenner.** In the winter ocean waves and the river clash here in a stormy drama. In the summer the mouth of the river is cut off from the ocean by temporary dunes. Salmon and steelhead runs attract crowds of seals hoping for delicious bites of their favorite food. In the spring seals hide in the river's mouth to give birth away from the sharp eyes of hungry sharks and whales. Ospreys in their treetop nests are some of the thousands of land and shore birds that feed and fly in this area.

Dinner: **River's End Restaurant,** Highway 1 at the north end of Jenner. (707) 865–2484. The perfect spot for a sunset view over the river and the ocean. A European chef turns out extraordinary cuisine, including Indonesian specialties, German veal dishes, oysters, crayfish, fresh seafood of all kinds, duck, wild game, caviar, and clam chowder. People come from the Bay Area just to have lunch and dinner here; reservations are absolutely necessary.

Lodging: **Murphy's Jenner Inn,** Highway 1, Jenner 95450. (707) 865–2377. Eleven comfortably casual rooms, some with river views, some with private decks and fireplaces; private homes also for rent.

Day 2

Morning

Breakfast: Continental breakfast at the inn, or a big American breakfast next door at **Jenner-by-the-Sea** restaurant (707–865–1192). Also, Sunday brunch at River's End Restaurant.

Drive back on Highway 116 to Guerneville, turning south on 116 past Forestville to **Kozlowski Farms,** 5566 Gravenstein/Highway 116 (707–887–1587), for luscious berries, jams, fresh fruits and pies—the ultimate Sonoma County farm store. Pick up a **Sonoma County Farm Trails** map at Kozlowski's to locate the many produce outlets and nurseries in these verdant rolling hills. Nearby are the **Green Valley Blueberry Farm,** 9345 Ross Station Road (707–887–7496); **Campbell's Green Valley Orchard,** 9753 Green Valley Road (707–823–3580), selling herbs, flowers, and Rome Beauty apples; **Carriage Charter,** 3325 Gravenstein Highway (707–823–7083), offering horse-drawn carriage rides; and **Bennett Valley Farm,** 6797 Giovanetti Road (707–887–9557), with dried flowers, garlic, and wreaths.

Lunch: Watch for the Russian steeple at **Topolos at Russian River Vineyards,** 5700 Gravenstein Highway. (707) 887–1575. Here the Topolos family has a great Greek restaurant on a shady patio and makes several varieties of wine; some taste faintly of apple, evocative of the orchardlands in which the vines were planted.

Afternoon

South on 116 are orchid nurseries and tree, herb, and fruit farms. **The Spinner's Wheel,** 6264 Fredricks Road (707–823–0245), south of Sebastopol, is an enchanting place; call ahead for a tour. Angora goats and several exotic varieties of sheep live here, their coats sheared and hand-spun into beautiful yarns. Great Pyrenees dogs greet you at the gate.

Between Sebastopol and Highway 101 are dozens of antiques shops.

Dinner: **Washoe House,** near Cotati, 2 miles south of Gravenstein Highway at the corner of Roblar and Stony Point roads. (707) 795–4544. The oldest roadhouse in California; prime rib, chicken, buffalo burgers: great fun.

Proceed south on Stony Point to Highway 101 and back to the Golden Gate Bridge.

There's More

Canoeing. Trowbridge Canoes, 20 Healdsburg Avenue, Healdsburg, 95448. (707) 433–7247.

Burke's Canoe Trips, 8600 River Road, Forestville. (707) 887–1222. Paddle the Russian River, stopping at quiet coves and sandy beaches along the way; easy and safe for all ages. The canoe companies shuttle you back to your car.

Johnson's Beach, wide stretch of sandy beach at Guerneville. (707) 869–2022. Site of the annual Russian River Jazz Festival.

Northwood Golf Course, 19400 Highway 116, Guerneville. (707) 865–1116. Eighteen holes in a redwood grove.

Fishing. Salmon runs on the Russian River occur late September through early November; steelheads follow, continuing through March. It's catfish in February and March, shad in April, several types of bass in the summer, plus crappie and bluegill. An excellent map to fishing access in the entire Russian River area is available from Russian River Region, P.O. Box 255, Guerneville 95446. (707) 869–9000.

Special Events

March. Russian River Slug Fest, Monte Rio. (707) 869–9000. Banana slugs compete in races and contests—it's true.

March. Russian River Wine Road Barrel Tasting. (707) 433–6935.

May. Russian River Wine Fest. (707) 433–6935.

September. Russian River Jazz Festival. (707) 433–6935. Huge crowds at the beach in Guerneville; big-name performers.

Other Recommended Restaurants and Lodgings

Guerneville

Ridenhour Ranch House Inn, 12850 River Road. (707) 887–1033. Next to Korbel Champagne Cellars, a turn-of-the-century redwood ranchhouse with comfortable rooms and a cottage; European chef and owner cooks incredible breakfasts.

The Estate, 13555 Highway 116. (707) 869–9093. A spacious, elegant country home, circa 1912: ten luxurious guestrooms, pool, spa; dinners some nights.

Duncan Mills

Casini Ranch Family Campground, 22855 Moscow Road. (707) 865–2255. Some 120 acres on the river, tent and RV camping, good fishing, small store, boat rentals.

Blue Heron Inn, 1 Steelhead Boulevard. (707) 865–2225. Lunch, dinner, and legendary brunches on the river; an old clapboard building surrounded by gardens; fresh fish, veggie specials.

Healdsburg

Charcuterie, 335 Healdsburg Avenue. (707) 431–7213. Deli sandwiches, pasta; casual cafe a few steps from the plaza.

For More Information

Healdsburg Chamber of Commerce, 217 Healdsburg Avenue, Healdsburg, CA 95448. (707) 433–6935.

Russian River Region Information Center, 14034 Armstrong Woods Road, Guerneville, CA 95446. (707) 869–9212.

Jenner Visitors Center, Highway 1, Jenner, CA 95450. (707) 875–3483. Maps; boat launch.

Sebastopol Chamber of Commerce, 265 South Main, Sebastopol, CA 95472. (707) 823–3032.

Southern Sonoma Valley

The circa-1841 Mission San Francisco Sloano de Sonoma.

On Country Roads

2 NIGHTS

Early California history · Wineries · Shopping · Hiking, biking, golf
Cheese, wine, produce · Mountain and valley parks

Between the rugged Mayacamas Mountains and the Sonoma Mountains, the 17-mile-long Sonoma Valley is a patchwork of vineyards and rich farmlands. Two-lane roads meander along rivers and creeks, through oak-studded meadows and foothills to country villages and to towns with entire neighborhoods that are National Historic Monuments. The Victorian and early California Mission eras come alive in museums and in hundreds of restored homes, inns, and commercial buildings all over the valley.

More than thirty premium wineries are located here, the birthplace of the California wine industry. Their production facilities and tasting rooms, in many cases, are of significant architectural and historical interest. Thousands of acres of vineyards create a tapestry of seasonal color and texture that cascades across the hills and streams out onto the valley floor.

Moderate climate and rich soil produce world-famous gourmet foods—cheeses, sausages, foie gras, orchard fruits and berries, nuts, and sourdough French bread. California wine country cuisine, a gastronomic genre all its own, attracts diners and chefs from afar.

Exploring the Sonoma Valley on quiet backroads by car, foot, or perhaps bike, you'll enjoy the landscape and discover some of Old California. After a day of winetasting, browsing in the shops, gourmet dining, and maybe a round of golf, a cozy bed-and-breakfast inn will be a welcome refuge.

Day 1

Morning

From the Golden Gate Bridge, drive north forty-five minutes on Highway 101 to the waterfront town of **Petaluma.** Take the Central Petaluma exit west into town, turning left on Petaluma Boulevard, then right on Western and right on Kentucky to **New Marvin's,** 145 Kentucky (707–765–2371). Sit at an oilcloth-covered table and tuck into a hearty breakfast of nutty banana waffles. You're in the heart of a unique historical district that includes the finest block of ironfront buildings in the western United States. One of California's largest cities in the 1860s and the Egg Basket of the World early in this century, Petaluma harbors a precious collection of restored Victorians. Before heading back to 101, drive through the neighborhoods west of downtown to see gingerbread-clad, turret-topped homes.

Drive 1 mile south on Highway 101 to the Sonoma/Napa Highway 116 exit, then turn east. Passing a marina where fishing boats and rowing shells ply the Petaluma River, you'll go 5 miles to the 116 East left turn. ROAD NARROWS and SLOW road signs mean you're officially in the Sonoma Valley wine country. Lush rolling pasturelands are dotted with black-and-white cows, dairy farms, and giant valley oaks. Undulating along on the curvy two-lane road, you'll turn right at a stop sign, still on 116, then emerge into a wide valley. Passing **Los Arroyos Golf Club** (707–938–8835)—an inexpensive, three-par, nine-hole course—turn left on Arnold Drive, heading north 8 miles, past vineyards, pony farms, country homes, and the **Valley of the Moon Winery** (707–996–6941), to the foresty village of **Glen Ellen.** On the way you'll see the tile roofs of the **Sonoma Golf Club** (707–996–4852); one of the most challenging courses in the state, it's a veritable botanical garden of trees, flowers, and waterways.

This is the **Valley of Moon,** named by its most famous (sometimes infamous) resident, Jack London, author of the classic adventure tales *Call of the Wild* and *The Sea Wolf.* You'll pass the **Jack London Bookstore and Research Center,** 14300 Arnold Drive (707–996–2888), across the road from a wonderful old gristmill, still creaking slowly over a rushing creek next to **Amedeo of Glen Ellen Ristorante,** 14301 Arnold Drive (707–996–3077), an indoor/outdoor Italian cafe.

When you see the large **London Lodge** banner, you've arrived in Glen Ellen, just a few blocks long. Turn left at the lodge, driving 1 mile up into dense oak forests, past **Glen Ellen Winery** (707–935–3000), to **Jack London State Historic Park** (707–938–1519). Once London's home ranch, the park is 800 magnificent acres of walking trails through groves of oaks, madrones, Douglas fir, redwoods, ferns, and explosions of wildflowers. There are shady picnic sites, mountain and valley views, a romantically spooky ruin, and a museum. Remnants of **Wolf House,** London's gigantic stone mansion, lie deep in a forest glade, at the end of a delightful short path through the trees (handicapped accessible by golf cart). Only walls and chimneys remain of the elaborately decorated and furnished home, which burned to the ground before London and his wife, Charmian, could enjoy it. Filled with London memorabilia and most of the original furnishings, his smaller home, the **House of Happy Walls,** is open to visitors.

Back in Glen Ellen, pick up a snack or a drink at **Shone's Country Store** (707–996–6728), on the main street, before crossing the stone bridge; then turn left on Warm Springs Road for a 6-mile drive. First you'll see **Glenelly Inn,** 5131 Warm Springs Road (707–996–6720), a peach-and-white confection built in 1916 as a railroad inn for train passengers from San Francisco who gamboled their summers away at nearby mineral springs resorts. If you're up for a strenuous bike ride and some breathtaking scenery, take the 15-mile Sonoma Mountain Road loop, starting and ending on Warm Springs Road. Feeling lazy and warm? Stop at **Morton's Warm Springs** (707–833–5511) for a picnic on sweeping lawns or a swim in one of three heated pools. You'll come into Kenwood, a tiny, overgrown hamlet of cabins and rustic homes, then meet up with Highway 12; still a two-lane country road, it's a main route through the county. **Smothers Winery,** 9575 Sonoma Highway (707–833–1010) is on the corner—yes, *the* Smothers Brothers—and **Kenwood Vineyards,** 9592 Sonoma Highway

(707–833–5891), is across the road. Even if you're not a winetaster, you'll want to visit Sonoma Valley tasting rooms. Wineries sell souvenirs and gifts, and some have extensive displays of historical memorabilia and art; most have picnic areas.

Lunch: Turn left onto Highway 12 and stop for a late lunch at **Cafe Citti**, 9049 Sonoma Highway. (707) 833–2690. A deli cafe with tables outdoors under the trees.

Afternoon

Nearby is a clutch of small shops. **Sonoma Grown**, at 9255 Sonoma Highway (707–833–1100), specializes in the amazing variety of food products produced here in the county—olives, jams, pastas, salsas, honey, cheese, and more. The **Iron Rose** (707–833–1153), next door, is a nursery and sculpture gallery. You'll see signs nearby for other wineries: **Chateau St. Jean** (707–833–4134), **Landmark** (707–833–1144), and **Kunde Vineyards** (707–833–5501).

Go north on Highway 12 for half a mile, then turn right on Adobe Canyon Road and drive 3 miles to **Sugarloaf Ridge State Park** (707–833–5712), a 3,000-acre green and golden jewel of mountains, redwood groves, creeks, wildflower-strewn meadows, and *views*. You may take a short walk or a strenuous hike, picnic in the pines, park your RV overnight, or camp out. In the late afternoon cool off with strawberry margaritas, alcoholic or non-, under a grape arbor at **Vineyards Inn**, 8445 Sonoma Highway (707–833–4500), a Mexican cantina and restaurant at the corner of Highway 12 and Adobe Canyon Road.

Dinner: **Oreste's Golden Bear**, at 1717 Adobe Canyon Road. (707) 833–2327. A casual Italian restaurant with a shady stone terrace beside a rushing stream, refreshing on a hot summer night.

Lodging: **Beltane Ranch**, 11775 Sonoma Highway, Glen Ellen 95442. (707) 996–6501. A big yellow ranch house at the foot of Hood Mountain. Rooms open to verandas overlooking vineyards and orchardlands. Owned decades ago by a San Francisco madam from Louisiana, the ranch has a southern look, with hospitality generously dispensed by innkeeper Rosemary Wood, who grew up here.

Day 2

Morning

Breakfast: At Beltane Ranch.

Proceed back through Kenwood on Highway 12 toward Sonoma, a 12-mile drive. You'll go through **Boyes Hot Springs,** where you may wish to stop for a look at the buildings and grounds of the **Sonoma**

Mission Inn, 18130 Highway 12 (707–938–9000), a pink, 1920s-style Mediterranean extravaganza of a luxury hotel and spa. It's five minutes farther to **Sonoma Plaza,** a typical Spanish town square, the largest and one of the oldest in California, laid out by General Mariano Guadalupe Vallejo in 1834. The site of many fiestas, parades, and historical events, it's a National Historic Landmark, and a beautiful one— huge bay and eucalyptus trees, a meandering stream with chattering ducks, a playground, picnic tables, the monolithic stone **City Hall,** and the **Visitor's Bureau,** 453 First Street East (707–996–1090).

Surrounding the plaza, and for several blocks around, are many historic buildings, including the **Mission San Francisco Solano de Sonoma,** circa 1841; **General Vallejo's home** and the barracks compound he built for his Mexican soliders; thick-walled adobes, Victorians, Classic Revival and Mission Revival structures; and more. Park your car, get out your camera, and explore the plaza and the streets and alleyways for a block or so in each direction. The visitor's bureau has good walking-tour maps.

Not to missed on the plaza: **The Wine Exchange,** at 452 First Street (707–938–1794), to taste and buy the wines of almost every winery in the Sonoma and Napa valleys; the **Sonoma French Bakery,** 468 First Street (707–996–2691), famous for sourdough bread; the **Arts Guild** gallery, 460 First Street (707–996–3115); **Kaboodle,** 447 First Street (707–996–9500), a feminine fairyland of country French gifts and accessories; and the **Sonoma Sausage Company**, at 453 First Street (707–938–8200), for German bread and exotic fresh sausages.

Lunch: Buy locally made cheese, meats, bread, and wine at the **Sonoma Cheese Factory and Deli,** 2 West Spain Street (707–996–1931), for a picnic in the plaza, or have Mandarin Chicken Salad or a burger in the **Feed Store Cafe and Bakery**'s patio just off the square, at 529 First Street West (707–938–2122).

Afternoon

Even if you're not interested in winetasting, you'll want to walk, bike, or drive 1.5 miles (take East Napa Street to Lovall Valley Road, then go left on Old Winery Road) from the plaza to the **Buena Vista Winery** (707–938–1266) and the **Hacienda Winery** (707–938–3220), both enchanting wine-country estates with old, vine-covered stone buildings, ancient trees, and rampant flower gardens. Tasting rooms are stocked with guidebooks, artwork, and museum-quality antiques. Buena Vista's Hungarian founder, Count Agoston Haraszthy, engaged in friendly winemaking competition with General Vallejo in the mid-1800s. The interconnected small roads on this western outskirt of town are pretty and quiet for walks, drives, and bike rides to several other wineries.

Dinner: **Eastside Oyster Bar and Grill,** 133 East Napa Street. (707) 939–1266. The fireplace creates a cozy atmosphere for fancifully prepared fresh seafood from both coasts; intimate in the winter, popular and fun on the patio in the summer.

Lodging: **Thistle Dew Inn,** 171 West Spain Street, 95476. (707) 938–2909. A six-room Victorian charmer just off the plaza. The innkeepers will spoil you with a gourmet breakfast, afternoon hors d'oeuvres, complimentary bicycles, and a hot tub in the garden.

Day 3

Breakfast: Thistle Dew Inn.

Leaving Sonoma, head south from the plaza on Broadway/Highway 12 for less than 1 mile, then turn left on Napa Road, another view-filled country byway. If you're extending your trip to the lower Napa Valley (see Northbound Escapes Three), turn left at the Highway 121 junction; otherwise turn right at the junction and proceed a couple of miles to the **Cherry Tree,** 1901 Fremont Drive (707–938–3480), just past the cow manure farm on your left (you'll sense it before you see it). At the Cherry Tree, pick up fresh black cherry juice and jalapeño-stuffed olives to take home. Go straight on through the Schellville–Highway 121 intersection and down the road to **Schug Carneros Estate** (707–939–9363), a winery tucked up against a low range of hills, a lost little corner of the valley. German-owned Schug makes a traditional California Chardonnay, a sparkling red wine, and a German-style Gewurztraminer, unusual for this area.

Continue on Highway 121 south at a slow pace along a 10-mile stretch of rolling hills. You'll soon see glimpses of wetlands at the top of San Pablo Bay. Stop at **Angelo's** (707–938–3688), a sausage and deli shop, and at the **World of** (exotic) **Birds and Llamas** (707–996–1477). You can take a scenic ride in an antique biplane at **Aero-Schellville** (707–938–2444). Turn right at the **Gloria Ferrer Champagne Caves** sign and drive up toward the hills to the tile-roofed Spanish hacienda built by the largest sparkling wine company in the world—Freixenet, based in Spain—at 23555 Highway 121 (707–996–7256). Gloria Ferrer has a luxurious tasting salon with a fantastic view. Many annual events are scheduled here, such as Catalan cooking classes and fireside concerts.

Back on Highway 121, you'll have a last chance to buy fresh fruits and veggies at a large produce stand, and there are two more wineries to check out. **Roche Carneros Estate** (707–935–7115) produces a crisp Chardonnay and a delicate salmon-pink Pinot Noir Blanc. It's a small, little-known operation, and the wines are hard to find other than here at the winery. A vine-draped arbor leads to **Viansa Winery** (707–935–4700).

On weekends there are car and motorcycle races at **Sears Point Raceway** (707–938–8448), at the junction of Highways 121 and 37, where you turn right, head west toward Marin County, and take Highway 101 south to the Golden Gate.

There's More

Walking tour. To see architectural styles circa 1860 to 1925, stroll an 8-block historic area in **Petaluma**. Detailed maps with historical notes are available from the Chamber of Commerce (707–762–2785).

Horseback riding. Sonoma Cattle Company. (707) 996–8566. Sugarloaf Ridge State Park. (707) 833–5712.

Bike rental. Sonoma Cyclery in Sonoma. (707) 935–3377. Good Time Bicycles in Boyes Hot Springs. (707) 938–0453.

Balloon rides. Once in a Lifetime. (707) 578–0580. Air Flambuoyant. (800) 456–4711.

Train Town, 1 mile south of Sonoma Plaza on Broadway/Highway 12. (707) 938–3912. A twenty-minute steamtrain trip through ten acres of landscaped park.

Sonoma County Wine Center and Winery, Rohnert Park, just north of Petaluma. (707) 527–7701. Educational tours, winetasting and sales, food demonstrations, wine industry displays.

More wineries. A visitor's guide to the Sonoma Valley, with all winery information listed, is available from the Sonoma Visitor's Bureau. (707) 996–1090.

Spas and mineral springs. Agua Caliente Mineral Springs. (707) 996–6822. Spa at Sonoma Mission Inn. (707) 938–9000. Sonoma Spa. (707) 939–8770.

Golf. Oakmont Golf Club, Santa Rosa. (707) 538–2454 or 539–0415.

Sonoma Valley Regional Park, Highway 12 between Arnold Drive and Madrone Road near Glen Ellen. Some 135 acres; picnicking; bike and walking trails.

Special Events

March. Heart of the Valley Barrel Tasting, Sonoma. (707) 996–1090.
April. Butter and Eggs Days, Petaluma. (707) 762–2785.
June. Annual Ox Roast, Sonoma. (707) 996–1090.

July. Old-fashioned Fourth of July Celebration, Sonoma. (707) 996–1090.

July. Sonoma Valley Wine Festival, Sonoma. (707) 996–1090.

August. Sonoma County Wine Auction, Boyes Hot Springs. (707) 996–1090.

August. Petaluma River Festival. (707) 762–2785.

September. Valley of the Moon Vintage Festival, Glen Ellen. (707) 996–1090.

October. Artrails of Sonoma County, throughout the county. (707) 996–1090.

October. World Wristwrestling Championships, Petaluma. (707) 762–2785.

November. Kenwood Wineries Open House. (707) 996–1090.

December. Christmas at the Sonoma Mission. (707) 996–1090.

Other Recommended Restaurants and Lodgings

Kenwood

Kenwood Inn, 10400 Sonoma Highway. (707) 833–1293. A mediterranean villa with pool and gardens, surrounded by vineyard views; unforgettable hearty breakfasts.

Sonoma

Victorian Garden Inn, 316 East Napa Street. (707) 996–5339. A dream of a turn-of-the century home a block from the plaza; pool, fireplaces, and full breakfast.

Sonoma Hotel, on the plaza, at 110 West Spain Street. (707) 996–2996. European-style country inn with Victorian charm, restaurant and bar, continental breakfast.

Pasta Nostra, 139 East Napa Street. (707) 938–4166. Lively, casual atmosphere; Italian food; indoors or garden patio with music; lunch and dinner.

Depot 1870 Restaurant, 241 First Street. (707) 938–2980. Looks like an inn in the South of France; mesquite-grilled meats, pasta, and seafood are served poolside or in small dining rooms; lunch and dinner.

Boyes Hot Springs

Sonoma Mission Inn Cafe, 18140 Sonoma Highway. (707) 938–9000. Hearty Northern Italian, upscale cafe; three meals.

Glen Ellen

RV park in Sugarloaf Ridge State Park takes RVs to 24 feet. (800) 444–7275.

For More Information

Petaluma Area Chamber of Commerce, 215 Howard Street, Petaluma, CA 94952–2983. (707) 762–2785.

Sonoma Valley Visitor's Bureau, in the plaza, 453 First Street East, Sonoma, CA 95476. (707) 996–1090.

Sonoma County Farm Trails, P.O. Box 6032, Santa Rosa, CA 95406. (707) 586–3276.

Schedule of events in Sonoma Valley. (707) 935–1111.

Lower Napa Valley

A ride in a hot-air balloon is a great way to see the wine country.

The Carneros, Napa, Yountville, Rutherford

_____ 1 NIGHT _____

Art and architecture · Wineries · Shopping · California cuisine
Vineyard walks · Gourmet picnics · Country lanes

Even those who decline to taste the grape will enjoy the museum-like exhibits and the architectural richness of wineries in the Napa Valley. Twenty-five miles long, just one-sixth the size of Bordeaux, this valley is home to the densest concentration of wineries in North America and to some of the state's most highly regarded California cuisine restaurants, several championship golf courses, dozens of charming bed-and-breakfast inns, and scenery that attracts visitors from all over the world.

Your escape begins in the Carneros wine-growing district at the top of San Pablo Bay, cooled by ocean breezes and summer fogs. Grapes ripen more slowly than in the hot, dry, upper valley, creating notable Chardonnays and Pinot Noirs. Vineyards and wineries here are relatively new in Napa's 150-year history of winemaking, and many tourists are unaware of the quiet lanes of the Carneros. (Carneros is one of the "appellations" into which the valley is divided. Just as in France, each area has a designated geographic appellation, producing grapes that differ in character according to topography, climate, and soil.)

There is time for some lesser-known sights near the town of Napa, a day in Yountville, and a meander down the Silverado Trail. Stretching from Napa 35 miles north to Calistoga, the trail winds along at the foot of high mountain ridges past venerable oaks, their trunks hoary with moss and tickled by buttercups. Sprinkled along the way are wineries and champagne cellars, gargantuan mansions, small stone cottages, luxurious hotels, and quaint inns, each in its own idyllic corner of the wine country.

Day 1

Morning

From the Oakland Bay Bridge, drive forty-five minutes north on Highway 80, *past* the Napa/Highway 37 exit, to the American Canyon exit a few miles north of Vallejo, turning west and connecting with Highway 221 north to Napa; staying to the left, you'll be on Soscol Avenue. From Soscol, take a left on Third, crossing the Napa River, and park a few blocks down, across from a bright blue Victorian, at 1517 Third.

Breakfast: **Alexis Baking Company,** 1517 Third Street, Napa. (707) 258–1827. Inventive breakfasts, the best pastries and desserts in the county, cappuccino, local color.

Need maps and brochures? The **Napa County Visitor's Center** (707–226–7459) is in the Napa Town Center, accessed from First Street, within a few blocks of the bakery.

Head west on First Street to Highway 29, then south two minutes to Highway 12, turning west. Within a minute, turn left on Cuttings Wharf Road and get lost for a while in the rolling vineyards and country roads of Carneros; biking is great on these empty lanes. Going west on Las Amigas, take a left on Buchli Station Road to **Bouchaine**

(707–252–9065), a winery specializing in Chardonnay and Pinot Noir; an appointment will be necessary. Farther west on Las Amigas, **Acacia Winery** (707–226–9991) produces superb Chardonnays. Going right on Duhig Road, you'll wind up back on Highway 12.

The supercolossal French château on the hill is **Domaine Carneros,** 1240 Duhig Road (707–257–0101), a French-American winery producing sparkling wines. Scamper up the quadruple staircase to the tasting room for a tour.

Cross the highway onto Old Sonoma Road; go left on Dealy Lane a couple of miles to a Spanish champagnemaker, **Cordorniu Napa Valley,** 1345 Henry Road (707–224–1668). The architecture here is New Age, to say the least, something like a spaceship partly hidden in a vineyard-draped hillside. **Carneros Creek Winery,** 1285 Dealy Lane (707–253–9463), is a small, friendly place with picnic tables under a vine-covered arbor.

Connect again with Highway 29 and head north five minutes to a left on Redwood Road, then 6.5 miles through redwood and oak forests to **Hess Collection,** 4411 Redwood Road, Napa (707–255–1144). A large and important European and American contemporary art collection resides here in a historic winery building. Take the self-guided tour and enjoy the gardens and the views.

Return to Napa, crossing over Highway 29 onto Trancas, and turn right on Jefferson; drive 2 blocks to Pasta Prego, in a shopping center on the left.

Lunch: **Pasta Prego,** 3206 Jefferson, Napa. (707) 224–9011. The best-kept secret and one of the best restaurants in the wine country; 1990s-style Italian cuisine, polenta with mushroom sauce, smoky grilled veggies, risotto, grilled local fish, poultry, meats, and many pastas. Noisy and fun; patronized by the "in crowd" of local winery families; dining is indoors in the cafe or on the outdoor patio.

Afternoon

On Highway 29 five minutes north of Napa is a monument-size white rooster, heralding **Red Hen Antiques,** 5091 St. Helena Highway (707–257–0822)—18,000 square feet housing the wares of more than forty dealers.

Proceed another five minutes to Yountville; across the highway near the old soldiers' home is **Domaine Chandon,** 1 California Drive (707–944–2892), a French-owned champagne cellar where you can enjoy the beautiful oak-studded grounds and learn about the *méthode champenoise* style of winemaking. A flute of champagne and complimentary hors d'oeuvres await in the tasting room; try the Blanc de Noirs, a blossomy pink champagne.

The tiny town of Yountville has a population of 14,000, half of whom are veterans in a retirement home. The few streets are lined with vintage cottages in overgrown country gardens. On Washington Street, the main drag, a blizzard of shops, restaurants, and inns make this a popular destination. You can bike or walk from here on a 5-mile frontage road running south and on Yountville Cross Road going east to the Silverado Trail.

The landmark building in Yountville is **Vintage 1870,** a massive pile of brick on twenty-two landscaped acres; once a winery, it's now many shops and cafes. You might come out of here with antiques, haute couture, or a book on winemaking. Try the apricot Danish at the **Pastry Shop** (707–944–2138), a European-style bakery. In **Groezinger Wine Merchants** (800–356–3970), more than one hundred locally produced wines are available to taste; shipping is available nationwide. **Wineoceros** (707–944–0827) sells every wine country T-shirt imaginable. Other shops sell toys, Victorian gewgaws, gourmet cooking accessories, fashions, art—more than enough to wear the numbers off your credit cards.

Nearby Vintage 1870, the **Overland Sheepskin Company** (707–944–0778) has sheepskin coats, leather jackets, and western hats. **Depot Gallery,** 6526 Washington (707–944–2044), has for three decades displayed the best of local artists' works. **Raspberry's**, at 6540 Washington (707–944–9211), is a gallery of art glass created by the country's most celebrated artists. And don't miss **Canard,** showing fine wildlife art, at 6550 Washington (707–944–0131).

Arrive at your lodgings in time to enjoy the gardens and perhaps a dip in the pool.

Dinner: For a snazzy, upscale atmosphere and renowned California cuisine, **Mustard's** (707–944–2424), two minutes north of Yountville on the highway.

Lodging: **Vintage Inn Napa Valley,** 6541 Washington Street, Yountville 94599. (707) 944–1112. An 80-room luxury garden hotel; elegant, spacious rooms with fireplaces, spa baths; 60-foot lap pool, tennis, buffet breakfast. Available on the grounds are a hot-air balloon and bikes.

Day 2

Morning

Breakfast: **The Diner,** 6476 Washington Street, Yountville. (707) 944–2626. Big, beautiful breakfasts, cornmeal pancakes, *huevos rancheros,* fresh local produce.

Driving north out of Yountville, you'll pass a sun-dappled city park and a fascinating old cemetery.

Just past Oakville Cross Road, stop at the **Oakville Grocery Company** (707–944–8802) for the makings of a French country picnic: pâtés, baguettes, Perrier, Yoplait, quiches, *fromages,* charcuterie, baby vegetables, salads.

Up the road, **St. Supery Vineyards and Winery,** 8440 St. Helena Highway, Rutherford (707–963–4507), is multifaceted. Here you can walk through a demonstration vineyard, see an art show, tour a lovely Queen Anne Victorian farmhouse, and enjoy elaborate exhibits about grape growing and winemaking. And taste wine, too.

Take a right on Rutherford Cross Road to **Rancho Caymus Inn,** a unique Spanish-style hacienda, a showplace for Mexican, Central American, and South American arts and crafts. Ask to see a room or two. They're decorated with specially commissioned wall hangings, rugs, hand-carved furnishings, and stained glass. The courtyard blooms with wisteria and bougainvillea. A walk from Rancho Caymus over the stone bridge to the Silverado Trail and back takes about an hour; you'll pass historic mansions, blooming orchards, and mossy oaks.

Drive to the Silverado Trail and turn left, then turn right up the hill to **Auberge du Soleil Resort,** 180 Rutherford Hill Road, Rutherford (707–963–1211), where you'll feel as though you've dropped suddenly into an olive grove in the South of France. Wisteria-draped arbors and riots of flowers beckon you past fat stucco walls into a tile-floored entry, flooded with light from the terraces where beautiful people dine al fresco on California cuisine. Enjoy the heartstopping view and ask to see a villa, for future getaways.

Lunch: Picnic under the oaks at **Rutherford Hill Winery.** (707) 963–7194. Just up the hill from Auberge de Soleil, with the same panoramic view. You can tour the winery's cool caves.

A little farther south, **Mumm Napa Valley** (707–963–1133), a French-American champagne cellar, has a pleasant terrace with wide vineyard views and a great gift shop.

Afternoon

Watch for the left turn to the **Silverado Country Club Resort,** 1600 Atlas Peak Road, Napa (707–257–0200), a 1,200-acre resort famous for its two eighteen-hole Robert Trent Jones golf courses. Towering eucalyptus, palm, magnolia, and oak trees line the drive leading to a huge, circa 1870 mansion. A curving staircase and period chandeliers grace the lobby; a terrace bar overlooks sweeping lawns, waterways, and gardens. Silverado has several restaurants, one of the largest tennis complexes in Northern California, and condominium accommodations.

Head south to Napa and back to the Bay Area.

There's More

Marine World Africa U.S.A., 495 Mare Island Way, Vallejo 94590. (707) 643–6722. Highway 80 on the north end of Vallejo at Marine World Parkway/Highway 37; 160-acre oceanarium and wildlife park; live shows with killer whales, sharks, dolphins, tigers, tropical birds; water-ski show on a fifty-five-acre lake.

Old Town Napa. On the west side of the Napa River, charming Victorian neighborhoods are bounded by Franklin, Division, Elm, and Riverside drives; behind Alexis Bakery, drive up Franklin and down Randolph.

Golf. Chardonnay Club, 2555 Jameson Canyon, Napa. (707) 257–8950. On the south end of Napa, on the Highway 80 connector; two links-style, eighteen-hole courses in a challenging landscape of ravines, hills, and vineyards; predictably windy.

Chimney Rock Golf Course, 5320 Silverado Trail near Napa. (707) 255–3363. Nine holes in the vineyards; playing conditions are variable.

J. F. Kennedy Municipal Golf Course, just north of Napa. (707) 255–4333. Eighteen challenging holes, water on fourteen; reasonable rates.

Ballooning. Floating silently in a hot-air balloon is an unforgettable way to see the wine country. Always scheduled for the early morning, balloon trips are usually accompanied by champagne, breakfast, and much revelry. Rates average $100 per person.

Napa Valley Balloons, P.O. Box 2860, Yountville 94599. (707) 253–2224. Launches at sunrise from Domaine Chandon Winery.

Adventures Aloft, P.O. Box 2500, Yountville 94599. (707) 255–8688.

Napa Valley Balloon Aviation, Yountville 94599. (707) 252–7067.

Napa Valley Wine Train. (707) 253–2111. Elegant restored dining and observation cars, a relaxing way to see the valley; lunch and dinner; no stops.

Napa Riverboat Company, 1400 Duhig Road, Napa 94559. (707) 226–2628. Cruising by sternwheeler on the Napa River.

Skyline Park, East Imola Avenue, Napa. (707) 252–0481. Hundreds of acres of hilly woodlands and meadows for hiking, horseback riding, picnicking, and RV and tent camping. Great for winter mushroom expeditions and springtime wildflower walks; find the waterfalls for a summer splash.

Hakusan Sake Gardens, junction of Highways 29 and 12 East. (707) 258–6160. Taste and tour at a sake factory.

Biking. Bryan's Napa Valley Cyclery, 4080 Byway East, Highway 29 at Trower on the north end of Napa. (707) 255–3377.

Special Events

March. Napa Valley Food and Wine Extravaganza, Greystone Cellars, St. Helena. (707) 963–1516. Renowned chefs and winemakers pair their specialties.

June. Concour de Elegance, Silverado Country Club, Napa. (510) 428–3355.

June. Napa Valley Wine Auction. (707) 963–5246. Wine aficionados from all over the world come for three days of parties, barrel tastings, and events at wineries; auction benefits local hospital.

September. Harvest Fest, Charles Krug Winery, St. Helena. (707) 253–2353.

November. Napa Valley Wine Fest. (707) 253–3563.

Other Recommended Restaurants and Lodgings

Yountville

Compadres, next to Vintage 1870. (707) 944–2406. Delightful outdoor patio under giant palms and oaks, zowie margaritas, good Mexican food.

Red Rock Cafe, under vine-draped arbors in front of Vintage 1870. (707) 944–2614. The best burgers and onion rings in the county, maybe the world; also in downtown Napa.

Napa Valley Lodge, Route 29 at Madison Street, on the north end of town. (707) 944–2468. A pretty, gardeny motel with spacious rooms, vineyard views, fireplaces, pool, spa, sauna.

Napa Valley Railway Inn, 6503 Washington Street. (707) 944–2000. In Victorian railroad cars, sumptuous suites with brass beds, skylights, and bay windows with garden and vineyard views.

French Laundry, corner of Washington and Creek. (707) 944–2380. Easy to pretend you're in Provence; single-entree French country menu in a lovely old stone building surrounded by gardens; reservations essential.

Napa

Inn at Napa Valley, 1075 California Boulevard. (707) 253–9540. All-suite, upscale hotel, very conveniently located at Highway 29 and First Street; full breakfast and cocktail hour included; golf packages.

The Fairways at Silverado, 100 Fairway Drive. (707) 255–6644. Two-bedroom condos on the golf course, long- or short-term rentals.

Napa Valley Reservations Unlimited, 1819 Tanen. (707) 252–1985.
Bed and Breakfast Exchange. (707) 942–2924.

Napa Valley

Tall Timber Chalets, near Yountville, at 1012 Darms Lane. (707) 252–7810. Circa 1940 cottages in a grove of trees; fresh, bright decor; sitting rooms, kitchens, continental breakfast; near wineries.

Rutherford

Auberge du Soleil Resort, 180 Rutherford Hill Road. (707) 963–1211. Five-star French country inn and restaurant, spectacular valley views, pool, spa, sauna, tennis.

For More Information

Yountville Chamber of Commerce, 6795 Washington Street, Yountville, CA 94599. (707) 944–0904. In Washington Square Center, north end of town.

Napa Valley Visitor's Bureau, 1556 First Street, Napa, CA 94559. (707) 226–7459.

Advice: It's wise to call wineries in advance. Not all are open to the public, but most will warmly welcome you for an appointment to tour and taste.

Upper Napa Valley

The Beringer Winery

Heart of the Wine Country

——————————— 2 NIGHTS ———————————

Hot springs · Art galleries · Winery architecture tour
Shopping · Mud baths · Vineyard picnic

A slower pace and fewer tourists characterize the upper end of the
Napa Valley, anchored by Calistoga, a hot springs resort town founded
in the 1840s. Steam rises from 200-degree mineral springs at a dozen
or so health resorts; some are scatterings of historic clapboard cottages
with simple facilities, while others are Roman-style spas with luxurious

lodgings. This is the place for rest and rejuvenation, for massages, mud baths, beauty treatments, and slow swims in warm pools. The mud-bath experience must be tried, at least once; be warned that après mud bath you won't feel like moving for quite a spell.

As you drive to Calistoga, through the valley bordered by the Maya-camas Range on the west and the Howell Mountain Range on the east, the tremendous variety of Napa Valley soils and microclimates becomes evident. It's fun to try the diverse wines produced from grapes grown on the dry hillsides, those from the valley floor, and es-pecially the wines from grapes grown on the "benches," the alluvial fans of soil and rocks eroded down from the mountainsides into trian-gles of rich bedding for vineyards whose grapes have produced wines besting the best in France.

Besides winetasting and hot-bath soaking in the upper valley, there's tons of shopping to do in St. Helena, plus biking, hiking, golf-ing, and ballooning; perhaps you'll be forced to return for another weekend or two.

Day 1

Morning

From the Golden Gate Bridge, drive north on Highway 101 to the Napa/Highway 37 exit, connecting with Highway 121 east to Highway 29 at Napa, then driving thirty minutes north to **St. Helena**—about ninety mintues altogether.

Breakfast: **Gillwoods,** 1313 Main Street. (707) 963–1788. Unique breakfast specialties and all-American favorites.

Of the plethora of specialty shops on Main, a few are of particular note. **Stillwaters,** 1228 Main (707–963–1782), is about traveling to ex-otic places and about fishing: bamboo rods, fish cookbooks, decoys, safari clothes, unique picnic accessories. **Main Street Books,** 1371 Main (707–963–1338), is stocked with regional guidebooks. English country garden goodies can be found at **Mosswood,** 1239 Main (707–963–5883).

The Gallery on Main Street, 1359 Main (707–963–3350), shows the best of local artwork. Just off Main at 1124 Pine, **Henry Evans Printmaker** studio (707–963–2126) produces sophisticated botanical linocuts created by a world-famous artist.

If you're a Robert Louis Stevenson aficionado, you'll find 8,000 pieces of his memorabilia at the **Silverado Museum,** 1490 Library Lane (707–963–3757). Next door, the **Napa Valley Wine Library** (707–963–5145) houses 6,000 books, tapes, and reference materials on the art of winemaking and the history of the valley.

Driving north from St. Helena, you'll see redwood forests grow darker and deeper, maples and oaks crowd closer to the roadside, creating canopies of leaves and branches overhead, brilliant canyons of color in the fall. Watch for **Beringer Winery's Rhine House** on the left, built in 1883, and **Greystone,** Christian Brothers' imposing monolith of a winery building. Both give excellent tours, but their location on the main highway keeps them exceedingly busy on weekends.

Lunch: **Brava Terrace,** just north of St. Helena at the Freemark Abbey complex, 3010 St. Helena Highway. (707) 963–9300. French bistro menu, delightful garden terrace, risotto, pasta, cassoulet, home-made ice cream.

Afternoon

While at Freemark Abbey, go into the **Hurd Beeswax Candle Factory and Store** (707–963–7211) to see wild and weird candles of every description being created for shipment worldwide.

Just up the road, the **Bale Grist Mill State Park** (707–963–2236) is a wooded glade with a 36-foot waterwheel beside a rushing creek. Walk from here into **Bothé–Napa Valley State Park** (707–942–4575) to find a lovely campground in Ritchie Creek canyon, a swimming pool and shady picnic sites under redwoods and firs along the creek. Both of these parks are home to the endangered spotted owl.

Proceeding north a short way, watch for mailbox #3358, **Frogs' Leap Winery** (707–963–4704). Call ahead for a tour of this boutique winery on the banks of Mill Creek. At the turn of the century, frogs were commercially raised in the creek for the frogs' legs lovers in San Francisco restaurants—they sold for 33 cents a dozen. Now the Sauvignon Blanc made here is characterized as "creamy, silky-thick lemon and bell pepper, trimly defined, finishing quite crisply."

Proceed on another ten minutes to Calistoga.

Dinner: **Valeriano's Ristorante** in the Mount View Hotel, 1457 Lincoln, Calistoga. (707) 942–0606. Notable Northern Italian cuisine in a casually elegant setting. Toddle across the hall to dancing and live entertainment in the lounge.

Lodging: **Mount View Hotel.** (707) 942–6877. Art deco–decorated rooms in a circa 1920 building on the main street, garden patio and pool, within walking distance to everything; spa facilities.

Day 2

Morning

Breakfast: **Johnny's** sidewalk cafe at the Mount View.

Set off on a walking tour of town, a compact grid of tree-shaded streets. The architecture is an eclectic conglomeration of Victorian, art deco, 1950s funky, Craftsman, and Greek and Mission Revival. Get a map and some orientation at the **Sharpsteen Museum,** 1311 Washington (707–942–5911), where an elaborate diorama re-creates the 1800s resort town. Exhibits are lifelike and colorful, and a huge collection of old photos recalls the people who came here a hundred years ago to "take the waters." Kids love the stagecoach and the unstuffy atmosphere of this museum, built and donated by a thirty-year veteran producer at the Walt Disney Studios; his Disney memorabilia is on display, too. Part of the museum is a charming Victorian cottage and gardens.

Just off the main street on Cedar, the green oasis of **Pioneer Park** on the Napa River has lawns, a gazebo, and a great kids' playground. Next door to the park, **The Elms,** 1300 Cedar (707–942–9476), is a bed-and-breakfast inn in a fanciful French Victorian mansion.

For a midmorning cappuccino, step into **Cafe San Marco,** 1336 Lincoln Avenue (707–942–4671); every variety of coffee and steamed milk specialty you can think of, as well as pastries, is served here. There are a dozen espresso bars in Calistoga, no doubt catering to the throngs of tourists who do the slow stroll of Lincoln Avenue every weekend in the summer and fall.

Galerie Chevrier, at 1219 Washington Street (707–942–6634), and **Donlee Gallery,** at 1319 Lincoln (707–942–0585), display large collections of well-known California artists' works.

Lunch: **All Seasons Cafe,** 1400 Lincoln. (707) 942–9111. Bistro cuisine and a major wine list; crabcakes, pasta, pizza, sandwiches.

Afternoon

A restored 1868 Southern Pacific train station on Lincoln houses the visitor's bureau and the **Calistoga Wine Stop,** 1458 Lincoln Avenue (707–942–5556), where you can choose from more than 1,000 Napa and Sonoma Valley wines and arrange for them to be shipped. **The All Season's Wine Shop,** inside the **All Season's Cafe** (707–942–6828), specializes in medal-winning wines.

Spend the rest of the day at one of Calistoga's health resorts being herbal-wrapped, enzyme-bathed, massaged, and soaked in mineral-rich mud; expect to feel like warm Jell-O when it's over.

Dinner. **Cafe Pacifico,** 1237 Lincoln. (707) 942–4400, Southwestern/ Mexican specialties, marvelous margaritas.

Lodging. **Mount View Hotel.**

Day 3

Morning

Breakfast: Choose from one of the coffeehouses.

Proceed a few minutes north on the Silverado Trail, north of Calistoga to **Chateau Montelena** (707–942–5105), at the foot of Mount St. Helena. Secluded in a piney wood, the winery is a spectacular castle built of French limestone brought around the Horn in 1880, enchantingly poised above a small lake surrounded by gardens and weeping willows, with a vineyard view. A Chinese junk floats serenely, and red lacquered gazebos provide private places for conversation and sipping of the renowned estate-grown Cabernets and Reislings, available only here. In 1972 a Chateau Montelena Chardonnay exploded the myth that French wines are best by winning a blind tasting against France's finest.

Head south on the Silverado Trail and turn right on Dunaweal Lane to **Clos Pegase** (707–942–4982), a russet-colored, postmodern extravaganza of a winery, the result of an international architectural competition. Besides winetasting here, you'll enjoy the vineyard views, sculpture garden, frescoed murals, and a slide show about the history of winemaking.

A minute farther on Dunaweal, the sparkling white Mediterranean aerie of **Sterling Vineyards** (707–942–3300) floats like an appartition high in the hills. For a small fee a tram will take you up for views from the sunny terraces.

Back on the Silverado Trail, continue south through the valley to a left on Meadowood Lane for a stroll on the grounds of the **Meadowood Resort Hotel** (707–963–3646), a posh country lodge reminiscent of the 1920s, residing regally on a rise overlooking 250 densely wooded acres, a golf course, and tennis and croquet courts.

Lunch: **Fairway Grill,** on the terrace at Meadowood. Or, for a picnic lunch, take a right on Zinfandel Lane, crossing over to Highway 29, and head south a few minutes to Oakville, stopping for gourmet goodies at **Pometta's Deli** (707–944–2365), at the Oakville Cross Road. Drive two minutes up this road to **Vichon Winery,** 1595 Oakville Grade (707–944–2811), to shady picnic tables on a hill overlooking the world.

Afternoon

Head south to the Bay Area (or turn to Northbound Escape Three and make this a *long* weekend).

There's More

Gliders. Calistoga Soaring Center, 1546 Lincoln Avenue, Calistoga, CA 94515. (707) 942–5592.

Spas. Golden Haven Hot Springs, 1713 Lake Street, Calistoga. (707) 942–6793. Complete spa facilities, mineral pool.

Lincoln Avenue Spa, 1339 Lincoln Avenue, Calistoga 94515. (707) 942–5296. Mud baths, body and beauty treatments, pools.

Roman Spa, 1300 Washington Street, Calistoga. (707) 942–4441. Mineral pools, beauty treatments, mud baths, enzyme baths, saunas, rooms around a tropical garden.

White Sulphur Springs, 3100 White Sulphur Springs Road, St. Helena 94574. (707) 963–8588. Some 330 acres of redwoods, creeks, hiking trails. Cottages, complete spa facilities.

Indian Springs Hot Springs Spa and Resort, 1712 Lincoln Avenue. (707) 942–4913. The oldest resort in town; mud baths, hot springs pool, beauty treatments, simple cottages.

Calistoga Village Inn and Spa, 1880 Lincoln Avenue, Calistoga. (707) 942–0991. Complete spa facilities in a country setting with vineyard views.

Napa Valley Museum, 473 Main Street, St. Helena. (707) 963–7411.

Old Faithful Geyser, 1299 Tubbs Lane, Calistoga. (707) 942–6463. Blows its top every forty minutes.

Petrified Forest, 4100 Petrified Forest Road, Calistoga. (707) 942–6667. Six million years ago a volcanic explosion turned redwoods to stone.

Robert Louis Stevenson State Park, 7 miles north of Calistoga on Highway 29. (707) 942–4575. Some 3,670 acres, 2,200 to 4,343 feet elevation, day use only; 5-mile trek to the top of Mount St. Helena for wide views of Northern California. Watch for the rare peregrine falcon; the fastest animal in the world, the falcon dives at speeds of up to 200 miles an hour.

Biking. Palisades Mountain Sports, 1330B Gerrard Street, behind the fire department. (707) 942–9687. Rentals.

Getaway Bicycle Tours, Calistoga. (800) 499–BIKE. Guided daytrips.

Backroads, 1516 Fifth Street, Berkeley 94710–1740. (800) 462–2848. Longer guided bike expeditions and inn tours.

Golf. Mount St. Helena Golf Course. (707) 942–9966. Nine holes, reasonable rates.

Special Events

July. Napa County Fair, Calistoga. (707) 942–5111.

September. Calistoga Vintage Air Fair. (707) 942–6333. Antique airplane fly-in and hangar dance.

October. Old Mill Days, Bale Grist Mill State Park. (707) 963–2236. Costumed docents grind grain and corn on the millstones and make bread; demonstrations of traditional trades and crafts, games, entertainment.

October. Calistoga Beer and Sausage Fest. (707) 942–6333. Local microbreweries.

December. Pioneer Christmas Celebration, Bale Grist Mill State Park. (707) 963–2236. Costumed docents help kids make traditional Christmas decorations; grain grinding, refreshments, entertainment.

Other Recommended Restaurants and Lodgings

St. Helena

Spring Street Restaurant, Spring at Oak. (707) 963–5578. Indoors in the historic bungalow or outdoors in a garden patio, American favorites loved by the locals.

Terra, 1345 Railroad Avenue. (707) 963–8931. In a historic stone building, warm and romantic; exotic California cuisine with French and Japanese accents, miraculous wine list.

Trilogy, 1234 Main. (707) 963–5507. Intimate, casual cafe; bistro cuisine for lunch and dinner; wine and appetizers on the patio.

Cinnamon Bear, 1407 Kearney Street. (707) 963–4653. A 1904 bungalow, 1920s antiques, four rooms with private baths, full breakfast, veranda for afternoon dozes.

Calistoga

Calistoga Inn, 1250 Lincoln Avenue. (707) 942–4101. Breakfast, lunch, and dinner; hearty country fare; chili, burgers, *huevos rancheros,* crabcakes, fresh fish, and homebrewed beers and ales. Also eighteen comfortable inn rooms.

Comfort Inn, 1865 Lincoln Avenue. (707) 942–9400. East end of town. Reasonably priced, simple, modern; pool, sauna, spa.

Napa

Bed and Breakfast Exchange. (707) 942–2924.

For More Information

Calistoga Chamber of Commerce, Old Depot, 1458 Lincoln Avenue, Calistoga, CA 94515. (707) 942–6333.

St. Helena Chamber of Commerce, 1080 Main Street, St. Helena, CA 94574. (707) 963–4456.

Advice: It's wise to call wineries in advance. Not all are open to the public, but most will warmly welcome you for an appointment to tour and taste.

Lake County Loop

The tasting room of the Fetzer Winery.

Clear Lake, Hopland, Ukiah

2 NIGHTS

Hot springs · Indian history · Fishing and water sports
Beer- and Winetasting · Country roads · Wildlife preserves

The mountains, lakelands, and wine valleys of Lake County and western Mendocino County are some of the least visited and most rewarding weekend destinations in Northern California. Traffic and tourist crowds occur only at Clear Lake when summer vacationers arrive with boats and fishing gear. In winter you'll see bald eagles and waterfowl that have come from Alaska and Canada to spend the season at the lake and at Anderson Marsh and Boggs Lake Preserve.

The smooth green flanks of 4,200-foot Mount Konocti, a dormant volcano, loom dramatically above Clear Lake's placid blue waters. Holding more fish per acre than any other lake in the United States, it's the largest natural lake in the state. Resorts, marinas, and campgrounds dot the 100-mile shoreline, and the lake is stocked regularly with warmwater fish, such as bass, crappie, trout, bluegill, and catfish. A lively competition for the big ones takes place at the Clear Lake Bass Tourney in February.

More discoveries: the surprising wine-country village of Hopland, champagne baths at Vichy Hot Springs, and a world-famous Indian museum in Ukiah.

Day 1

Morning

From the Golden Gate Bridge, drive north on Highway 101 to the Napa/Highway 37 exit, connecting with Highway 121 east to Highway 29 at Napa, then driving thirty minutes north to Calistoga—about ninety minutes altogether. Stop for picnic supplies along the way or in Calistoga. The **All Seasons Cafe,** 1400 Lincoln Avenue, Calistoga (707–942–9111), makes up gourmet box lunches including utensils and wine.

Follow Highway 29 through town and five minutes beyond to **Robert Louis Stevenson State Park** (707–942–4575). If you're up for a morning hike, set out into 3,000 wild acres of hillside forest trails; a steep scramble to 4,343 feet, the summit of Mount St. Helena, rewards with views of the entire Napa Valley.

From here to Middletown is a scenic drive like no other, on a roller-coaster road through stream canyons and woods scented with bay and pine. Big-leaf maples strike red in the fall, and oaks golden yellow, along many sideroads, where bikers and walkers love the quiet. You'll emerge in a valley of walnut, pear, and kiwi orchards; tumbledown farmhouses; scrub oaks; and rocky meadows. Vast vineyards were planted here in the past decade, creating an increasingly more prominent wine region. Passing through Middletown, watch for the GUENOC WINERY sign and make the 5.5-mile drive on Butts Canyon Road to **Guenoc Estate Vineyards and Winery,** 2100 Butts Canyon Road (707–987–2385). Surrounded by gracious verandas and gardens, the former home of nineteenth-century British actress Lillie Langtry was lovingly restored by current owners, who've established the winery and vineyards on thousands of acres stretching to Napa County.

Lunch: Picnic here in the vineyards on Guenoc Lake or at Anderson Marsh State Historic Park.

Afternoon

Proceed on Highway 29 to Lower Lake, taking the Highway 53 exit to **Anderson Marsh State Historic Park** (707–994–0688). The 900 acres you see from here to the horizon are the wetlands habitat for herons, pelicans, ducks, grebes, coots, cormorants, bald eagles, and hundreds more species of waterfowl. The sight of a bald eagle fishing for its dinner is a moment to remember. Numerous ancient Native American sites are here, some dating from 8000 B.C., when the shores and swamps surrounding Clear Lake were almost exactly as they are today. At the historic **Anderson Ranch House** is a small museum and visitor's center; ask for directions to the re-created Pomo village and ceremonial roundhouse. To see the natural sights, hike through **Redbud Audubon Society's McVicar Preserve** or rent a boat at Garner's Resort (707–994–6267) or Shaw's Shady Acres (707–994–2236).

Back on Highway 29, it's another twenty minutes to the right turn on Soda Bay Road, then a 5-mile descent to **Konocti Harbor.** In the shadow of Mount Konocti, **Konocti Harbor Resort and Spa** is a sprawling lakeside resort and marina, with two large swimming pools, tennis courts, minigolf, playgrounds, and a lot more. After enjoying some of the recreational opportunities, have a twilight cocktail on the deck overlooking the action of the marina. Get ready for plenty of live action indoors; *big* country-and-western stars perform here all year long.

Dinner: **Konocti Landing Restaurant.** (707) 279–4286. Seafood, steak, lobster, hearty American fare.

Lodging: **Konocti Harbor Resort and Spa,** 8727 Soda Bay Road, Kelseyville 95451. (800) 862–4930. Rooms, beach cottages, condo units, family packages; complete health spa (707–279–4261) with body and beauty treatments, exercise classes, lap pool.

Day 2

Morning

Breakfast: In the resort coffee shop.

On the way to Lakeport on Highway 29 is **Konocti Winery,** on Thomas Drive (707–299–8861), and **Kendall-Jackson Winery and Vineyards,** at 600 Mathews Road (707–263–5299), both open for tasting every day. Lakeport, a busy summer-vacation town, has a few historic buildings and an old-fashioned band shell and playground in a grassy lakefront park.

From here it's 18 miles on a zigzaggy mountain road, a 2,500-foot ascent up and over the craggy **Mayacamas Range** to Hopland, a route not recommended for large RVs or for stormy days—light snow is not uncommon on this road in midwinter. The road descends on the west side of the mountains into a peaceful vineyard valley, finally crossing an arm of the Russian River, entering Hopland on Highway 101.

Lunch: Purchase picnic goodies in the **Fetzer Tasting Room** gourmet deli, 13500 Highway 101, Hopland (707–744–1737), and settle into one of several woodsy picnic venues around the Fetzer complex. Or go up the street to **Hopland Brewery and Beer Garden,** 13351 South Highway 101 (707–744–1361). Red Tail Ale, Peregrine Pale Ale, Black Hawk Stout, and other exotic brews are fun to try; the lunch menu, served in the century-old pub or outside on a sunny deck, features hearty sausages, burgers, chili, and salads. Brewing operations are open to view, and if you're here on a Saturday night, hang around for the live music and dancing. The joint really jumps during Hopland's Octoberfest celebration.

Afternoon

Hardly 1 mile long, **Hopland** could be the cutest one-horse town you've ever seen, an enclave of art galleries, antiques shops, winery tasting rooms, and small cafes, wrapped snuggly around with vineyards and farmlands.

The ivy-covered Fetzer tasting room is also a large store specializing in food products from the wine country: mustards; jams, jellies, and pickles; cheeses; fresh garlic; olive oil and vinegars; and regional cookbooks and guidebooks. A wide variety of Fetzer's wines, from table wines to estate reserves, are available to taste, buy, and ship home, including a new line of organically grown varieties.

Adjacent to Fetzer, **Made in Mendocino** (707–744–1300) sells art, weavings, jewelry, and fine crafts produced in the region.

If you dare, take your chances at the **Cheesecake Lady,** 13325 Highway 101 (707–744–1441), for espresso and guess-what.

Like an elderly lady, perfectly preserved and in splendid Victorian dress, the **Thatcher Inn,** Highway 101, Hopland 95449 (800–266–1891), takes up ½ block of Hopland's main street. The hundred-year-old hotel, with peaked dormers and sweeping verandas, shelters an elegant restaurant, bar, dining terrace, swimming pool, and twenty elaborately furnished rooms with private baths. The bar is distinguished by one of the country's largest collections of single malt scotch whiskeys; the library, by 4,000 volumes, one of which will keep you reading in an armchair by the green marble fireplace.

Drive north to Ukiah on Highway 101 and take a right on Vichy

Springs Road, 2 miles through pear orchards to Vichy Hot Springs, arriving in time for a relaxing late-afternoon soak in the warm, bubbly mineral-water baths or the pool.

Dinner: **North State Cafe,** 801 North State Street, Ukiah. (707) 462–3726. Sophisticated specialties in a casual setting, exotic pizzas from the brick oven, pasta, fresh fish, local poultry, meats, and produce.

Lodging: **Vichy Hot Springs,** 2605 Vichy Springs Road, Ukiah, 95482. (707) 462–9515. Since 1854, a country resort famous for carbonated mineral-water springs. From 25,000 feet below the surface of the earth, the magical waters rush forth, sixty-five gallons a minute, filling a large swimming pool and several tubs. Simple, spacious rooms have verandas overlooking sweeping lawns, meadows, and gardens.

Day 3

Morning

Breakfast: A substantial continental breakfast in the sunny dining room at Vichy Springs. Stoke up for a morning hike in the surrounding 700 acres of woods, meadows, streams, and hillsides.

The main attraction in Ukiah, formerly a lively logging town, is the **Grace Hudson "Sun House,"** at 431 South Main Street (707–462–3370), an impressive museum complex housing American Indian baskets, artifacts, and paintings. The late Hudson painted the faces and the domestic life of native Pomo Indians, and her ethnologist husband assembled the extraordinary collection, one of the most important in the Northern Hemisphere. Open to inspection, their home is a wonderful redwood Craftsman-style bungalow. A tree-shaded park surrounds the museum buildings.

Head south to the Bay Area, about two hours away. The Russian River follows you down the highway; watch for access points if you're of a mind to play along the riverbanks. And if you can't bear to return to the city, refer to Northbound Escape One.

There's More

Clear Lake State Park, 3.5 miles northeast of Kelseyville on Soda Bay Road. (707) 279–4293. Some 565 acres; RV, camper, and tent sites. Behind the visitor's center look for great blue herons on the banks of Kelsey Creek; the large nests in the treetops are heron rookeries.

Boggs Lake Preserve, at Middletown. Take Highway 175 to Cobb, then a left on Bottle Rock Road; proceed 6.5 miles, then take a right onto Harrington Flat Road and drive for 1 mile. A 141-acre tract of fir and pine forest with a unique vernal pool, a lakeland habitat for 141 species of birds, including wintering wildfowl and songbirds, plus a myriad of common and endangered wildlflowers. Early May to mid-June is best for flowers; wintertime, for osprey and bald eagles. Tours April through June. Information: Nature Conservancy, 785 Market Street, San Francisco 94103. (415) 777-0487.

Gliders. Crazy Creek Soaring, Middletown. (707) 987-9112. Scenic glider rides.

Golf. Hidden Valley Lake Golf Course, Highway 29, 5 miles north of Middletown. (707) 987-3035. Eighteen-hole championship course.

Clear Lake Riviera Golf Course, 10200 Fairway Drive, Kelseyville. (707) 277-7129. Eighteen holes and a restaurant.

Hoberg's Forest Lake Golf Club, Highway 175 and Golf Road. (707) 928-5276. Nine holes.

Indian crafts. Owl's Flight, 6292 Highway 20, Lucerne. (707) 274-7734. Native American crafts, jewelry, art, games, supplies.

Parasailing. On the Waterfront, 60 Third Street, Lakeport. (707) 263-6789.

Special Events

April. Spring Wine Adventure, Lake County Wineries. (707) 525-3743.

May. Native American Cultural Day, Anderson Marsh. (707) 994-0688. Dancing, displays, demonstrations of traditional arts and crafts.

June. Lakeport Revival Classic Car Show. (707) 525-3743. Parade, dance.

July. Lake County Rodeo, Lakeport. (707) 525-3743.

August. Blackberry Festival, Anderson Marsh. (707) 994-0688. Homemade pies, demonstrations of traditional trades, arts and crafts, entertainment, games, tours.

October. Octoberfest, Lakeport and Hopland. (707) 263-7231.

Other Recommended Restaurants and Lodgings

Clearlake

El Grande Inn Best Western, P.O. Box 4598. (707) 994-2000. On the lake; forty-four very nice rooms and suites, pool, sauna, spa, garden courtyard, restaurant, bar.

Nice

Featherbed Railroad Company, 2870 Lakeshore Boulevard. (707) BR–GUEST. On Clear Lake; rooms in railroad cabooses; pool.

Middletown

Harbin Hot Springs, 18424 Harbin Springs Road. (707) 987–2477. Hot, warm, and cold mineral pools; sundecks, sauna, gym; 1,160 acres of nature trails; camping, restaurant, store.

Lakeport

Forbestown Inn, 825 Forbes Street. (707) 263–7858. Built in 1863, a Victorian masterpiece chock-full of antiques and designer touches. Hearty breakfast, pool, spa; 1 block from the lake.

Park Place, 875 Lakefront Boulevard. (707) 263–0444. Lunch and dinner, fresh produce, seafood, pasta, burgers, steak; casual, with windows overlooking the city park and the lake.

For More Information

Lake County Visitor's Center, 875 Lakeport Boulevard, Lakeport, CA 95453. (707) 525–3743.

Greater Ukiah Chamber of Commerce, 495 East Perkins Street, Ukiah, CA 95482. (707) 462–4705.

Mendocino County Vintner's Association, P.O. Box 1409, Ukiah, CA 95482. (707) 463–1704.

MISTIX (state park campground reservations). (800) 444–7275.

The Redwood Route

The Gingerbread Mansion, one of the premier Victorian homes on the West Coast.

Seacoast Towns, Path of the Giants

_____ 2 NIGHTS _____

Logging towns • Rivers and seacoast • A Victorian village
Ancient redwoods • Seafood cafes • California history

The drive up Highway 101 to the seaside logging town of Eureka is a respite from summer's heat and a cozy adventure on foggy winter weekends. You'll stop along the way to see the redwoods and play on the Eel River. California's coastal redwoods are the world's tallest living things. Walking beneath a 300-foot forest canopy among these silent giants from the age of the dinosaurs is an unforgettable experience.

Eureka and smaller coastal towns look much as they did in their Victorian heyday—streets lined with gracious old homes and elaborate gingerbread-trimmed hotels. From partaking of bed-and-breakfast inns, fresh seafood, logging and Indian history, wildlife sanctuaries, and sea air to fishing for the mighty salmon, biking on forest paths, and going river rafting or beachcombing, you'll find that there's more than a weekend's worth of enticements here.

Expect foggy mornings, even in the summer, and winter rains December through March. These tremendous northern woods are true rainforests, thriving on drizzle and damp. But don't let drippy weather keep you at home. Fishing is best from October through March, and Eureka is misty and romantic then, too.

Day 1

Morning

Begin the 280-mile trip at the Golden Gate Bridge, going north on Highway 101 for 80 miles to **Healdsburg.** Take the Central Healdsburg exit and go 2 blocks north to the plaza, the palm-shaded green heart of the wine regions of the Alexander and Dry Creek valleys (see Northbound Escape One).

Breakfast: **Healdsburg Coffee Company,** 312 Center Street, on the plaza. (707) 431-7941. Cappuccino, muffins, fresh pastries, and many breakfast goodies.

Back on 101, head north. Crisscrossed by the Russian River, the serene **Alexander Valley** opens up, its folded foothills carpeted with vineyards and scattered with giant oaks and poufs of yellow broom. At **Cloverdale** you'll begin to see redwood groves and logs piled up at sawmills on the roadside. Slowing up through Cloverdale (a notorious speed trap), notice old stone landmark buildings and Victorians, as well as the very 1950s **HiFi Drive-In** (707-894-2811), on the north end of town, one of the first soft-serve ice cream joints in California.

Between Cloverdale and Leggett you'll share the road with logging trucks as the highway winds along the rugged, forested spine of the Coast Range. Mountains become jagged and canyons deep. Redwoods, pines, maples, and madrone crowd the hillsides, vivid in the fall. Above Leggett watch for the **Redwood Tree House,** a fun tourist trap with a good collection of guidebooks and maps. The vestibule is formed from the burned-out shell of a giant sequoia; the tree is still alive and thriving.

Hartsook Inn, 900 Highway 101, Piercy, CA 95587 (707-247-3305), 8 miles south of Garberville, is another stretch-your-legs opportunity. In a grove of towering redwoods, the inn has been famous for fresh trout dinners since the 1920s. Take a peek at the old photos in the lobby and walk down to the river, the south fork of the Eel, past simple vacation cabins; families spend their summers here, fishing and swimming in the river.

Twenty-three miles north of Leggett, you'll see a sign for the **Benbow Road,** a pretty byway running close along the Eel, making a nice little drive, walk, or bike ride, ending up at the **Benbow Inn,** 445 Lake Benbow Drive, Garberville (707–923–2124). Built in 1925, the inn is a Tudor monolith overlooking a twenty-six-acre summer lake. Here you can fish and rent a canoe; for a refreshing sidetrip, go with the park rangers (707–946–2311) on a one-hour interpretive canoe tour to absorb some natural history and see osprey, turtles, herons, and belted kingfishers.

Now on to the **Avenue of the Giants,** a world-famous 33-mile scenic drive, the highlight of your visit to redwood country. The avenue bypasses the highway and its many attractions are well marked; turnouts and parking areas access short loop trails into the forest. Some 51,222 acres of spectacular redwood groves along the Eel and its south fork are contained here in **Humboldt Redwoods State Park** (707–946–2311). These are the biggest of the 2,000-year-old beauties remaining in a 30-mile-wide belt of coastal redwoods stretching from Monterey to Oregon.

Pick up picnic goodies at one of the small groceries along the first few miles of the avenue, then begin your tour at the **Visitor's Center** (707–946–2311), about 4 miles from the south end of the avenue. Here you'll get oriented by a movie, exhibits, and trail maps. Ask for advice on the lengths and types of walks and drives you'd like to take in the park. Docents will show you a special binder of trail maps, pointing out new trails and those that may be closed due to weather or maintenance.

Not to be missed is the **Rockefeller Forest** in the **Big Trees** area, a 5-mile drive in on Mattole/Honeydew Road. Since the former champion sequoia Dyerville Giant, 362 inches in diameter, fell in rain-saturated ground in the spring of 1991, the new champ is a 363-footer in the Rockefeller Forest. Tiptoeing along boardwalks and spongy pathways in the damp, cool stillness at the foot of these magical giants, you'll hear only the bustle of chipmunks. Under a fragrant green canopy hundreds of feet above your head, the shade on the forest floor is deep and dark, even on a hot summer's day. Wildflowers—trilliums, wild iris, and redwood orchid—spring from a carpet of moss and fern, while brilliant blue Stellar's jays flash through the branches overhead. A spooky rush of air signals the flight of a black raven; the shiny and silent 2-foot-long ravens are aggressive guardians of their

1,000-year-old forest. A short trail leads to a sandy riverbank, for sunbathing, wading, picnicking, and fishing.

Lunch: Have your picnic here or at Bull Creek Flats.

Afternoon

Returning toward the highway on the Mattole/Honeydew Road, watch for the sign to **Bull Creek Flats,** a sunny pebbled beach and picnic area at a lovely bend in the river; wild lilacs bloom here in great purple clouds in the spring. In the rainy season the river runs with salmon and steelhead. Summer fishing—carp and eels—is for fun, not for food.

One hundred miles of trails in Humboldt Park are maintained for walkers, backpackers, bikers, and horseback riders. Meanderings will turn up old homesteaders' cabins and a plethora of campgrounds, some for RVs and others consisting of simple sites in the backcountry. Apple blossoms bloom in orchards planted by early settlers. In fall big-leaf maples, alders, and buckeyes turn red and gold. In the farthest outback are bobcats, black-tailed deer, foxes, ring-tailed cats, and even black bears.

Reaching Eureka by day's end, you'll be warmly welcomed by Doug Vieyra, the mustachioed proprietor of the **Elegant Victorian Mansion,** 1406 C Street, Eureka 95501 (707–444–3144). Lily Vieyra will hand you a glass of wine and take you on a tour of the house, perhaps the finest of Eureka's great treasure trove of Victorian bed-and-breakfast inns. Built in 1888, it's an extravagantly antiques-filled Queen Anne surrounded by a garden of 150 antique roses; there are four large, comfortable rooms. The Vieryas offer saunas, massages, croquet, vintage movies, fireplace chats, and a library of guidebooks.

Dinner: **The Sea Grill,** 316 E Street. (707) 443–7187. In historic Old Town on Humboldt Bay; biggest seafood menu in town, legendary salad bar, steak; reservations necessary.

Stroll around under the gaslights in nineteenth-century **Old Town** for a last whiff of sea air before bedtime. It's 12 blocks to the mansion.

Day 2

Morning

Breakfast: Lily's hearty eggs benedict and Dutch pancakes, with fresh fruits and juices.

A font of local sightseeing and historical information, Doug will clue you in to secret spots to visit in the area. With an architectural/scenic walking-tour map, start the day with an exploration of the surrounding Victorian neighborhood, ending up in Old Town. On the waterfront, home port to more than 500 fishing boats, are several blocks of 1850–1904 Queen Anne, Eastlake, and Classic Revival buildings. The Victoriana is enhanced by parks, fountains, playgrounds, and shaded benches for resting between shopping, photo snapping, and museum discoveries.

Not to be missed is the **Indian Art Gallery,** 241 F Street (707–445–8451), where Northwestern Indian artists exhibit and sell their works. The **Clarke Memorial Museum,** at Third and E streets (707–443–1947), a 1920s Italian Renaissance-style former bank with a glazed terra-cotta exterior, houses an extraordinary collection of Indian basketry, antique weapons, maritime artifacts and photos, furniture, and memorabilia of early Humboldt days. The **Carson Mansion,** at Second and M streets, said to be the most photographed home in America, is a wedding cake of an Italianate/Queen Anne mansion built in the 1880s by a lumber baron; it's a private club, and the interior is off-limits to the public.

Lunch: **Bristol Rose Cafe** in the Eureka Inn off the elegant main lobby, Seventh and F streets. (707) 442–6441. Rub shoulders with loggers and tourists. Or, for a picnic lunch, go to **Sequoia Park,** Glatt and W streets, in fifty-two acres of virgin redwoods with a zoo, a kids' playground, formal gardens, walking paths, and a duck pond.

Afternoon

From June through September a seventy-five-minute cruise of the bay, departing from the foot of C Street, can be had on the *M.V. Madaket* (707–444–9440), a wooden steamer built in the 1920s. You'll get a narrated tour of historical and natural sights around the bay, passing oyster farms, flocks of aquatic birds, and the third largest colony of harbor seals in the West. If it's a clear, mild day, try the cocktail cruise, leaving at 4:00 P.M.

One of the magic places in Eureka that will catch and keep you longer than you planned to stay, the **Blue Ox** (800–248–4259) is an old mill at the foot of X Street, 3 blocks north of Fourth. This is a museumlike job shop and sawmill that makes custom trim for Victorian buildings, using the same machines that were used to create the originals. Owner Eric Hollenbeck collected machines from junked mills and from the briarpatches of Mendocino County, restoring dozens of them for turning columns, carving rosettes, and forming wooden gutters. In the huge main building, you can take a self-guided tour on catwalks above the workers; call ahead to see if Eric happens to be giving one of his special personal tours. A loggers' camp, a bird sanctuary, and other attractions make this a worthy stop.

Dinner: **Hotel Carter Restaurant,** 301 L Street, Eureka. (707) 444–8062. Opulent Victorian decor, California cuisine, and nouvelle Italian specialties; scallops in garlic, lemon, and herbs; oysters with basil and chèvre; filet mignon in Burgundy wine; grilled breast of duck in Zinfandel-blueberry sauce; extensive wine list.

Lodging: Fall into a big, comforter-covered bed here at the **Carter House Country Inn.** (707) 445–1390.

Day 3

Morning

Breakfast: **The Samoa Cookhouse,** on Woodley Island in the bay. (707) 442–1659. Reached by the Highway 255 bridge on the north edge of Old Town, this is the last surviving lumber camp cookhouse in the West. In the dining room, where giant breakfasts are served from 6:00 A.M., historical photos and logging artifacts add to the turn-of-the-century atmosphere. Woodley Island affords breezy seaside walks, bike rides, and views of the bay and Eureka; watch for the egret rookery in cypress trees on Indian Island.

From the Samoa Cookhouse take scenic Highway 255 north fifteen minutes around Humboldt Bay to **Arcata,** home of Humboldt State University. This is another old logging town with unique attractions, such as the **Historic Logging Trail** in Arcata's 600-acre **Community Forest** (707–822–7091). Enter Redwood Park at the corner of Fourteenth and Union, following Redwood Park Road to the parking lot. On foot, take Nature Trail #1 on the west side of the parking lot and follow signs and a map that's provided to see logging sites and equipment from a century ago. A few old-growth sequoias remain in these groves, but most are second-growth.

Arcata Marsh and Wildlife Sanctuary, at the foot of I Street in Arcata (707–822–7091), is a birdwatcher's mecca. For the best photography settle into one of the bird blinds. Guided nature walks are scheduled on Saturdays, rain or shine.

Twenty-two miles south of Eureka, take the Ferndale exit, driving 5 miles west across the Eel through flat, green dairylands to **Ferndale.** Just two long streets of glorious Victorian buildings, the entire tiny town is a State Historic Landmark. To attract tourists and cheer themselves through long, damp winters, residents have painted more than 200 of their homes and businesses in a cacophony of bright colors. Art galleries, antiques shops, ice cream parlors, and cafes abound. The **Gingerbread Mansion,** at 400 Berding Street (707–786–4000), is one of the premier Victorian masterpieces on the West Coast. Dressed in bright yellow and peach with cascades of lacy white trim, and surrounded by whimsical formal gardens, the gigantic hundred-year-old beauty is ½ block long. Nine elaborately decorated rooms have claw-foot tubs (one room has two tubs, toe to toe) and the mansion has four parlors. This was the only Victorian in town to survive undamaged a monster earthquake in 1992; Ferndale has since been completely restored.

Ferndale sparkles all over and decorates to the max at Christmastime. The lighting of the tallest living Christmas tree in America, a parade, a Dickens's Festival, and concerts are among the blizzard of holiday activities.

Lunch: **Diane's Cafe and Espresso,** next to Foggy Bottoms Antiques, 553 Main Street, Ferndale. (707) 786–4950. Sandwiches, salads, soups, homemade desserts.

Afternoon

Head back to the Bay Area, stopping along the way to walk again under the great redwoods.

There's More

Fishing. K Street and the F Street piers; the south jetty, 11 miles south of Eureka on 101; the north jetty, 6 miles from the west end of Samoa Bridge, for surf and rock fishing, lingcod, salmon. Trolling and shorecasting for salmon and steelhead in coastal lagoons between Trinidad and Orick, north of Eureka; clamming on several nearby beaches. The Eel, the Mad, the Van Duzen, the Little River, and Redwood Creek all are near Eureka; the Klamath, a little farther. River runs of king and silver salmon start after the rains have begun in October. Steelhead runs begin in late November. Twenty lakes in Humboldt County are stocked with trout. To check for fishing conditions, call North Coast Fishphone (707–444–8041) or Eel River Headquarters (707–946–2311).

Celtic Charter Service, 5105 Woodland Way, Eureka 95501. (707) 442–7580. From Woodley Island Marina, Phil Glenn takes you out on his sportfishing boat, daily from May to September, for salmon and rock cod fishing and for whale-watching.

Rivers West Fishing Expeditions, P.O. Box 53, Redcrest. (707) 722–4159. A veteran jetboat operator customizes camping, fishing, and sightseeing jaunts on local rivers.

Golf. Eureka Municipal Golf Course, 4750 Fairway Drive, Eureka. (707) 443–4808. Eighteen holes.

Tennis: Eureka High School, 1915 J Street. Five courts.

Highland Park, Highland and Glen streets. Four courts.

Mad River Salmon and Steelhead Hatchery, 2 miles south of Blue Lake on Hatchery Road.

Winter fun. Horse Mountain cross-country skiing, sledding. Take Highway 299 to Titlow Hill Road.

Scenic drive along wild Humboldt County rivers. Take Highway 36 along Van Duzen and Mad rivers to Ruth Lake in Trinity County (three to four hours) or beyond to Red Bluff (five to six hours).

Tour. Trees to Sea Interpretative Tours, 2006 Street Maru, McKinleyville, CA 95521. (707) 839–8066. Five- and seven-hour guided tours of Eureka and Humboldt County.

Special Events

February. Annual Trinidad Clam Beach Run, Patrick's Point State Park, Trinidad. (707) 677–3448. One thousand runners and walkers; 8.5-mile route ending at the beach.

March. Annual Oyster Shooter Eating Contest and April Fools' Day Eve Ball, 102 F Street. (707) 445–3970.

April. Rhododendron Festival, Eureka. (707) 442–3738.

April. Dolbeer Steam Donkey Days, Fort Humboldt State Historic Park. (707) 445–6567. Logging competition; operation of steam donkeys, locomotives, and equipment; rides.

May. Avenue of the Giants Marathon. (707) 442–1226.

June. Scandinavian Festival and Barbecue, Main Street, Ferndale. (707) 786–9853. Dancing, food, a parade, and festivities for descendants of Scandinavian lineage and for visitors; food, music, and fun.

June. Rodeo and Western Celebration, Garberville. (800) 338–7352.

August. Humboldt County Fair and Horse Races. (707) 786–9511.

December. Truckers' Parade, downtown Eureka. (707) 443–9747. Some 150 big rigs decorated in Christmas lights; logger-style floats. You've never seen anything like this parade.

Other Recommended Restaurants and Lodgings

Eureka

Bay City Grill, 508 Henderson Street. (707) 444–9069. Bistro-style menu, fresh seafood, great salads, upbeat, lively.

Cafe Waterfront Oyster Bar and Grill, 102 F Street at First. (707) 443–9190. Bay view, Victorian decor, casual; seafood, pasta, chicken, beef.

Ramone's Bakery, 209 E Street. (707) 445–2923. Where the locals go for cappuccino, killer bagels, and scones.

Lazio's, 327 Second Street. (707) 443–9717. Great seafood since 1944.

Camellia Cottage, 1314 I Street. (707) 445–1089. French country–style.

Eureka Inn, Seventh and F streets. (707) 442–6441. Hundred-room hotel with a pool, spa, and three restaurants.

Red Lion Inn, 1929 Fourth Street. (800) 547–8010. 175 nice motel rooms in town, pool, restaurant, and bar.

Eureka KOA Kampground, Highway 101, 4 miles north of Eureka. (800) 462–KAMP.

E-Z Boat Landing and Trailer Park, 4 miles south of Eureka at King Salmon turnoff. (707) 442–1118. All services; good clamming and sportfishing.

Garberville

Knight's Restaurant, Myers Flat on the Avenue of the Giants. (707) 943–3411. Casual cafe serving all day and evening, basic good food, impeccable, comfortable.

For More Information

California State Park Campsite Reservations. (800) 444–2775.

Redwood Empire Association, 785 Market Street, Fifteenth Floor, San Francisco, CA 94103. (415) 543–8334.

Eureka/Humboldt County Convention and Visitor's Bureau, 1034 Second Street, Eureka, CA 95501. (800) 338–7352.

Eureka Chamber of Commerce, 2112 Broadway, Eureka, CA 95501. (707) 442–3738.

Ferndale Chamber of Commerce, 248 Francis Street, Ferndale, CA. (707) 786–4477.

Sonoma County Sojourn

One of the many farms featured on the Sonoma County Farm Trail map.

On the Way to Bodega Bay

——————————— 1 NIGHT ———————————
Beach walks · Waterfront cafes · Harbor life
Pasturelands · Antiques shopping · Birdwatching

From the Gravenstein Apple Capital of Sebastopol, through Sonoma County's rolling pastures, to the major fishing port of Bodega Bay, there is much to fill a weekend. On the way to the wild beaches of the central coast and the lively harbor town, relaxing meanders on country roads are enlivened with frequent stops for antiques and art-gallery browsing, sightseeing, and coastal contemplation in cafes.

Day 1

Morning

Drive north from the Golden Gate on Highway 101 for forty-five minutes to Cotati, turning west on Highway 116 to Sebastopol. You'll pass more than a dozen antiques shops on the way into town; stop if you dare at the **Antique Society,** 2661 Gravenstein Highway South (707–829–1733), the county's largest antiques collective. **Julien's Sebastopol Antiques**, at 1190 Gravenstein Highway South (707–836–0595), has nine rooms of goodies.

Breakfast: **East West Cafe,** 128 North Main, Sebastopol. (707) 829–2822. Simply the best local produce in inventive breakfasts; vegetarian specialties.

Set off through the orchardlands of western Sonoma County on the **Bodega Highway,** after 6 miles taking a right turn on the Bohemian Highway to **Freestone. The Wishing Well Nursery,** 306 Bohemian Highway, Freestone (707–823–3710), is like no other nursery. Surrounding a 200-year-old hotel are acres of fabulous plants and flowers, outdoors and in greenhouses. Exotic birds, fancy chickens, ducks, swans, peacocks, pheasants—you name it—twitter in cages, glide on ponds, and strut around as if they owned the place. Decorating the grounds are statuary remnants of Bernard Maybeck's turn-of-the-century Palace of Fine Arts in San Francisco. **Trude's Antiques** (707–823–3710) is in the same building; a player piano accompanies your antiques discoveries in the large shop.

Continue on the Bodega Highway a few miles to the wide-spot-in-the-road town of **Bodega,** 2 miles west of Bodega Bay; take a left on Bodega Lane. The old school on the hill that looks vaguely familiar is the **School House Inn,** 17110 Bodega Lane (707–876–3257), a comfortable bed-and-breakfast establishment. When Alfred Hitchcock filmed *The Birds* in 1962, this was the school where the black beauties lined up menacingly on the schoolyard jungle gym and chased the children down the road. Near the inn is St. Teresa's Church, circa 1860, and a few antiques and gift shops. On the highway watch for **Bodega Landmark Studio Collection,** 17255 Bodega Highway (707–876–3477), a regional center for art and fine crafts of all kinds.

Lunch: **Lucas Wharf Restaurant,** 595 Highway 1, Bodega Bay. (707) 875–3522. Dine at a sunny window table overlooking the action of the wharf and the harbor. Fresh local seafood: clam chowder, Dungeness crab, salmon, mussels, sand dabs—the list goes on.

Afternoon

Whale-watching cruises and deep-sea fishing party boats leave from the wharf, headquarters for Bodega Bay's harbor and the home port for many northern coast fishing vessels. Fishermen unload their catch and shoppers choose from local and imported fresh seafood at **The Tides Wharf Fresh Fish Market** (707–875–3554). It's crab in the fall, herring in the spring, salmon in the summer—and rock and ling cod all year.

On the north end of town, turn left on Eastshore Road, then right on Westshore Road, circling the bay. Notice a swampy area on your right, near an old boat skeleton, where blue herons often stalk about in the reeds. Fishing boats and sailboats are lined up at **Spud Point Marina** (707–875–3535), and there's a long fishing pier where you can try your luck. At **Westside Park** (707–875–2640), you can picnic, dig for clams and bait, and launch a boat. Most days sailboarders flit like butterflies in the harbor breezes.

There's a sign for the **University of California Bodega Marine Laboratory** (707–875–2211), open to tours on Friday afternoons. About .5 mile of coastline and surrounding marine habitat is protected and studied; the exhibits and working research projects—such as aquafarming of lobsters—are fascinating.

At the end of the road, park and get out onto the bluffs of **Bodega Head** (707–875–3540), a prime whale-watching site. Footpaths from here connect to 5 miles of hiking and horseback-riding trails in grassy dunes.

Back on Eastshore Road near the highway, stop in at the **Branscomb Gallery**, 1588 Eastshore Road (707–875–2905). There are three floors of galleries with sea views, featuring local and internationally known artists, wildlife etchings, seascapes, and vineyard scenes, one of the best galleries in gallery-rich Sonoma County. Next door is **Lucy's Whale of a Cookie and Pastry Place,** 1580 Eastshore Road (707–875–2280); Lucy bakes small batches of cookies, muffins, and breads all day long. At **Candy and Kites,** 1425 Highway 1 (707–875–3777), get you-know-what for your beach walks. The **Ren Brown Collection**, 1781 Highway 1 (707–875–2922), features works from California and Japan—wood blocks, etchings, silkscreens.

From Bodega Bay north to Bridgehaven, the **Sonoma Coast State Beach** (707–875–3483) is 13 miles of sandy beaches and coves accessible in a dozen or so places; dramatic rocky promontories and seastacks, tidepools, and cliffsides make this a thrilling drive. You can camp at **Wright's Beach** or **Bodega Dunes** (800–444–7275). For rock fishing and surf fishing, **Portuguese Beach** is a good choice; for beachcombing and tidepooling, try **Shell Beach.** Surf fishing is good at **Salmon Creek Beach** (campsite reservations, 800–444–7275), a beautiful dune area planted with European grasses. The creek is dammed up with sand, forming a lagoon inhabited by throngs of seabirds. At the north end of the beaches, **Goat Rock,** a notoriously dangerous place to swim, is popular for seashore and freshwater fishing at the mouth of the Russian River; seals like it, too. This coastline is home to more than 200 species of sea- and shorebirds. You don't need to be an official birdwatcher; they're easy to see in saltmarshes, mudflats, tidepools, and bays—great blue herons, white and brown pelicans, gulls, ospreys, even peregrine falcons.

At **Bridgehaven,** where the Russian River meets the sea, are a simple restaurant and lodgings (see Northbound Escapes Eight).

Dinner: **Ocean Club Restaurant** at Bodega Bay Lodge, Highway 1 on the south end of Bodega Bay, near Bodega Harbour Golf Links. (707) 875-3525. Fresh Sonoma County seafood, poultry, cheeses, and produce on a California cuisine menu.

Lodging: **Bodega Bay Lodge.** (707) 875-3525. Perched on a protected spot overlooking Bodega Bay and bird-filled marshes; all rooms with views and decks, some with fireplaces. The lobby has a giant stone fireplace and two 500-gallon aquariums filled with tropical fish; fresh, contemporary decor, pool, spa, sauna, exercise room, complimentary bikes, golf packages.

Day 2

Morning

Breakfast: Complimentary continental breakfast in the Ocean Club Restaurant. Later in the morning the **Sandpiper Dockside Cafe,** on the water at 1410 Bay Flat Road (707-875-2278), is the place to tuck into eggs with home fries, *huevos rancheros,* or crab omelets.

From the lodge take a morning walk at **Doran Beach Regional Park** (707-875-3540), a 2-mile curve of beautiful beach separating Bodega Bay and Bodega Harbor. Clamming and surfing are good here, as is sailboarding on the harbor side, and there are RV and tent camping sites. Birdwatchers hang out in the marshes to see sanderlings, plovers, and herons.

Head out of town, south on Highway 1 through Bodega Bay to the Valley Ford cutoff/Highway 1 road just west of Bodega, to Valley Ford. You'll drive past lush green hills, dairy farms, and ranches to the town of **Tomales,** a 2-block-long headquarters for crabbing, clamming, and surf fishing at **Dillon Beach** and in the skinny finger of **Tomales Bay,** between the mainland and the peninsula of Point Reyes National Seashore. A number of nineteenth-century buildings remain near the intersection of Main Street and Dillon Beach Road; the Church of the Assumption, just south of town, was built in 1860.

The town of Dillon Beach, 4 miles west of Tomales, consists of a collection of Craftsman-style beach cottages from the 1930s; on the beach are some of the richest tidepools on the entire coastline. You can walk on the dunes or drive 1 mile south to Lawson's Landing, where hang-gliders often ride the winds. Camping, boating, and fishing equipment and advice are available at **Lawson's Landing Resort** (707–878–2204). At low tide in the winter, catch a clammer's barge out to the flatlands around Hog Island in Tomales Bay. Hog Island and nearby Duck Island are private wildlife sanctuaries frequented by harbor seals.

Lunch: **Old Town Cafe,** 26950 Highway 1, Tomales. (707) 878–2526. A false-front, hundred-year-old building, antiques bedecked. Sandwiches, homemade soup, fresh fish. Across the street is the **U.S. Hotel,** 26885 Highway 1 (707–878–2742), a circa 1860 bed-and-breakfast inn. If inn guests have checked out, ask for a tour of the museumlike hotel.

Afternoon

To connect with Highway 101 south to the Golden Gate, drive east on Tomales Road, a eucalyptus-lined lane winding through coastal farmlands; it's 15 miles to **Petaluma.** If you have some of the afternoon remaining, pick up a walking-tour map at the Chamber of Commerce, 215 Howard (707–762–2785), and sightsee in the riverport town.

There's More

Golf. Bodega Harbour Golf Links, 21301 Heron Drive, Bodega Bay. (707) 875–3538. Eighteen holes on a links-style course designed by Robert Trent Jones; challenging; windy; spectacular views.

Sportfishing. The Challenger, 1785 Highway 1, Bodega Bay. (707) 875–2474.

New Sea Angler and Jaws, at the Boathouse, 1145 Highway 1, Bodega Bay. (707) 875–3495.

Horseback riding. Sea Horse Stables, 2660 Highway 1, Bodega Bay. (707) 875–2721. Two-hour guided dune ride.

Special Events

April. Bodega Bay Fisherman's Festival, Bodega Bay. (707) 875–3422. Thousands come for the blessing of the fleet and boat parade, outdoor fair, food, entertainment, and arts and crafts.

June. Sonoma-Marin Fair, Petaluma Fairgrounds. (707) 763–0931.

August. Sonoma County Wineries Association Auction. (707) 579–0577.

August. Old Adobe Fiesta, Petaluma. (707) 762–2785.

August. Petaluma River Festival. (707) 762–5331. A hundred craft and food booths, steamboat and sternwheeler rides, entertainment.

August. Sebastopol Apple Fair. (707) 586–FARM.

October. Sonoma County Harvest Fair, Santa Rosa. (707) 545–4203.

November. Festive Bay Days, Bodega Bay. (707) 875–3777. Seasonal festival; Santa arrives.

Other Recommended Restaurants and Lodgings

Bodega Bay

Inn at the Tides, 800 Highway 1. (707) 875–2752. Luxury accommodations with sea views, fireplaces, lap pool, spa, sauna.

The Bay Hill Mansion, 3919 Bay Hill Road. (707) 875–3577. Modern rendition of a Queen Anne, six view-filled rooms, full breakfast.

Sea Horse Guest Ranch, 2660 Highway 1. (707) 875–2721. A 700-acre working ranch on Salmon Creek; three guestrooms.

Bodega Coast Inn, 421 Highway 1. (707) 875–2217. Forty-four simple, contemporary rooms, each with ocean view and balcony, some with fireplaces and spas.

Valley Ford

Dinucci's, downtown on Highway 1. (707) 876–3260. For decades a destination in itself. Huge home-style Italian dinners; seafood and steaks; a friendly long bar.

For More Information

Vacation Homes. (707) 875–4000. Vacation home rentals.

Petaluma Chamber of Commerce, 215 Howard Street, Petaluma, CA 94952. (707) 762–2785.

Bodega Bay Chamber of Commerce, 855 Highway 1, Bodega Bay, CA 94923. (707) 875–3422.

Jenner to Point Arena

The beaches of Sonoma County make for great horseback riding.

North Central Coastline on Highway 1

_____ 1 NIGHT _____

Rugged coastline · Rocky beaches · Russian history
Whale-watching · Fishing harbors · Seacoast villages

Day 1

Morning

From the Golden Gate Bridge, drive north on Highway 101 to the Guerneville Road exit on the north end of Santa Rosa, an hour's drive.

Go west on Guerneville Road to Highway 116, proceeding west to Guerneville along the lush riparian corridor of the **Russian River.**

Breakfast: **Sweet's Cafe and Bakery,** 16251 Main, Guerneville. (707) 869–3383. Belgian waffles, omelets, homemade croissants, espresso.

Proceed to the Highway 1 junction, turning north toward **Jenner.** Here the mild, meadowy headlands of the southern Sonoma coastline turn abruptly steep. The 11-mile stretch of road between Jenner and Fort Ross winds cruelly along a narrow marine terrace with precipitous bluffs on one side—some 900 feet above the shore—and high cliffs on the other side. This is a challenging, spectacular drive; take your time, and take advantage of pullovers and vista points.

From the west end of the parking lot at **Fort Ross State Park,** 19005 Highway 1 (707–847–3286), walk down to the small, protected beach below the fort. As you breathe in fresh sea air before starting your explorations of the fort, think about the Russians who arrived in 1812, accompanied by Aleut fur hunters. They came to harvest otter and seal pelts and to grow produce for their northern outposts. Their small settlement of hand-hewn log barracks, blockhouses, and homes, together with a jewel of a Russian Orthodox church, was protected with high bastions and a bristling line of cannons, just in case the Spanish decided to pay a call. At the visitor's center are exhibits, films, and guidebooks. Inside the restored buildings are perfectly preserved rifles, pistols, tools, furniture, and old photos. The "crib-style" architecture uses hand-adzed logs notched together and fastened with oakum, a jute-rope-and-tar combination. Several times a day costumed docents put on a demonstration of domestic activities.

Back on the highway, if you're ready for a snack, stop at the **Fort Ross Store and Deli** (707–847–3333) for an ice cream cone. Then go on to **Salt Point State Park** (707–847–3221), 6,000 acres of sandy beaches, tidepools, high cliffs, sunny meadows, and hiking and biking trails: a good place to beachcomb, scuba dive, or get a little exercise. Campground sites on both sides of the road are private and protected. The dense forestlands of Salt Point are inhabited by gnarly pygmy pines and cypress, their ghostly gray, mossy trunks tickled by maidenhair ferns. Seven miles of coastline are characterized by long, sandy beaches: rocky coves with tidepools rich in wildlife; and many breeding and nesting locations for birds, such as at **Stump Beach,** where a large number of cormorants reside.

Kruse Rhododendren State Park (707–847–3221) should not be missed in the months of April, May, and June, when wild rhododendron glades up to 15 feet high are brilliant with bloom under redwood, oak, and madrone branches. It's a 1-mile dirt road into the park; a trail sign shows easy and challenging trails.

Lunch: **Sea Ranch Lodge,** 60 Sea Walk Drive, off Highway 1. (707) 785–2371. Sandwiches, salads, and whale-watching in the glass-sided restaurant. All with ocean views, rustic lodge rooms seem to float in wildflowery meadows.

Afternoon

The Sea Ranch Lodge is headquarters for a unique residential development that pioneered the use of extensive open space and architectural restraint. Widely scattered, naturally weathered wood houses on the headlands and hillsides are barely visible; some have sod roofs. A string of quiet, sandy coves and rocky beaches are accessible for several miles along the Sea Ranch coast; **Shell Beach, Pebble Beach,** and **Black Point Beach** are the best.

When you see the lace curtains and wooden porches of the eighty-seven-year-old **Gualala Hotel,** you've made it to the town of Gualala, your final destination for the day. Once a logging center, Gualala is now an art colony and headquarters for steelhead and salmon fishing.

Several shops in the **Seacliff Center,** on the south end of town, are worth browsing. **Once upon a Time** (707–884–4910) specializes in imported dolls, art glass, and "chainsaw sculpture," an art form unique to the redwood forest areas. A yarn and sweater store, **Marlene Designs** (707–884–4809), has contemporary hand-knit sweaters glowing with vivid colors, not the styles your grandmother used to knit. Prowl around town a bit to find art galleries and antiques shops.

Dinner: **Gualala Hotel,** P.O. Box 675, Gualala 95445. (707) 884–3441. Family-style Italian dinners, fresh fish, and steaks, all in a lively, friendly atmosphere. Come in early for a tall one at the long bar, where local fishermen and tourists rub elbows beneath a museumlike array of photos of early days and fishing on the Gualala.

Lodging: **Seacliff,** P.O. Box 697, Gualala 95445. (707) 884–1213. Contemporary suites with fireplaces, spas, and private decks overlooking **Gualala Beach;** a prime whale-watching and fishing spot.

Day 2

Morning

Breakfast: Eggs and bacon with a sea view at the **Sandpiper,** at the south end of town. (707) 884–3398.

Drive north to **Point Arena.** At the south end of the main street, turn west on Port Road, following it to the **Point Arena Public Fishing Pier,** which thrusts 330 feet out into the water from the edge of a cove seemingly protected by high cliffs on either side. The original wooden pier was dramatically smashed to pieces in 1983, along with all of the buildings in the cove. In the **Galley at Point Arena** restaurant, Port Road, Point Arena (707–882–2189), are photos of the storm as it ripped and roared. Fishing, crabbing, and whale-watching are good from the pier; tidepooling and abalone hunting, from the rocks.

Walk up to the **Wharf Master's Inn,** on the hill behind the pier. Built in the 1870s for wharf masters who watched over the port until the 1920s, this is the town's most elaborate building, a fantasy of turned posts, scroll brackets, and fancy window moldings. Just below, the **Coast Guard House,** P.O. Box 117, Point Arena (707–882–2442), now a bed-and-breakfast inn, is a classic California Arts and Crafts–style house built in 1901 as a lifesaving station.

Rollerville Junction, 3 miles north of Point Arena, is the westernmost point in the continental United States, the site of many a shipwreck; ten vessels went down on the night of November 20, 1865. The 115-foot **Point Arena Lighthouse** (707–882–2777) was erected here in 1870, then reerected after the 1906 San Francisco earthquake. The lighthouse is the all-time best location for California gray whale-watching; December through April are the prime months. Scramble around in the lighthouse and visit the museum of maritime artifacts below.

Few people know that the three small homes at the **Point Arena Coast Guard** facility are available to rent; neat and clean, with kitchens, they're perfect for a family or several couples.

Proceed north on the highway to **Elk,** a tiny community perched on cliffs above a spectacular bay. You'll recognize the **Greenwood Pier Inn** complex, 5928 Highway 1 in Elk, by the multitude of blooming flowers and trees. Take your time poking around in the gardens and in the **Country Store** and **Garden Shop at Greenwood Pier Inn** (707–877–9997).

Lunch: **The Roadhouse Cafe,** 606 Highway 1, Elk. (707) 877–3285. Hamburgers and sandwiches.

Afternoon

Drive back to the Bay Area by way of Highway 253 through Boonville and the beautiful Anderson Valley (see Northbound Escape Nine), or retrace your Highway 1 route.

Special Events

Feb–May. Gualala Arts Music Series. (707) 884–1138.
March. Gualala Whale Festival. (707) 884–3377.
July. California Winetasting Championships, Anderson Valley. (707) 877–3262.

Other Recommended
Restaurants and Lodgings

Point Arena

Wharf Master's Inn, 785 Port Road, P.O. Box 674. (800) 932–4031. New inn surrounding a landmark house from the mid-1800s; court-yards, private decks, firpelaces, spas, ocean views, upscale decor.

Galley at Point Arena, located at Point Arena Pier. (707) 882–2189. Chowder, snapper sandwiches, homemade pies, bar, whale-watching.

Elk

Greenwood Pier Inn, 5928 Highway 1. (707) 877–9997. Redwood castles on a cliff with wonderful coastline views; fireplaces, decks, amazing gardens, privacy. In a complex with a shop, plant nursery, and cafe.

Jenner

Fort Ross Lodge, 20705 Coast Highway 1. (707) 847–3333. Comfort-able ocean-view rooms and suites, some with fireplaces, spas; reason-able.

Sea Coast Hideaways, 21350 Highway 1. (707) 847–3278. Vacation home rentals.

Timber Cove Inn, 21780 Highway 1. (707) 847–3231. Eclectic rooms have fireplaces, decks, and hot tubs or Jacuzzis. On a whale-watching, ocean-viewing point; good restaurant; three-story stone fireplace in the lounge; romantic—a place for runaways.

Gualala

Old Milano Hotel, 38300 Highway 1. (707) 884–3256. Romantic rooms in a bed-and-breakfast inn, which features a renowned restau-rant and lovely gardens overlooking the sea.

For More Information

Sonoma County Convention and Visitor's Bureau, 10 Fourth Street, Santa Rosa, CA 95401. (707) 575–1191.

California State Park Reservations, (800) 444–7275.

Advice: Driving can be hazardous on the twists and turns of High-way 1, and it's not recommended that you attempt it after dark or dur-ing storms. Farm animals and deer in the road can be a scary, and maybe deadly, surprise as you're coming around a blind curve.

Mendocino and the Anderson Valley

The roads of Sonoma County offer ideal conditions for cyclists.

Romance by the Sea, Country Pleasures

_____ 2 NIGHTS _____

Victorian village · Galleries galore · Seafood · Wineries
Hidden coves · Redwood groves · Fishing, beachcombing

Floating like a mirage on high bluffs above a rocky bay, Mendocino seems lost in another century. The entire town is a California Historical Preservation District of early Cape Cod and Victorian homes and steepled clapboard churches. Though thronged with tourists in summer, the look and feel of a salty fisherman's and lumberman's village somehow remain.

Old-fashioned gardens soften weather-worn mansions and cottages; picket fences need a coat of paint; dark cypress trees lean into the sea breezes. Boutique and art-gallery shopping is legendary, charming bed-and-breakfast inns abound; in fact, there are more B&Bs per capita in and around Mendocino than anywhere else in California.

For a contrast to the rocky and rugged Highway 1 coastline, you'll head inland on the last day, meandering through a deep redwood forest to the sunny meadows and country wineries of a valley not much visited, not much changed in a hundred or so years.

Day 1

Morning

Head north from the Golden Gate Bridge on Highway 101 to Santa Rosa, an hour's drive (it's about three and a half hours from the bridge to Mendocino).

Breakfast: Take the downtown exit and go under the freeway to the **Omelette Express,** 112 Fourth Street in Old Railroad Square, Santa Rosa. (707) 525–1690. Every omelet imaginable, wooden tables, hanging ferns, historical photos.

Proceed ten minutes north on 101 to the River Road exit, heading west toward the coast, then north at the Highway 1 junction at **Jenner.** On the roller-coaster road from here to Mendocino, make frequent stops to enjoy cliffhanging views of rocky coves, salt-spray meadows, redwood and pine forests, and a necklace of tiny fishing villages and loggers' towns along the way (see Northbound Escape Eight).

Lunch: **Salt Point Bar and Grill,** 23255 Highway 1, just north of Timber Cove. (707) 847–3238. Solarium windows overlooking gardens and Ocean Cove; mesquite-grilled specialties, fresh fish, salad bar, barbecue.

Afternoon

After you arrive in Mendocino, revive with a bracing walk along the bluffs, the grassy headlands that surround the town. The trail traces the very edge of the cliffs, above swaying kelp beds where otters tap-tap-tap their abalone shells and harbor seals play. The sea churns and boils through rocky arches and dark grottoes. Sandy, driftwoody beaches and tidepools are accessible and safe, unless it's stormy. December through April you may see whales offshore. From the bluffs are views of a deep river valley as it meets the sea at **Big River Beach**, and looking back at the town's skyline, you can imagine when horse-drawn carriages were parked in front of the Mendocino Hotel and ladies with parasols swept along the boardwalk in their long gowns.

Good old days in mind, now is the time to visit the **Kelley House Museum** on Main Street (707–937–5791). A sunny yellow house built in 1852, it's set back from the street next to a huge water tower and a pond surrounded by an old garden. Among the historical photos in the Kelley House are those of burly loggers hand-sawing ancient redwoods. Both the loggers and the redwoods are now endangered, imparting a bittersweet aspect to the contemplation of life as it was in Mendocino's heyday. Lumber for shipbuilding and for construction of the Gold Rush city of San Francisco brought Easterners here in the mid-1800s; it took them six months by ship from the East Coast to reach this wilderness of mighty river valleys and seacoast, inhabited only by Indians and fur trappers.

On Main Street's headlands is **Ford House** museum (707–937–5397), built in 1854. A scale model of Mendocino in the 1890s shows the dozens of tall water towers that existed at that time; more than thirty towers, some double- and triple-deckers, are distinctive features of the skyline today.

Have a sunset cocktail at the **Mendocino Hotel,** a gloriously overdecorated gathering place since 1878. A rough-and-tumble logging town until the 1930s, Mendocino languished quietly for several decades after the lumbermen left, only to be reborn as an art colony and, eventually, a tourist destination. The Mendocino Hotel underwent a $1 million restoration in the 1980s.

Dinner: **MacCallum House Restaurant and Grey Whale Bar,** 45020 Albion Street, Mendocino. (707) 937–5763. Haute cuisine in a rambling Victorian mansion. Oysters, *gnocchi,* lobster, fresh salmon, duck in blackberry sauce; sophisticated menu and wine list.

Lodging: **Joshua Grindle Inn,** 44800 Little Lake Road, Mendocino 95460. (707) 937–4143. One of the oldest homes in town, a circa 1880 beauty on two cypress-bordered acres overlooking the town. Spacious New England–style rooms in the main house; plus very private accommodations in the water tower and the "chicken coop." Escapees from corporate life, Jim and Arlene Moorehead are gleeful in their incarnation as innkeepers. Their lively spirit and the friendly ghost of Joshua Grindle pervade; guests return again and again.

Day 2

Morning

Breakfast: Baked pears, quiche, frittata, and fresh apple and orange juices, as well as merry conversation, at the old harvest table at Joshua Grindle Inn.

Browsing the boutiques and galleries in Mendocino village can take an hour or a week, depending on your love of discovery. At 400 Kasten is the **Mayhew Wildlife Gallery** (707–937–0453), where paintings and prints of whales, dolphins, seabirds, and seascapes are featured. Next door is wild and crazy **Eclectic** (707–937–5951), a gallery of Mexican art; walk through the shop to the sculpture garden in back. On to **Gallery Fair,** at Kasten and Ukiah streets (707–937–5121), a bright yellow building from the 1870s housing fine jewelry, art deco furniture, and paintings.

Tiptoe into the **Gallery Bookshop,** at the corner of Kasten and Albion (707–937–2665), a crowded rabbit's warren of bookshelves, frequented by seriously browsing resident artists and writers.

When you see clouds of swirling birds, you're near **Papa Birds,** 45040 Albion Street (707–937–2730), a shop selling hundreds of birdfeeders, birdhouses, and bird paraphernalia. Their outdoor feeders attract feathered types. Just up the street is the **Nicky Boehme Gallery,** 45055 Albion (707–937–2048), showing the work of a famous local artist who paints the boats, harbors, and seagoing scenes of California and Oregon; you can get affordable print reproductions of the original paintings.

Main Street shops of note are the **Highlight Gallery** (707–937–3132), for burlwood sculpture; the **Irish Shop,** 45050 Main (707–937–3133), for winter coats and sweaters; and **Mendocino Mercantile** (707–882–3017), a barnlike structure housing several shops selling art glass, ceramics, and gifts. Farther down the street is a feminine fantasy, the **Golden Goose** (707–937–4655), two floors of European antiques, country-luxe bed and table linens, and a children's boutique for heirs and heiresses.

Lunch: **Chocolate Mousse Cafe,** corner of Kasten and Ukiah streets. (707) 937–4323. A cottage in a garden. Smoked salmon, Blackout Cake, wine-poached chicken, bread pudding, extensive Mendocino County wine list; popular all afternoon for cappuccino and dessert.

Afternoon

Overgrown country gardens will draw you up and down the sidestreets and alleys; look for the two old cemeteries, not in the least spooky, whose headstones are fascinating relics of the days when European sailors, Russian soliders, and Chinese workers lived here.

Three miles north of Mendocino, turn west into **Jug Handle State Reserve** (707–937–5804), a 700-acre park notable for an "ecological staircase" marine terrace rising from sea level to 500 feet. Each terrace is 100,000 years older than the one below, a unique opportunity to see geologic evolution. The plants and trees change from terrace to terrace, too, from wildflowers and grasses to wind-strafed spruce, second-growth redwoods, and pygmy forests of cypress and pine.

Mendocino Coast Botanical Gardens, 18220 Highway 1, Fort Bragg (707–964–4352), 1 mile south of Fort Bragg on Highway 1, is seventeen acres of plantings, forest, and fern canyons, with 2 miles of paths leading through lush gardens to the ocean.

Noyo Harbor, at the mouth of the Noyo River, is headquarters for a large fleet of fishing trollers and canneries. Barking and posing, sea lions lounge on the wooden piers, waiting for the return of the boats at day's end. **The Wharf** bar (707–964–4283) is a great place for a sundown cocktail or cup of tea and a calamari appetizer.

Now proceed into Fort Bragg, a lumbering and fishing town founded in 1857.

Dinner: **Coast Hotel Cafe,** 101 North Franklin Street. (707) 964–6446. Checkered tablecloths give no hint of a sophisticated menu and large wine list. Oysters, jambalaya, twenty pastas, fresh fish in imaginative sauces, house-smoked ribs. Warm and cozy on a cold night; live jazz on weekends.

Lodging: **Grey Whale Inn,** 615 North Main, Fort Bragg 95437. (707) 964–0640. Built as a hospital in 1915, the rooms and public spaces of this three-story landmark are spacious, with high windows looking to the sea or inward through the trees to town. Rooms have sitting areas with armchairs, deep tubs, some fireplaces, lots of books. A penthouse suite with double Jacuzzi tub and private deck with ocean view is the highest point in Fort Bragg.

Day 3

Morning

Breakfast: A big buffet in the tiny dining room or in your room at the Grey Whale Inn. Owner Colette Bailey wins prizes at the county fair for her coffeecakes and fruit breads; you'll get to try them, along with breakfast casseroles, fresh fruit, bottomless pots of coffee, and big-city newspapers.

Walk out the back door of the inn to take a long stroll along the waterfront on the **Old Coast Road.**

Drive south of Mendocino 20 miles to Albion, then take Highway 128 inland. For 12 or so miles, the road tunnels through vast groves of second-growth redwoods and ferny glens, part of a 673-acre parcel of riverfront property purchased by the Save-the-Redwoods League. Throughout the tract, fishing, swimming, and exploring are available to the public.

Three miles south of Philo is **Hendy Woods State Park** (707–937–5804), where you'll walk beneath a shady canopy in virgin redwood groves, some of the largest and oldest trees remaining in the state. Here the wide, calm **Navarro River** is enjoyed by fisherpersons, canoers, kayakers, picnickers, and sunbathers.

Beyond the village of **Navarro** are the vineyards and orchardlands of the **Anderson Valley,** where small wineries and produce stands merit frequent stops. In the octagonal wooden building on your right is **Greenwood Ridge Vineyards,** 5501 Highway 128, Philo (707–895–2002), where you can try medal-winning Pinot Noirs and Cabernets. The mountain backdrop, pond, and gardens make this a good place to picnic. Across the road are the **Kendall-Jackson Winery** (707–895–3232) and the **Navarro Winery** (707–895–3686).

At **Gowan's Oak Tree** produce stand, 6350 Highway 128 (707–895–3353), kids stay busy in the playground while their parents taste apple cider and choose berries, local apples, giant garlic, and veggies to take home.

At **Obester Winery,** 9200 Highway 128, Philo 95466 (707–895–3814), taste Chardonnay, Reisling, and homemade vinegars and olive oil; you can picnic and pick your own produce here.

Lunch: **Boonville Hotel,** P.O. Box 326, Boonville. (707) 895–2210. On the main street of a town with a language all its own called "boontling." Southwestern, California, and Italian cuisine by a French-trained chef who picks herbs and vegetables from the hotel garden. Pizza with goat cheese, fresh fish with avocado-lime salsa, *huevos con chorizo.* Popular bar; indoor and outdoor dining.

Afternoon

Across the road from the hotel, at the **Boont Berry Farm** (707–895–3576), you'll have a last chance to pick up fresh juices, fruits, and local wines. If you're a beer aficionado, check out the **Anderson Valley Brewing Company,** 14081 Highway 128 (707–895–2337), in the basement of the **Buckhorn Saloon.** At the south end of town, at 14300 Highway 128, is the **Rookie-To Gallery** (707–895–2204), which has an extraordinary collection of contemporary ceramics and fine art jewelry.

Take the Dry Creek Road exit into Healdsburg, stopping just north of the plaza at **Costeaux French Bakery,** 417 Healdsburg Avenue (707–433–1913), for memorable bread and pastries. If it's dinnertime, **Matuszek's Restaurant,** 345 Healdsburg Avenue (707–433–3427), near the northwest corner of the plaza, has a pleasant, gardeny terrace; Czech specialties; and hearty European cuisine.

Head south to the Golden Gate.

There's More

Skunk Train, Laurel and Main Streets, Fort Bragg. (707) 964–6371. Historic diesel and steam logging trains make round trips between Fort Bragg and Willits, taking a riverside route through scenic redwood forests; deli foods and snacks available at midpoint. Kids love this.

Van Damme State Park, 2 miles south of Mendocino. (707) 937–4016. Home of the Pygmy Forest—strange, stunted dwarf trees and flowering shrubs. Camping; great beach.

Russian Gulch State Park, 2 miles north of Mendocino. (707) 937–5804. Small, scenic campground; walking trails.

MacKerricher State Park, 3 miles north of Fort Bragg. (707) 937–5804. Camping, a long beach, tidepools. Ranger-led hikes and tours, ocean fishing, mussel-taking, abalone diving, walking and biking trails. Lake Cleone is stocked with trout.

Paul Dimmick Wayside Campground, 6 miles east of Highway 1 on Highway 128. (707) 937–5804. Very pretty, small wooded campground.

Special Events

March. Whale Festival, Mendocino. (707) 961–6300. Chowder- and winetasting, tours and talks.

April. Wildflower Show, Boonville Fairgrounds. (707) 964–3153.

May. Heritage Days, Mendocino. (800) 726–2780. Parade, film festival, historical activities.

July. Mendocino Music Festival, P.O. Box 1808, Mendocino 95460. (707) 964–3153. Classical and jazz.

July. World's Largest Salmon Barbecue, Fort Bragg. (707) 964–6598.

September. Mendocino Art Center Open Studio Tours. (707) 937–5818.

Other Recommended Restaurants and Lodgings

Mendocino

Mendocino Hotel, 45080 Main Street. (800) 548–0513. Victorian rooms in the main hotel; luxurious garden suites across the way. Garden cafe and dining room dependably good for breakfast, lunch, and dinner.

Little River Inn, Highway 1, Little River, 95456. (707) 937–5942. In the same family since it was built in the 1850s, a white wedding cake of a house that's expanded to become a sizable resort with one of the best restaurants in the area, a nine-hole golf course in the redwoods, and tennis. The bar is a favorite locals' meeting place. Rooms behind the inn have porches overlooking a beautiful beach and bay.

Whitegate Inn, 499 Howard. (707) 937–4892. A dream of a Victorian bed-and-breakfast establishment, right in the village.

Cafe Beaujolais, 9161 Ukiah Street. (707) 937–5614. Nationally known; country-chic; breakfast, lunch, and dinner. Pizza with chicken sausage and pear barbecue sauce; Thai shrimp salad; black bean chili omelet. Always a surprise; worth the trip to Mendocino.

Restaurant 955, 955 Ukiah. (707) 937–1955. California cuisine, fresh fish.

Elk

Harbor House Inn, 5600 South Highway 1. (707) 877–3203. Classic Craftsman-style mansion, spectacular cliffside location, notable restaurant, lovely rooms.

Boonville

Toll House Restaurant and Inn, 15301 Highway 253. (707) 895–3630. On a 360-acre ranch, a circa 1910 ranchhouse and rooms; real luxury with laid-back atmosphere.

Fort Bragg

North Coast Brewing Company, 444 North Main. (707) 964–2739. Nachos, burgers, salads; lively, casual.

For More Information

Mendocino Coast Accommodations (inns, hotels, bed-and-breakfast places, cottages, homes). (707) 937–1913.

Mendocino Coast Reservations, (707) 937–5033.

Fort Bragg–Mendocino Chamber of Commerce, 332 North Main Street, Fort Bragg, CA 95437. (707) 961–6300.

Coastal Visitor's Center, 990 Main Street, Mendocino, CA. (707) 937–1938.

California State Park Reservations. (800) 444–7275.

Advice: Driving can be hazardous on the twists and turns of Highway 1, and it's not recommended that you attempt it after dark or during storms. Farm animals and deer in the road can be a scary, and maybe deadly, surprise as you're coming around a blind curve.

Marin Waterfront

A short ferry ride will take you to Angel Island State Park.

Sausalito, Tiburon, and Larkspur

_____ 1 NIGHT _____

Sea views • Waterfront cafes • Mountaintop walks
Wildlife sanctuaries • Island idyll • Boutique shopping

_____

On the north side of the Golden Gate, Marin County is a "banana belt," sunny and warm all summer when San Francisco is socked in with fog. It's nice to get away for a couple of quiet days in Marin's small, seaside towns.

Sausalito tumbles down steep, forested hillsides to the edge of the bay. Sophisticated shops, sea-view restaurants, and marinas lined with yachts and funky houseboats share postcard views of the San Francisco skyline.

A residential community of vintage mansions and luxury condos, Tiburon occupies a spectacular peninsula surrounded by the quiet waters of Richardson Bay, where kayakers paddle and sailboarders fly about. Raccoon Straits, a narrow, windswept channel carefully navigated by sailboats and ferries, runs between Tiburon and Angel Island, which is a state park.

Shopping, walks in the salty air, and fine dining are primary activities on this trip, with a Mount Tamalpais sidetrip on the way home.

Day 1

Morning

Immediately to the north of the **Golden Gate Bridge,** take the Alexander Avenue exit, descending down into **Sausalito;** Alexander becomes Bridgeway, the main street. Turn left at the first light, at **Princess Street;** go up the street and make a U-turn, then a right at the same light, and turn immediately into a public parking lot. Some of the best shops in town are located on Princess. At **Studio Saga,** 16 Princess (415–332–4242), the jewel-like colors of soft, silky handwovens envelop you—sweaters, coats, fringed scarves. **Something Special,** at 28A Princess (415–332–0338), specializes in glass oil lamps, potpourri, and brightly colored stuffed gamebirds.

Breakfast: **Seven Seas,** 682 Bridgeway, Sausalito. (415) 332–1304. From 8:00 A.M. every breakfast specialty you can think of, best in town, indoors or on the patio.

In midtown, where a hundred or so shops and restaurants are concentrated, is a small city park with palm trees and huge elephants with streetlights on their heads, leftovers from San Francisco's 1915 Exposition. Behind the park is a dock where ferries come and go to San Francisco and Tiburon. Across the street the **Village Fair,** 777 Bridgeway, is a four-story, hillside rabbit's warren of shops.

The **Bearded Giraffe,** at 1115 Bridgeway (415–332–4503), specializes in books, tapes, art, and crystal "for lighting the inner lamp." **Fine Woodworking,** at 1201 Bridgeway (415–332–5770), exhibits the work of more than 50 Northern California artists and craftspeople. Off Bridgeway the **Armchair Sailor,** at 42 Caledonia (415–332–7505), has books, charts, games, and art for the nautically inspired. Two miles north of midtown, the **Heathware Ceramics Outlet,** 400 Gate 5 Road off Bridgeway (415–332–3732), is worth a stop for seconds from a major producer of stoneware.

Heading north on Bridgeway, watch for the sign for **Bay Model,** 2100 Bridgeway at Spring Street (415–332–3871), a one-and-a-half-acre, hydraulic working scale model of the San Francisco Bay Delta, a fascinating research tool used by the U.S. Corps of Engineers; call ahead to find out when the tides in the model are scheduled for activity. The natural and cultural history of the bay are traced in exhibits—wetlands, wildlife, shipwrecks, antique equipment—plus there are videos to watch and video games to play; kids love it.

Nearby at **Open Water Rowing,** off Bridgeway at 85 Liberty Ship Way (415–332–1091), take a kayaking lesson on Richardson Bay between Sausalito and Tiburon; all ages find it easy to learn and a great way to get a gull's-eye view of wildlife on the bay. Along the Sausalito shoreline in this area is a series of yacht harbors, marinas, and houseboat moorings. The houseboats, permanently located at the north end of town, are a phenomenon in themselves and fun to see.

Drive south out of town to Highway 101 to the Tiburon exit, taking Tiburon Boulevard south along Richardson's Bay to **Tiburon.**

Lunch: **Sam's Anchor Cafe,** 27 Main. (415) 435–4527. One of several harborfront restaurants with views of the San Francisco skyline, Belvedere Island, and Angel Island. Ferries, yachts, and seagulls slide by; time slides by, too, as you sip a beer on the sunny deck and tuck into clam chowder, fresh crab, and fish of all kinds. Casual, with a frisky bar crowd at times. Weekend brunches are a reason to spend the day at Sam's.

Afternoon

One-block-long **Main Street** and **Ark Row,** a curvy tree-lined road at the west end of Main, are both chockablock with art galleries and shops. Between the two streets is the **Corinthian Yacht Club;** it's OK to walk in through the gate and take a look at the fancy yachts.

You'll find seascapes and posters at the **Wooden Pelican,** 7 Main (415–435–1407). **Windsor Vineyards,** 72 Main (415–435–3113), will ship gift boxes of wine with your name on the bottles. **Westerley's,** 46 Main (415–435–4233), has old-fashioned penny candy, bubblegum cigars, chocolate sardines, and licorice pipes. The **Designer Watch Shop,** 28 Main (415–435–3732), sells cheapo copies of every name-brand watch; your friends will never know the difference.

From Main, walk north on Tiburon Boulevard 3 blocks to the **Boardwalk** shopping center, where tucked into an alleyway is **Shorebirds,** 1550 Tiburon Boulevard (415–435–0888), a shop worth searching out. It's a gallery/gift store displaying sophisticated, one-of-a-kind jewelry pieces; locally crafted ceramics and woodware; European toys; paintings; and nautical gifts.

From downtown Tiburon to the north end of Richardson Bay is a beautiful waterfront walk, 2 miles one way, on a flat, paved path; there are benches along the way and a huge lawn for Frisbee tossing and sunbathing. The path is popular with joggers, rollerbladers, bikers, and tykes on trikes. At the north end of the path is the **Richardson Bay Audubon Center and Wildlife Sanctuary,** 376 Greenwood Beach Road (415–388–2524). Thousands of sea- and shorebirds, accompanied by harbor seals in the wintertime, inhabit this 900-acre preserve. A self-guided nature trail and a bookstore are adjacent to **Lyford House,** a lemon-yellow landmark Victorian open to the public.

Reachable by a short ferry ride from Main Street (Red and White Fleet, 415–435–2131), **Angel Island State Park** (415–435–3522) is just offshore. Take a ten-minute cruise over and walk or bike around the breezy perimeter road for wide views of the Bay Area. Historic buildings remain from World War II, when 5,000 soliders a day were processed before leaving for the Pacific. Between 1910 and 1940 hundreds of thousands of Asians were detained on the island, awaiting admission into the United States.

Dinner: **Guaymas,** 5 Main, Tiburon. (415) 435–6300. Spectacular waterfront location; nouvelle Southwest/Mexican food; lively bar and outdoor terrace.

Lodging: **Tiburon Lodge,** 1651 Tiburon Boulevard, 94920. (415) 435–3133. The only hotel in town; walking distance to everything; eclectic decor; some suites with spas.

On weekends, dance to live bands at **Christopher's** on the waterfront, 9 Main (415–435–4600).

Day 2

Morning

Breakfast: **Sweden House,** 35 Main. (415) 435–9767. Breakfast by the bay with the denizens of Tiburon. Swedish pastries, eggs, and everything else.

At the west end of Main Street, **Belevedere Island** is a wooded hilltop almost completely surrounded by water, an exclusive neighborhood of mansions from several eras. It's an architectural sightseeing adventure to drive or walk the steep, narrow lanes; the homes, the gardens, and the ocean views—wow!

From the east end of Main Street, take Paradise Drive around the west side of the Tiburon Peninsula, a narrow, winding road through forestlands on the edge of the bay. After 1 mile, before Westward Drive, watch for the **Nature Conservancy Uplands Nature Pre-**

serve, also known as the **Ring Mountain Preserve,** 3152 Paradise Drive (415–435–6465), a ridgetop, 377-acre piece of wilderness with walking trails and wonderful views. It's less than 1 mile's walk to the summit on a trail edged with knee-high native grasses dotted with wildflowers in the spring. Bay trees, madrones, live oaks, and buckeyes provide shade in meadows inhabited by several endangered plant species, including the **Tiburon Mariposa Lily,** existing nowhere else in the world; blooming all through the spring on a stalk about 2 feet tall, the lily has a tan, cinnamon, and yellow bowl-shaped flower. On the hilltop you'll have a 360-degree view of San Francisco Bay, Mount Tam, and Marin County, across the Richmond–San Rafael Bridge over Berkeley to the East Bay hills.

Proceed on Paradise Drive 2 miles to Highway 101 at Corte Madera, then go north for five minutes to the Larkspur exit, to the west side of the freeway opposite the Larkspur ferry terminal, parking at **Larkspur Landing Shopping Center,** a complex of forty stores and restaurants.

Lunch: **A Clean, Well-lighted Place for Books,** at Larkspur Landing. (415) 461–0171. A casual cafe with a bistro menu, in one of the Bay Area's biggest and best bookstores. Open until 11:00 P.M. on the weekends, ACWLPB is popular for after-the-movies people-watching.

Afternoon

Shop to your heart's content, then drive south on 101 to the Panoramic/Highway 1 exit south of Mill Valley, turning west and winding several miles up on the east side of **Mount Tamalpais State Park** (415–388–2070). You can't miss Mount Tam—it's the 2,500-foot mountain peak that you can see from everywhere in Marin. Park at the Pan Toll Ranger Station and Visitor's Center, get a trail map, and walk a bit on one of several hiking trails that start here; the shortest one is the **"Twenty-Minute Verna Dunshea Trail"** circling the peak. Views are beyond description, and it's often sunny up here when it's foggy everywhere below. Dominating the Marin Peninsula, the mountain looms high above the Pacific Ocean, the Marin headlands, San Francisco Bay, and the rolling hills of the Marin and Sonoma County farmlands. Easily accessible by car or mountain bike or on foot or horseback, Mount Tam's natural wonders are legion—canyons, forests, streams and meadows, waterfalls, and wildflowers—and offer opportunities for wild-and-wooly mountain biking or easy downhill walking.

Perhaps you'll want to stop for a sunset cocktail on the deck at **Mountain Home Inn,** 810 Panoramic Highway (415–381–9000) if you have a designated driver for the trip back to San Francisco.

There's More

Bay Area Discovery Museum, 557 East Fort Baker, Sausalito. (415) 332–9646. A hands-on museum for kids, in turn-of-the-century buildings at East Fort Baker, accessible from the Alexander Road just north of the Golden Gate Bridge.

China Camp State Park, RR 1, P.O. Box 244, San Rafael 94901. (415) 456–0766. North of San Rafael take the Civic Center exit off Highway 101 to North San Pedro Road, heading east. A 1,640–acre waterfront park on San Pablo Bay, with beach, hiking trails, a small museum, and primitive camping.

Ferries. Tiburon, Sausalito, and Larkspur are accessible by ocean-going ferry.

Angel Island Ferry. (415) 546–2700.

Blue and Gold Fleet. (415) 781–7877.

Red and White Ferries. (415) 332–6600.

Kayaking. Bluewaters Ocean Kayak Tours. (415) 456–8956. Bird-watching and natural history kayak trips for beginners.

Special Events

April. Opening Day of Yacht Season, Tiburon and Sausalito water-front. (415) 435–5633. Pleasure craft decorated and blessed; a beautiful and exceedingly high-spirited day on the bay.

June. Humming Toadfish Festival, Bay Model, Sausalito. (415) 332–0505. Entertainment, games, food, in celebration of a famous fish.

September. Art Festival, Bay Model, Sausalito. (415) 332–0505.

October. Bay Area Cajun and Zydeco Music, Dance, and Food Festival, San Rafael. (415) 472–7470.

October. Marin Center Fall Antiques and Art Show, San Rafael. (415) 472–7470.

October. Italian Film Festival, San Rafael. (415) 472–7470.

December. Lighted Yacht Parade, Sausalito. (415) 332–0505.

Other Recommended Restaurants and Lodgings

Sausalito

Scoma's, 588 Bridgeway. (415) 332–9551. On the water at the south end of town, in a baby blue clapboard building. Dependably good seafood.

Sushi Ran, 107 Caledonia. (415) 332–3620. Trendy, contemporary sushi bar and restaurant.

Casa Madrona Hotel and Restaurant, 801 Bridgeway. (415) 332–0502. Circa 1880 landmark inn, luxurious rooms with fireplaces. One of the Bay Area's finest restaurants, California and continental cuisine, bay views.

Golden Gate Youth Hostel, Fort Barry. (415) 331–2777. Single or shared dorms; accessible by public bus.

Alta Mira Hotel and Restaurant, 125 Bulkley Avenue. (415) 332–1350. The breathtaking view from the terrace makes a sunset cocktail or Sunday brunch an event.

Tiburon

New Morning Cafe, 1696 Tiburon Boulevard. (415) 435–4315. Indoors or out, lunch and breakfast, the best.

Larkspur

Scoma's, 2421 Larkspur Landing Center. (415) 461–6161. Good seafood, lively bar, view of ferry landing and the bay.

The Lark Creek Inn, 234 Magnolia Avenue. (415) 924–7767. Internationally famous chef, American heartland and nouvelle cuisine, garden patio, vintage architecture.

San Rafael

Panama Hotel and Restaurant, 5 Bayview Street. (415) 457–3993. Eccentric, fun atmosphere; simple, comfortable inn; popular restaurant serving seafood, pasta, exotic specialties.

Bed and Breakfast Exchange of Marin. (415) 485–1971.

For More Information

Marin County Chamber of Commerce, 30 North San Pedro Road, San Rafael, CA 94903. (415) 472–7470.

Sausalito Chamber of Commerce, P.O. Box 566, Sausalito, CA 94977. (415) 332–0505.

Belevedere-Tiburon Chamber of Commerce, 96 Main, Tiburon, CA 94920. (415) 435–5633.

Point Reyes and Inverness

McClure Beach is a great place to explore.

The National Seashore

2 NIGHTS

Natural Seashore • Beachcombing • Birdwatching
Wildflower walks • Oyster farms • Inns by the sea

More than a few weekends are needed to discover the many joys of
the Point Reyes National Seashore, comprising 71,000 miraculous acres
on the edge of the continent: two fingerlike peninsulas pointing
jaggedly into the Pacific; the long, shallow biodiversity of Tomales
Bay; the big curve of Drakes Bay, where Sir Francis set foot those cen-

turies ago; and oyster farms, clamming beaches, tidepools, and wildlife sanctuaries.

From February through early summer, the meadows and marine terraces of Point Reyes are blanketed with California poppies, dark blue lupine, pale baby-blue-eyes, Indian paintbrush, and a few varieties of wildflowers existing only here. Dominating the landscape is the green-black Douglas fir forest of Inverness Ridge, running northwest to southeast alongside the San Andreas earthquake fault. The summit of Mount Wittenberg, at 1,407 feet, is reachable in an afternoon's climb.

Subject to summer fogs and winter drizzles, Point Reyes is a favorite destination not only for those who love a sunny day at the beach but for intrepid outdoor types who follow cool-weather nature hikes with cozy evenings by a fireplace in a vintage bed-and-breakfast inn.

Day 1

Morning

Drive north from the Golden Gate Bridge on Highway 101 to the Sir Francis Drake/San Anselmo exit, proceeding west forty-five minutes on a winding two-lane road; your destination is the **Point Reyes National Seashore Visitor's Center** (415–663–1092), at Olema. Near Highway 101 on Sir Francis Drake Boulevard, stop at Safeway in the Bon Air Shopping Center for picnic supplies.

Breakfast: **Victoria Pastry,** 292 Bon Air Center. (415) 461–3099. Offspring of a seventy-five-year-old traditional Italian bakery in San Francisco, espresso and pastries, open 7:00 A.M.

Five miles before Olema is **Samuel P. Taylor State Park** (415–488–9897), a 2,600-acre piece of forested canyon along Lagunitas Creek, a popular place for mountain bikers, horseback riders, and hikers.

Exhibits, guidebooks, and trail maps at the Point Reyes Visitor's Center will help orient you to the diverse ecosystem and the many destinations within the National Seashore. According to the day's weather, you may choose beachcoming and sunbathing (or fog-bathing) at **Limantour Beach** on Drakes Bay; backpacking to overnight sites; or easy walks or bike rides on popular meadowland paths, such as the 4.4-mile **Bear Valley Trail** to Arch Rock overlook at the beach—a sunny picnickers' meadow and restrooms are located halfway. This is the most popular and one of the most beautiful trails, leading through forest tunnels, along creeks, and through meadows, ending on a bluff 50 feet above the sea.

Birdwatching is excellent in the 500-acre **Limantour Estero Re-**

serve, west of Limantour Beach. You get to **Drakes Estero,** a much larger saltwater lagoon, from Sir Francis Drake Boulevard on the west side. This rocky intertidal area is a giant tidepool and bird sanctuary, rich with such wildlife as anemones, sea stars, crabs, and even rays and leopard sharks.

Lunch: Picnic on the beach or in a trailside meadow.

Afternoon

Energetic hikers can make the steep but short ascent on Sky Trail to the summit of Mount Wittenberg, and beach bums will choose from many coastal access trails. The long sandy stretch of Point Reyes Beach is accessible in two places by car.

Short, easy walks near the visitor's center include **Kule Loklo,** the Miwok Village, where an ancient Indian site has been re-created; the **Woodpecker Trail,** a self-guided nature walk leading to the park rangers' Morgan horse ranch and a Morgan horse museum; and the **Earthquake Trail,** less than 1 mile, where you'll see photos of the effects of the 1906 earthquake and signs explaining earth movement.

Dinner: **Station House Cafe,** Main Street, Point Reyes. (415) 663–1515. Eclectic, hearty California food; pot roast, duck breast with cherry sauce, fresh fish, pecan pie; dinner served until 11:00 P.M. in the bar; live entertainment three nights a week. Kick up your heels to country music at the **Western Saloon** on Main Street (415–663–1661).

Lodging: **Point Reyes Seashore Lodge,** 10021 Highway 1, P.O. Box 39, Olema 94950. (415) 663–9000. Just south of Point Reyes. Elegantly re-created turn-of-the-century lodge, fireplaces, spas, elaborate continental breakfast.

Day 2

Morning

Breakfast: At the Point Reyes Lodge.

Give your hiking legs a break and spend the morning shopping and cafe lounging in the town of **Point Reyes Station.** Many hundred-year-old buildings remain on the main street of the old railroad town founded in the 1800s. The **Black Mountain Weavers,** on Main Street (415–663–9130), is a co-op gallery of fine woven rugs, sweaters, and tapestries, plus jewelry and art. The **Borge Gallery,** 221 B Street (415–663–1419), specializes in California landscapes. Equestrians will go into **Cabaline Saddle Shop** on Main Street (415–663–8303), for English and western saddlery and clothing. Also on Main is **Toby's Feed Barn** (415–663–1223)—fresh flowers, plants, produce, T-shirts, and hay for your horse.

Lunch: From Point Reyes, drive north on Highway 1 along the shoreline of Tomales Bay a few miles to **Nick's Cove,** 23240 Highway 1, Marshall. (415) 663–1033. Rustic, aromatic, on the wetlands of the bay, barbecued oysters and seafood galore, a list of beers as long as your arm, lots of fun.

Afternoon

On your way back to Point Reyes, then around to Inverness, take a walk or swim in the quiet waters of **Heart's Desire Beach** in **Tomales Bay State Park** (415–669–1140).

A resort village since 1889, Inverness, population 1,000, is a daytrippers' reststop and a community of country cottages on steep wooded slopes at the northern end of **Inverness Ridge** overlooking Tomales Bay. There are seafood cafes, bed-and-breakfast inns, a small marina, and not much else but eye-popping scenery.

Discovered by Spanish explorers in the 1600s, Tomales Bay is 13 miles long, 1 mile wide, and very shallow, with acres of mudflats and salt- and freshwater marshes. Commercial oyster farms line the western shore. More than one hundred species of resident and migrating waterbirds are the reason you'll see anorak-clad, binocular-braced birdwatchers at every pullout on Highway 1. Perch, flounder, sand dabs, and crabs are catchable by small boat. The San Andreas earthquake fault runs beneath Tomales Bay; in 1906 20 feet of the peninsula dropped beneath the bay waters.

Dinner: **Manka's Inverness Restaurant,** 30 Calendar Way, Inverness. (415) 669–1034. A 1917 fishing lodge nestled under the pines; game and fresh fish grilled in an open fireplace, house-cured meat and poultry, homegrown produce; comfortably cozy, candlelit atmosphere, notable chefs; reservations essential.

Lodging: **Manka's Inverness Lodge.** Rustic-luxe rooms in the lodge; cabins with fireplaces.

Day 3

Morning

Breakfast: Continental breakfast by the fire at the lodge. Later, European-style pastries and cappuccino at the **Knave of Hearts Bakery,** 12301 Sir Francis Drake Boulevard, Inverness (415–663–1236).

Walk or bike from Manka's north on Sir Francis Drake Boulevard to the Pierce Point Road; take a right and park in the upper parking lot at **McClure Beach.** It's a 7-mile round-trip around **Tomales Point** and along the coastline. Spring wildflowers float in the meadows; whales spout December through February. A herd of elk live in the grassy fields of **Pierce Ranch** on the tip of the peninsula. These windswept moors remind some visitors of Scotland.

McClure Beach is wide, sandy, backed by high cliffs, and dotted with rocks and great tidepools. Bluffs framed by groves of Bishop pine look like Japanese woodcut prints; these pines are found only in a few isolated locations on the California coast.

Point Reyes Lighthouse, at the end of Sir Francis Drake Boulevard, 15 miles south of Inverness, is reachable by 400 steps leading downhill from a high bluff. Many shipwrecks occurred off the **Point Reyes Headlands** until the lighthouse was built in 1870. Englishman Sir Francis Drake cruised into **Drakes Bay** in 1579; the dramatic cliff-rimmed bay is accessible from Drakes Beach Road off Sir Francis Drake Boulevard. At **Drakes Beach** are a visitor's center, picnic tables, and a great sandy beach. During whale-watching season, December through spring, a shuttlebus may be operating between the lighthouse and the beach. Some 20,000 California gray whales travel the Pacific coastline going south to breed in Mexican waters, and then return with their babies to the Arctic.

Lunch: **Barnaby's by the Bay,** 12938 Sir Francis Drake Boulevard, 1 mile north of Inverness at the Golden Hind Inn. (415) 669–1114. Two decks overlooking a marina, fresh fish, salads, barbecued oysters, jazz on weekends; you'll be tempted to stay here for the rest of the day.

Head back to the Bay Area.

There's More

Horseback riding. Five Brooks Trailhead. (415) 663–8287. Three miles south of Olema.

Bear Valley Stables. (415) 663–1570.

Mount Vision hike. From downtown Inverness walk up Inverness Way, past the school and through the pedestrian gate; bear right at the Y and left through a gate at the next Y. You'll reach the summit in about ninety minutes; dizzying views of Tomales Bay all along the way and views of the ocean and the world at the top!

Oysters. Tomales Bay Oyster Company, 5 miles north of Point Reyes Station on Highway 1. (415) 663–1242. Founded in 1914; fresh oysters and other live shellfish.

Special Events

July. Coastal Native American Summer Big Time, Point Reyes National Seashore. (415) 663–1092. Demonstration of crafts, skills, music, dancing.

October. Acorn Festival, Point Reyes. (415) 663–1092. Celebrations and festivities of the Miwok Indians.

Other Recommended Restaurants and Lodgings

Point Reyes Station

Chez Madeleine, 10905 Star Route 1. (415) 663–9177. Very French, very wonderful dining; cassoulet, roast chicken, fresh fish, escargots.

Inverness

Inns of Point Reyes, P.O. Box 145. (415) 485–2649. Referral service for several inns.

Point Reyes Hostel. (415) 663–8811. Off Limantour Road, 6 miles from Bear Valley Road in the National Seashore.

Blackthorne Inn, 266 Vallejo. (415) 663–8621. Five charming rooms.

Dancing Coyote Beach B and B, P.O. Box 98. (415) 669–7200. Four Southwest-style cottages, decks, views, fireplaces, kitchens.

Golden Hind Inn, 12938 Sir Francis Drake Boulevard. (415) 669–1389. Bay view and poolside rooms, some fireplaces, kitchens, fishing pier, restaurant, bar; reasonable.

Olema

Olema Ranch Campground, .25 mile north of Highway 1 and Sir Francis Drake Boulevard. (415) 663–8001. RV facilities, tent sites, gas, store.

San Anselmo

Bed and Breakfast Exchange of Marin, 45 Entrata. (415) 485–1971.

For More Information

Marin County Chamber of Commerce, 30 North San Pedro Road, San Rafael, CA 94903. (415) 472–7470.

Audubon Canyon Ranch. (415) 383–1644. A private, nonprofit research organization that owns Olema Marsh and other nature preserves.

South Coast Marin

There's always time for a relaxing stroll on the beach.

Stinson Beach, Bolinas, Olema

——————————— 1 NIGHT ———————————
Sandy beaches · Hiking trails · Seafood cafes · Wildlife preserves

It's a short drive to the 3-mile-long sandy shores of Stinson Beach, often warm and sunny when the Bay Area is fogged in. Nearby is the quiet village of Bolinas, at the southern end of the Point Reyes National Seashore trail system. Extensive lagoons and wetlands in the area support hundreds of species of sea- and shorebirds and ducks. Beachcombing, nature hikes, cafe sitting, and photo snapping are your main activities on this overnight escape.

Day 1

Morning

Drive north from the Golden Gate on Highway 101, turning west at the Stinson Beach/Highway 1 exit just south of Sausalito. You'll connect with Panoramic Highway, a winding two-lane road over **Mount Tamalpais,** the "Sleeping Maiden" whose 2,600-foot profile dominates western Marin County. Weekends only, have breakfast on the top of the world at **Mountain Home Inn,** 810 Panoramic Highway (415–381–9000). The road drops steeply from here, through oak and evergreen forests, down to the tiny burg of **Stinson Beach**, headquarters for daytripping and vacationing at the beach on **Bolinas Bay** in the **Golden Gate National Recreation Area** (415–868–0942). One of the state's first home subdivisions founded the summer-vacation colony in 1906, the year of the big one in San Francisco.

Lunch: **Stinson Beach Grill,** 1 block from the beach on Highway 1. (415) 868–2002. Fresh seafood, pasta, Southwest cuisine; fifty varieties of beer. Dine indoors or on the sunny deck; breakfast, lunch, and dinner.

Afternoon

The waters off Stinson are surprisingly warm in the winter, due to a unique rising to the surface of the tropical undercurrent. In a protected mini-banana belt, the beach and the town enjoy a Mediterranean climate all year. Resting in eucalyptus and Monterey pines, thousands of monarch butterflies like the winters here, too. Surfboards, boogieboards, and wetsuits can be rented, and bathing suits purchased, at **Live Water Surf Shop,** 3450 Highway 1 (415–868–0333). If nude sunbathing is your choice, **Red Rock** beach is the place to go (1 mile south of Stinson Beach, watch for a parking area off the highway below reddish cliffs, access by steep trail).

Among the galleries and shops is **Claudia Chapline Gallery,** at 3445 Highway 1 (415–868–2308), showing a wide variety of locally produced fine art. **Stinson Beach Books,** 3455 Highway 1 (415–868–0700), has regional guidebooks, maps, and best-sellers for beach bums.

Dinner: **The Sand Dollar,** Highway 1 at Stinson Beach. (415)

868–0434. People come all the way out here just for dinner; small, friendly, crowded; superb fresh seafood and more; bar.

Drive north on Highway 1 for 5 miles to Bolinas. At the north end of the lagoon, watch for a left turn—there will be no sign—onto Olema/Bolinas Road, skirting the west side of the lagoon. Wharf Road is the main street of town.

Lodging: **Thomas' White House Inn,** 118 Kale Road, Bolinas 94924. (415) 868–0279. Be sure to call for directions. Bed-and-breakfast accommodations in a New England-style clapboard house; wonderful sea views from rooms and garden.

Day 2

Morning

Breakfast: Bountiful continental breakfast at Thomas' White House Inn and/or unforgettable organic-ingredient pastries, breads, pies, and espresso at **Bolinas Bay Bakery and Cafe,** 20 Wharf Road, Bolinas (415–868–0211).

Lost in the 1960s, Bolinas is a quiet country village inhabited by artists, craftspersons, and weekenders. Some nineteenth-century buildings remain from a summer colony in the 1800s.

Bolinas Lagoon is 1,200 acres of saltmarsh, mudflats, and calm seawaters harboring myriad wildlife. Great blue herons and egrets, migrating geese and ducks—as many as 35,000 birds have been spotted in a single day. Harbor seals hang out at the mouth of the lagoon.

On Bolinas's shoreline is **Duxbury Reef,** 1 mile of shallow tidepools exposed at low tide. At the north end of the reef is **Agate Beach,** a small county park.

Drive 4 miles northwest from Bolinas on Mesa Road to the **Point Reyes Bird Observatory** and field station (415–868–1221) to see research projects, a small museum, and a short self-guided nature trail. There's a lot going on here, and you're welcome to take a look.

One mile farther on Mesa Road is **Palomarin Trailhead,** at the southern end of Point Reyes National Seashore; this trail leads to four freshwater lakes that are waterfowl habitats, as well as to the small **Double Point** bay, where harbor seals breed and tidepools are inviting to look into; you're not allowed to touch. Three miles from the trailhead, watch for **Bass Lake,** a secret swimming spot.

Lunch: The **Olema Farm House Restaurant,** Highway 1 at Sir Francis Drake Boulevard, Olema. (415) 663–1264. Fifteen minutes north of Bolinas on Highway 1. Seafood, steak, pasta, espresso—indoors or out.

Afternoon

Headquarters for hikers, horseback riders, and campers heading for Point Reyes National Seashore, Olema has a few structures remaining from the mid-1800s. Nearby forty-acre **Olema Marsh** (415–868–9244), a birdwatchers' mecca, is privately owned but can be enjoyed from the side of the road.

Head back south on Highway 1 and stop, just south of the Bolinas exit, for a visit at **Audubon Canyon Ranch** (415–868–9244), an educational and research center open to the public from March through July on weekends and holidays. In the tops of redwoods and pines in deep, wooded canyons, herons and egrets make their nests, and hundreds of thousands of monarch butterflies spend the winter here in a grove of eucalyptus trees. A short trail leads to fixed telescopes for nest-watching; you can also walk on two nature trails.

Retrace your route back to the Golden Gate Bridge, or drive back on Highway 1 (see below).

There's More

Muir Beach: An alternate route to or from Stinson is on Highway 1 around the base of Mount Tamalpais, a supercurvy, spectacular seacoast road providing access to Muir Beach and, on the slopes of the mountain, Muir Woods National Monument (415–388–2595). Located at Redwood Creek lagoon, a spawning stream lined with maples and alders, the often windy beach is long and sandy with tidepools; a World War II gun emplacement, the Muir Beach Overlook is now a county park. Muir Woods, 3 miles north of Highway 1 on Muir Woods Road, is the only remaining old-growth redwood forest near San Francisco.

Other Recommended Restaurants and Lodgings

Bed and Breakfast Exchange of Marin. (415) 485–1971.

Muir Beach

Pelican Inn, several miles south of Stinson Beach on Highway 1. (415) 383–6000. Re-creation of a sixteenth-century English country inn; small, comfy rooms; full breakfast.

Bolinas

Blue Heron Inn and Restaurant, 11 Wharf Road. (415) 868–1102. Lunch, dinner; simple lodgings.

155 Pine, P.O. Box 62. (415) 868–0263. A private cottage overlooking the ocean; short walk to the beach.

For More Information

Marin County Chamber of Commerce, 30 North San Pedro Road, San Rafael, CA 94903. (415) 472–7470.

Southbound Escapes

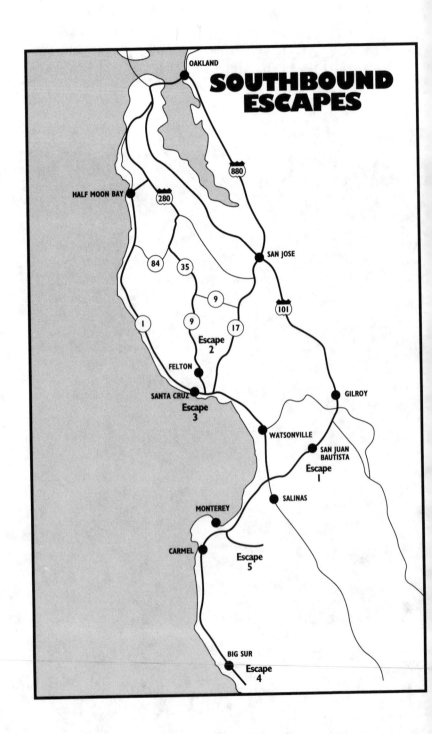

SOUTHBOUND ESCAPES

OAKLAND

880

HALF MOON BAY

280

84

35

SAN JOSE

9

101

1

9

17

Escape 2

FELTON

SANTA CRUZ

Escape 3

GILROY

WATSONVILLE

SAN JUAN BAUTISTA

Escape 1

SALINAS

MONTEREY

CARMEL

Escape 5

BIG SUR

Escape 4

Old California, the Central Valley

The Mission San Juan Bautista, the largest of all California mission churches.

San Juan Bautista and the Pinnacles

_____ 1 NIGHT _____

Mission town · Antiques · Nature trails, rocky climbs
Mexican food · Garlic galore · Salinas Valley

Between the tawny Gabilan Mountains on the east and the coastal range of the Santa Lucias on the west, vegetable fields surround a handful of small farming towns in the Salinas Valley. The Salinas River curls and twists around the valley, finally relaxing into Monterey Bay. Meadows and foothills are carpeted with lupines and poppies in the spring, turning to knee-high yellow mustard, then to golden grasses all summer.

Here John Steinbeck lived and wrote of the struggles and romances of early farm families. Father Junípero Serra founded his largest mission, around which grew a town that's not much changed in a hundred years. Thrusting dramatically up in rocky spires, Pinnacles National Monument goes lush and green when winter rains reinvigorate the waterfalls and rushing streams.

Day 1

Morning

From the Oakland Bay Bridge, drive south on Highway 880 to Highway 101, for about ninety minutes, to Gilroy, edging out of the smog into the oak-studded, rolling hills of San Benito County. Wisping in over the coast range, morning fogs cool the dusty summer heat of the valley.

The scent of fresh garlic announces **Gilroy,** home of the **Gilroy Garlic Festival,** attended by 150,000 lovers of the stinking rose. About 10 miles south of the Highway 152 junction, watch for a huge red barn on your left. On weekends here there's a big fleamarket and farmer's market, a barbecue, and an antiques fair.

Take the Highway 156 exit to **San Juan Bautista,** often called San Juan, a Spanish village since the late 1700s, in the arms of the Gabilan Range. Park at the first available space; you'll walk everywhere in this tiny town. Go to the grassy plaza on the north side of town and start at the heart and soul of San Juan, the magnificent **Mission San Juan Bautista,** at Second and Mariposa streets (408–623–2127). Founded in 1787, it's the largest of all California mission churches, with three aisles and a glorious 40-foot-high ceiling of grayed beams in traditional viga-latilla formation. Light floods the cathedral, making vibrant the rust-and-blue painted decoration, most of it created in 1816 by a Boston sailor who worked at the mission in exchange for room and board. It's OK to stand at the back, near the giant entry doors, before and during the masses, when local families mingle and chat, little girls flit about in their ruffled best dresses, and their brothers jet up and down the aisles. The soft singing voices of the congregation float out the open door into the sunshine of the plaza.

Many original statues, paintings, and carvings remain. The carving of St. John the Baptist behind the main altar was brought from Mexico in 1809, a superior example of the style. Surrounding the cathedral are a series of rooms, once living quarters for the padres, housing a museum of early Indian, Spanish Colonial, and Victorian artifacts, including one of the best collections of Mission furniture in the world. You'll see a small kitchen with iron pots in an open firpelace, from which 1,200 people were fed three times a day.

The mission gardens are dense with old cacti, aromatic lavender, and climbing roses. Behind the church under ancient olive trees, 4,300 Indians and early pioneers are buried. The cemetery and the plaza overlook vast, flat fields and the **San Andreas earthquake fault,** here at the south end of the Santa Cruz Mountains. A seismograph sits in a glass box, recording every tremor.

Lunch: **Jardines de San Juan,** 115 Third Street. (408) 623–4466. A Mexican restaurant with a big, popular garden patio. Guitarists strum, breezes ruffle the fig and maple trees, people-watching is excellent; it's tempting to stay for a second margarita. Lunches and dinners are served at umbrella tables or indoors in art-filled dining rooms.

Afternoon

The plaza is circled by historic buildings open to inspection. The **Plaza Stable,** a barn museum of horse-drawn carriages and wagons, dispatched coaches for seven stage lines in the 1860s. San Juan was on a main route between San Francisco and Los Angeles, with silver and gold miners trading, resupplying, and traveling through town; as many as eleven coaches a day arrived, with about seventeen passengers each.

Restored and completely furnished, the **Plaza Hotel** was the first place the dusty travelers headed, to get a beer or something stronger in the bar and to book a room for the night. The owner of the hotel, Angelo Zanetta, built himself a magnificent dwelling on the plaza; the structure now houses an outstanding collection of early California furnishings and personal items—the **Zanetta House.**

The red-tile-roofed **Castro House** was owned by a family from the Donner party who struck it rich in the Gold Rush; behind the house is a 150-year-old pepper tree shading lovely gardens. Fat-trunked pepper trees, mimosa, and black walnuts shade the few streets constituting the village; lushly overgrown old-fashioned gardens romp and ramble around the buildings.

Twelve antiques stores await discovery, plus small shops of every description, delightfully untrendy. At the **San Juan Crate and Packing Company,** 404 Third Street (408–623–4159), are regional gourmet food products, garlic braids, and wreaths; the establishment will pack and mail for you. **Buchser Farms,** 318 Third Street (408–623–4430), sells wine and antiques, a great combination. **Tops,** 5 Second Street (408–623–4441), offers semiprecious stones and rare rocks in a museumlike store. And **Kushi Weaving Mission Gallery,** 35 Muckelemi Street (408–623–2051), is a source of miraculous woven clothing and gifts. When you can't walk another step or browse another shop, have an icy margarita or an iced tea and some guacamole in anticipation of dinner at Felipe's.

Dinner: **Felipe's Restaurant and Bar,** 313 Third Street. (408) 623–2161. Where the locals go for the best Mexican and Salvadorean food in town; live music on weekends.

Lodging: **Country Rose Bed and Breakfast Inn,** 455 Fitzgerald Avenue, 95046. (408) 842–0441. Drive ten minutes north on Highway 101 to San Martin, taking the Masten exit west to three mailboxes, turning right to reach the inn. Beneath gigantic spreading oaks, Rose's place is a shady 5-acre oasis in the middle of vegetable fields, a stone's throw from the western side of the Santa Cruz Range. Five quiet, private, spacious rooms with baths, some fireplaces; the largest is a suite with Jacuzzi tub and steam shower.

Day 2

Morning

Take a morning walk on nearby country lanes; explore the five-acre farmyard.

Breakfast: In the garden terrace dining room, with a merry blaze in the fireplace when it's cool, Rose serves you Dutch apple pancakes, fresh local fruits, and stories of her celebrity guests. If you stayed overnight in San Juan, the best place in town for breakfast is **Donkey Deli,** 322 Third Street (408–623–4521), serving cappuccino and homemade Danish on the garden patio. (*Sidetrip:* From Rose's, it's just a half-hour over a beautiful mountain road, Highway 152, to the Monterey coast.)

It's an hour's drive from Rose's—through Hollister on Highway 25—to **Pinnacles National Monument,** Paicines (408–389–4485). Spires and crags rising dramatically out of the valley are what's left of an ancient volcano; the other half of the volcano lies 195 miles to the southeast, thanks to the San Andreas Rift Zone. All through the winter and spring, and in the fall after the rains have come, the 1,600-acre wilderness park attracts rock climbers, hikers, cave explorers, and picnickers. Short, easy paths make ferny creeks and mountain views accessible. At the visitor's center, a jewel of a stone building constructed in the 1930s by the Civilian Conservation Corps, pick up trail maps and chat with the rangers. They'll head you toward the Bear Gulch waterfalls, a swimming hole, and a short trail to spooky caves. Midsummer can be extremely hot and dry, with temperatures in the hundreds. A nice private campground at the entrance to the park has a swimming pool: **Pinnacles Campground** (408–389–4462).

Lunch: **La Casa Rosa,** 107 Third Street, San Juan Bautista. (408) 623–4563. A taste of old Spanish days in San Juan; hearty American food in an antiques-filled, pink clapboard house built in 1858. Try the Old California Casserole and the chicken soufflé. Famous treats to take home—chutney, preserves, pickles.

Don't leave town without a loaf of Portuguese bread, panetone, brownies, and a pie from **San Juan Bakery,** 319 Third Street (408–623–4570).

Afternoon

Head back to the Bay Area, stopping along the way to buy wine at **Mirassou Winery,** 3000 Aborn Road, San Jose (408–274–4000), owned by America's oldest winemaking family. Dozens of wineries are located in the Salinas, Gonzales, and Soledad areas. A directory and map of the Salinas Valley/Monterey wine country is available by calling (408) 375–9400.

There's More

Steinbeck House, 132 Central Avenue, Salinas. (408) 424–2735. The perfectly preserved, turreted Victorian where Steinbeck was born and raised, a mecca for his devotees. Unfortunately, not open to the public except for lunch Monday–Friday; small gift shop open seven days. An annual Steinbeck Day includes walking tours of the town and a special lunch at the house.

Christopher Ranch, 305 Bloomfield Avenue, Gilroy. (408) 847–1100. The ultimate source for garlic.

Golf. Ridgemark Golf and Country Club, 3800 Airline Highway, Hollister. (408) 637–8151. Golf, tennnis, lodging, restaurant.

Hollister Hills State Vehicular Recreation Area, 7800 Cienega Road, Hollister 95023. (408) 637–3874. Some 2,400 acres and campground for motorcycles and four-wheel drive vehicles.

Special Events

May. American Indian Spring Market, San Juan Bautista. (408) 623–2379.

July. Gilroy Garlic Festival, Gilroy. (408) 842–1625. Huge food fair featuring garlic dishes, entertainment, arts and crafts, even garlic ice cream.

July. California Rodeo, Salinas. (408) 757–2951. America's best cowboys and cowgirls compete.

August. Downtown Micro Brewery and Antique Collectibles Festival, Salinas. (408) 842–6964.

August. Hispanic Cultural Festival, San Juan Bautista. (408) 848–5780.

September. All-Indian Market, San Juan Bautista. (408) 623–2379.

September. Fine Arts and Crafts Show, San Juan Bautista. (408) 623–2454. Some 300 artisans and crafters.

September. Casa DeFruta Wine Festival, Hollister. (408) 842–9316.

December. Candlelight processions, La Posada, San Juan Bautista. (408) 623-2454.

Other Recommended Restaurants and Lodgings

Salinas

Crayons, 172 Main Street. (408) 759–9355. Trendy bistro cafe and bar; lunch, dinner, Sunday brunch.

San Juan Bautista

Mission Farm RV Park, 400 San Juan-Hollister Road on the southeast corner of town, 95045. (408) 623–4456. Old barns, a store, all facilities, simple surroundings in a walnut orchard.

San Juan Inn, 410 Alameda Street. (408) 623–4380. A forty-two-unit motel.

For More Information

San Juan Bautista Chamber of Commerce, 402A Third Street, P.O. Box 1037, San Juan Bautista, CA 95045. (408) 623-2454.

Advice: Midsummer temperatures in San Juan can reach a hundred degrees or more, so bring a hat. Evenings are cool, as sea breezes rise and fog creeps in from the coast.

Santa Cruz Mountains

The fabulous narrow-gauge railroad at Roaring Camp and Big Trees.

Redwoods, Wineries, Salty Air

_____ 1 NIGHT _____

Redwoods, rivers • Country wineries • Cabin in the mountains
Beaches • A train ride • Shopping for antiques and veggies

The Santa Cruz Mountains are an hour away and a world away from
the metropolitan Bay Area. Ancient redwood groves, sunny riverbanks, and quiet little resort towns afford peaceful getaway days. Discover rustic boutique wineries, known for their dark Pinots and

German varietals. Take a ride on a rollicking steamtrain, chugging up into redwood country or all the way down to the beach.

Cruising the mountain roads of Santa Cruz County can turn up dusty antiques shops, wildflowery meadows, and cowboy cafes. If there's a lane that doesn't show on the map, take it. And don't forget your corkscrew.

Day 1

Morning

From San Francisco drive south on Highway 280, taking Highway 84 west, connecting with Highway 35 south to Highway 9 south, around **Castle Rock State Park** (408–867–2952) to Boulder Creek.

Breakfast: **Country Harvest Bakery,** Brandy Station Building, Boulder Creek. (408) 338–4157. Good old-fashioned breakfasts on the town's main street.

One of California's gold-medal makers of Pinot Noir and Chardonnay, **David Bruce Winery** (408–354–4214), is on Bear Creek Road east of Boulder Creek; it's open for tasting on the weekends and by appointment during the week. (Calling ahead for touring and tasting appointments is well worth the effort. Proprietors of small wineries sometimes ask for this advance notice, not for exclusivity but to reserve plenty of time to spend with you.) **Byington Winery and Vineyard** (408–354–1111) is on Bear Creek, too; it offers dizzying views of Monterey Bay from the picnic grounds.

Riverside parks, beaches, and swimming holes on the San Lorenzo River are at **Boulder Creek Park,** east of Boulder Creek, on Middleton; **Ben Lomond County Park,** on Mill Street (408–336–9962); and **Highlands County Park,** in Ben Lomond (408–336–8551), with a pool and tennis courts.

Between Boulder Creek and Ben Lomond, a string of redwood burl and antiques shops may compel you to stop.

Head west toward the sea on the beautiful Felton-Empire Road, 8 miles west to **Bonny Doon Vineyard,** 10 Pine Flat Road (408–425–3625). The winemaker has made his wines famous with crazy labels like Clos de Gilroy, Le Cigare Volant, Big House Red, and Old Telegram. Hang out in the redwood grove on Soquel Creek and try his European "ice wines," produced in just a handful of American wineries, one of the unusual types of wine you'll find here.

Also on Felton-Empire Road is **Hallcrest Vineyards** (408–335–4441), specializing in organic Gewurztraminers, Rieslings, and grape juices.

Back on Highway 9 heading south, you can't miss **Brookdale**

Lodge, 11570 Highway 9 (408–338–6433), a funky summer-vacation inn built in 1900 and eccentrically expanded in the succeeding decades. A creek runs through the dining room, called the Brook Room.

Just south of Felton on Graham Hill Road is **Roaring Camp and Big Trees Narrow-Gauge Railroad** (408–335–4484), a re-creation of an 1880s logging town, complete with covered bridge, general store, and a wonderful narrow-gauge steamtrain.

Lunch: **Roaring Camp.** Chuckwagon barbecue—charcoal-broiled steak, chicken, burgers, and cider in a forest glade. Or opt for your own picnic on the mountain.

Afternoon

Take the steamtrain up through redwood forests to the summit of **Bear Mountain,** the steepest railroad grade in North America. A second route runs along the San Lorenzo River down to Santa Cruz Beach.

From Roaring Camp walk into **Henry Cowell State Park,** 101 North Big Trees Park Road, Felton (408–335–4598). Most of the trails are short and easy, such as **Redwood Grove Nature Trail** to the **Big Trees Grove,** providing a rare opportunity to see first-growth redwoods. Several trails connect for walks in 1,800 acres of stream canyons, meadows, forests, and chaparral-covered ridges along the meandering San Lorenzo River and Eagle Creek, under a railroad trestle, through the ponderosas on Pine Trail, and to an observation deck overlooking the Monterey/Santa Cruz coastlines and the Santa Cruz Mountains. Besides BIG redwoods and pines, you'll see sycamore, elders, madrone, manzanita, California poppies, dove, quail, waterfowl, deer, and maybe poison oak.

Dinner: **Tyrolean Inn,** 9600 Highway 9, Ben Lomond. (408) 336–5188. German-Austrian and American food.

Lodging: **Griffin's Fern River Resort,** 5250 Highway 9, Felton, 95018. (408) 335–4412. Nice little red housekeeping cabins, some fireplaces, on four acres of lawns, trees, and fern gardens. Private sandy river beach. Adjacent to Cowell Park and Roaring Camp.

Day 2

Morning

Breakfast: **Heavenly Cafe,** 6250 Highway 9, Felton. (408) 335–7311. Big American breakfasts; the place to see and be seen in Felton.

Head on down from the mountains to the seashore, connecting with Highway 1 at Santa Cruz, and turning south. Refresh with a walk or a sunbath on one of the many beaches on the Santa Cruz County coastline, perhaps at **Seacliff State Beach** (408–688–7146), just across the highway from Aptos, five minutes south of Santa Cruz. On Sunday afternoons you can join a guided tour to see fossilized remains of multimillion-year-old sea creatures; toothbrushes are supplied for your own archaeolgical recovery.

Take a short drive to **Devlin Wine Cellars,** at the end of a country road, 3801 Park Road off Soquel Drive just south of Soquel (408–476–7288). Devlin makes the luscious dessert wine Muscat Canelli and several other varieties; picnickers are welcome in thirty acres of redwoods.

Bargetto Winery, 3535 North Main Street, Soquel (408–475–2258), overlooking Soquel Creek, makes fruit wines and vinegars—raspberry, olallieberry, and apricot.

Lunch: **Gayle's Bakery and Rosticceria,** 504 Bay Avenue, Capitola. (408) 462–1127. Take the Soquel/Capitola exit west off Highway 1, proceeding to the corner of Bay and Capitola Avenue. Homemade pasta, salad, pizza, sandwiches, spit-roasted meats; bakery is famous for pies, cheesecake, breads, and pastries.

Afternoon

The foothill and valley area behind Aptos and Soquel is dotted with small farms producing a huge variety of fresh fruit, vegetables, and flowers. **Von's Garden,** 2701 Monterey Avenue, Soquel (408–462–4255), sells fresh and dried flowers, orchids, exotic plants, vegetables, and herbs. For five varieties of apples, pumpkins, and fall vegetables, go to **Valencia Ranch,** 2760 Valencia Road, Aptos (408–684–0400). **The Apple Barn,** 1765 Hames Road, Aptos (408–724–8119), has seventeen kinds of apples, plus fresh juice and cider.

For the two-and-a-half-hour drive back to San Francisco, head back on Highway 1 to Santa Cruz, connecting with Highway 17 north.

There's More

Big Basin Redwoods State Park. (408) 338-6132. Thousand-year-old redwoods, fern canyons, the Bay Area's most wonderful waterfalls; round-trip hike to the falls takes four to five hours; 50 miles of shorter trails. The Sea Trail drops from mountain ridges to Waddell State Beach through dense woodlands, along Waddell and Berry creeks;

waterfalls, sea and mountain views, 11 miles one-way. Bike, horse rentals.

Forest of Nisene Marks State Park, in the highlands of Soquel, Aptos Creek Road, Aptos. (408) 335–9145. Densely forested wilderness on Aptos Creek; popular with runners, bikers, horseback riders, and hikers. Picnic areas.

Public transportation. Santa Cruz County's buses. (408) 425–8600. All with bike racks, the buses stop at parks and small towns in the mountains.

Farm Trails, 141 Monte Vista Avenue, Watsonville 95076. Free map of produce farms, ranches, and shops in Santa Clara and Santa Cruz counties.

Special Events

April. Amazing Egg Hunt, Roaring Camp. (408) 335–4484. Some 10,000 eggs.

May. Art and Wine Festival, Boulder Creek. (800) 833–3494.

May. Civil War Memorial, Roaring Camp. (408) 335–4484. Reenactment of Civil War battles and camp life, the largest encampment in the United States.

June. Redwood Mountain Faire, Felton. (800) 833–3494.

July. Race through the Redwoods, Boulder Creek. (408) 335–2612.

July. Jumpin' Frog Contest, Roaring Camp. (408) 335–4484.

August. Artist's Weekend, Soquel. (800) 833–3494.

October. Roaring Camp Harvest Fair. (408) 335–4484. Beautiful 1880s crafts, demonstrations, pumpkin carving, free pumpkins.

Other Recommended Restaurants and Lodgings

Capitola

Seafood Mama, 820 Bay Avenue. (408) 476–5976. At the Crossroads Center, 1 block from Highway 1. Fresh fish and shellfish from both coasts; mesquite grill.

Boulder Creek

Boulder Creek Lodge and Conference Center, 16901 Big Basin Highway. (408) 338–2111. A few minutes west of Boulder Creek on Highway 236. Condo units, eighteen-hole golf course, tennis, swimming pools—all in a glorious green setting surrounded by redwoods.

Watsonville

Pajaro Dunes, 2661 Beach Road. (800) 7–PAJARO. Condos and homes to rent on a long sandy beach.

Santa Cruz KOA Kampground, 1186 San Andreas Road. (408) 722–0551. Has 240 tent and RV sites, cabins; pool, store, hot tubs, all facilities; lively atmosphere, near beaches.

Ben Lomond

Tyrolean Inn and Cottages, 9600 Highway 9. (408) 336–5188. Seven simple cottages, walking distance to town and river, German/American restaurant.

Santa Cruz

Babbling Brook Inn, 1025 Laurel Street. (800) 866–1131. Country French inn, lovely gardens, full breakfast; ask for the room near the creek.

Felton

Smithwoods RV Park, 4770 Highway 9 (408) 335–4321. Some 1.5 miles south of Felton; store, pool, all facilities.

For More Information

San Lorenzo Valley Chamber of Commerce, Boulder Creek, CA 95006. (408) 335–2764.

Santa Cruz Winegrowers, P.O. Box 3222, Santa Cruz, CA 95063. (408) 458–5030. Free brochure and map describing nineteen wineries.

Santa Cruz Visitor's Bureau, 701 Front Street, Santa Cruz, CA 95060. (408) 425–1234.

MISTIX. (800) 444–7275. State campground reservations.

Highway 1 to Santa Cruz

This lighthouse along West Cliff Drive houses a surfing museum.

Cruising the Coast, Beaches, and the Boardwalk

_____ 2 NIGHTS _____

Butterflies, beaches, bikes, hikes • Lions of the sea
Discoveries on the Coast Road • Shopping for art, antiques, and veggies

A real California beach town, Santa Cruz is kinda honky-tonk, kinda artsy, kinda irresistible in its seaside setting. A spanking new downtown full of shops and restaurants replaces the near-total devastation of an earthquake in 1989.

Your Highway 1 route runs alongside the coast, the landscape changing from peaceful farm country and rocky coves to small waterfront villages and wide sandy beaches.

Day 1

Morning

Drive south from San Francisco on Highway 280, then west on Highway 92 toward **Half Moon Bay,** a forty-five-minute trip (if it's Friday afternoon, triple the travel time). In a few minutes the scent of eucalyptus signals that your getaway to the coast has begun. The road passes down through a deep gorge; tree farms and commercial flower fields patchwork the meadows. Besides ocean fishing, the important endeavor in this town is flower and vegetable growing. An annual **Pumpkin Festival** in October draws hundreds of thousands of revelers and their children.

Take a right at the Highway 1 junction and drive 4 miles north to **Pillar Point Harbor,** turning right, opposite the harbor, at the stoplight. Scurry in to **Cafe Classique,** at the corner of Granada and Sevilla (415–726–9775), and kick-start your day with cappuccinos, monster muffins, and croissants. Take a walk around on the Pillar Point wharf and along the waterfront to see fishing boats and yachts. The tiny seafood cafes and bars here are popular with locals trying to avoid the touristy downtown of Half Moon Bay; on a winter's day a booth next to the wood stove at **Ketch Joanne** (415–728–3747) can be a warm experience.

Head south on Highway 1 for 15 miles to the **Pescadero State Beach** sign (415–726-6238) (if you're a runner, this is a good place to do what you do); then turn left, going 2 miles to the minitown of **Pescadero,** circa 1850, continuing for .5 mile to **Phipps Ranch** (415–879–0787). Park under the giant oak and get out your camera. Phipps Ranch is a combination produce market, farm, plant nursery, and menagerie of exotic birds and farm animals. Among the cacophony of sounds are parrots' squawks, green and orange canaries' songs, and peacocks' trumpetings. There are fancy chickens, big fat pigs, a variety of bunnies, and antique farm equipment. You can pick your own berries or buy them at the produce stand.

Back on the highway, proceed south; it's 22 miles to **Davenport,** where you'll have lunch. On the way are the 115-foot-tall **Pigeon Point Lighthouse** (415–879–0633), serving as a unique youth hostel, and a scattering of beautiful beaches, tide pools (the best ones are just north of the lighthouse), wind-bent cypresses, wildflower meadows, and fields of veggies.

Stop at **Ano Nuevo State Reserve** (415–879–0595), to see the elephant seals. A .5-mile walk through grassy dunes brings you to an unforgettable sight: dozens of two-ton animals lounging, arguing, maybe mating, cavorting in the sea, and wiggling around on the beach. December through March is the mating season, when they're particularly active; make a reservation for a tour at this time. As many as 2,500 seals spend their honeymoons here, and there is lots of other wildlife to see in the dunes and on the beaches.

Lunch: Arrive starved at the wonderfully weathered **New Davenport Cash Store Restaurant and Inn,** on Highway 1 at Davenport. (408) 425–1818. Tuck into grilled chicken sandwiches, homemade soup, omelets with homemade chorizo, big killer brownies, and fresh fruit from nearby farms. The gift shop sells guidebooks, jewelry, and a surprising array of African trinkets and crafts. Upstairs is a casually comfy bed-and-breakfast operation. If art glass is one of your interests, don't miss the **Lundborg Studios** (408–423–2532) (down the road a block or so—ask for directions), a mecca for aficionados of Tiffany-style lamps and art deco paperweights.

Afternoon

A few miles farther on the highway, **Pescadero Marsh,** at Pescadero Road on the east side of the road (415–726–6238), is 588 acres of uplands and wetlands, an important stop on the Pacific Flyway. More than 200 species of waterfowl and shorebirds make this a must-stop for avid birders, or for anyone wishing to walk or hike the wilderness trails.

Two miles north of Santa Cruz, **Wilder Ranch State Park,** 1401 Coast Road, Santa Cruz (408–423–9703), has been a 5,000-acre working ranch since the 1800s. Stroll in and out of the old barns, homes, and gardens.

Turn into the **Natural Bridges State Beach** (408–688–3241), bear to the right, and park in the lot. There is a short boardwalk leading through a eucalyptus forest to the **California Monarch Butterfly Preserve.** Depending on the time of year—early October through March is best—you'll see hundreds of thousands of butterflies hanging in the trees and moving about in great golden clouds.

Cliff Drive starts here at Natural Bridges and winds above the ocean right into and through Santa Cruz; walkers, bikers, joggers, and passengers in baby strollers love it. Stop at the **Mark Abbott Memorial Lighthouse** (408–429–3429) for views of the city, sea, and sea lions. Almost every day there are surfers in "Steamers Lane" below. Go into the lighthouse to see a small surfing museum, the only one in the world.

Almost completely flattened by an earthquake in October 1989, downtown Santa Cruz is now risen from the splinters and piles of brick into 29 blocks of boutiques, coffeehouses, and galleries—more than 200 stores in all. A few: **Bookshop Santa Cruz,** at the new three-story St. George Hotel building at Pacific and Front (408–423–0900), is one of the largest bookstores in Northern California; the **Santa Cruz Art League,** 526 Broadway (408–426–5787), has three galleries and a shop selling fine arts and crafts; **Santa Cruz Brewing Company,** 516 Front Street (408–429–8838), offers a microbrewery with touring and tasting of porter, lager, root beer, and seasonal brews.

Dinner: **Indian Joze,** 1001 Center Street, Santa Cruz. (408) 427–3554. Indoor/outdoor cafe in leafy surroundings. Middle Eastern, Mediterranean, and Asian specialties of the day might include calamari saté, red snapper in curry, and pecan pie. Decor is bright and light, with squid mobiles and folk art.

Lodging: **Château Victorian,** 118 First Street, Santa Cruz 95060. (408) 458–9458. Hidden away on a sidestreet, just ½ block from the beach and boardwalk, a hundred-year-old passionate purple Victorian featuring a sunny garden and seven rooms with fireplaces. Interiors are opulently of the era, the big continental breakfast is satisfying, and proprietors Franz and Alice-June are charmers (be sure to ask them how they met). Over late afternoon wine and hors d'oeuvres, Alice-June will fill you in on sights and restaurants.

Day 2

Morning

Breakfast: In the dining room or on the deck at Château Victorian. Platters of fruit, croissants, muffins, homemade goodies.

After your early-morning walk on 1-mile-long **Santa Cruz Beach,** get to the **Santa Cruz Beach Boardwalk** (408–423–5590) before everybody else does. It's a kick to see the color and excitement of the West Coast's last remaining boardwalk amusement center. Try the Buccaneer Bay miniature golf course: volcanoes erupt, pirates threaten, cannons fire. If you hear screaming, it's probably coming from the $5 million roller coaster, the Hurricane, guaranteed to make you forget your name. A 1911 carousel and the Giant Dipper coaster are National Historic Landmarks. Get rid of your spare cash in the Casino Arcade or just sit on the boardwalk and watch the bikinis and the sailboats glide by.

The **Santa Cruz Municipal Wharf** (408–429–3628) is all about fishing off the pier, shopping in tourist traps, browsing the fresh-fish markets, eating chowder and shrimp cocktail in waterside cafes, and watching the sea lions, pelicans, and passing boats. Deep-sea fishing trips and bay cruises start from here.

Lunch: **Beach Street Cafe,** on the corner of Beach and Cliff streets. (408) 426–7621. The walls are literally covered with prints by Maxwell Parrish, a famous pre–art deco artist. Bistro food, espresso.

Afternoon

Drive along Cliff Drive to **Capitola Village,** 4 miles south. An oceanside resort since 1861, Capitola Village remains a quaint art colony, one-tenth the size of and less commercial than Santa Cruz. Swimmers, waders, and sunbathers can enjoy **Capitola Beach,** sheltered by two high cliffs, and **Soquel Creek,** rushing right through town into the sea. Restaurants with outdoor patios are lined up at beachfront on **The Esplanade,** and there are a few blocks of boutiques, art galleries, and beachwear shops. Highlights include the **Chocolate Bar,** 205 Capitola Avenue (408–476–1396), selling fresh, hand-dipped treats; **Draginwood,** 216 Capitola Avenue (408–475–0915), featuring crystals and magical gifts; **Capitola Dreams,** 118 Stockton Avenue (408–476–5379), selling bikinis and wild beachwear; and at **Oceania,** 204 Capitola Avenue (408–476–6644), offering painted wood gewgaws from Thailand. For a hundred stores in an indoor mall, go up the hill to the Capitola Mall, on Forty-first Avenue (408–476–9749).

Join in a volleyball game on the beach, or walk south toward **New Brighton Beach** (408–475–4850) to take a look at the fossilized remains of million-year-old sea creatures found on the cliffsides. From here you can walk at least 15 miles of sandy beach, all the way to the Pajaro River.

Dinner: **Antoine's,** 200 Monterey Avenue, Capitola. (408) 479–1974. Cajun and French food, gumbo, oysters, jambalaya, good wine list; upstairs overlooking the village.

After dinner, amble over to **Balzac Bistro,** 112 Capitola Avenue, Capitola (408–476–5035), for a cappuccino or to **Zelda's,** at 203 Esplanade (408–475–4900), for live jazz.

Lodging: **Capitola Inn,** 822 Bay Avenue, Capitola 95010. (408) 462–3004. Convenient, with a pool, some kitchens and fireplaces, free beach shuttle.

Day 3

Morning

Breakfast: **Zelda's** (see above) on the esplanade; home-fry scramble, blackened snapper with eggs. Sit by the window or on the deck while the early-morning sea turns from rosy to silver-blue as it laps Capitola's scruffy old fishing pier. Capitola Beach and most public beaches in the area are cleaned nightly; even in the summer they start out trash-free and pearly white every day.

On the north side of Highway 1 just south of Capitola lies the village of Aptos, where you'll find **Aptos Antiques,** behind the Bay View Hotel on Soquel Road (408–662–2421); this is an antiques collective in a huge old barn, fun to get lost in.

Lunch: **The Veranda at the Bay View Hotel,** 8041 Soquel Drive, Aptos. (408) 685–1881. California cuisine, corn fritters with Smithfield ham, shiitake mushroom ravioli, Southwest caesar salad, roast pork and chicken, fresh fish.

Afternoon

Stop at **Antonelli Brothers Begonia Gardens,** 2545 Capitola Road between Capitola and Santa Cruz (408–475–5222). This is a showplace of more begonias than you can imagine, at their blooming best in late summer and fall—hanging begonias, ferns, and indoor plants of all kinds. There are picnic tables in the Hanging Begonia Room.

Before heading back to the Bay Area, pick up some Santa Cruz County wine to take home. From Highway 1 take the Front Street/Downtown exit; go left on River Street and left on Potrero to **Storr's Winery** tasting and sales, at the Old Sash Mill, 303 Potrero Street (408–458–5030).

There's More

Bach Dancing and Dynamite Society, P.O. Box 302, El Granada, CA 94018. (415) 726–4143. At Miramar Beach, 2.5 miles north of Half Moon Bay. Begun in a private home years ago, Sunday-afternoon jam sessions evolved into big-name jazz and classical concerts, with catered lunches and dinners. These long, lazy, musical afternoons by the sea, across from the very strollable Miramar Beach, are popular; purchase tickets in advance.

Butano Park Redwoods. (415) 879–0173. Take Pescadero Road 2 miles past Pescadero, turn right on Cloverdale Road; 5 miles to park entrance. An 11-mile loop over wilderness trails; short, steep hike to Ano Nuevo Island lookout.

Long Marine Laboratory and Aquarium, near Natural Bridges State Park. (408) 459–2883. A university research facility open to the public.

Biking. Santa Cruz County Cycling Club. (408) 423–0829. Daytrips, map of area bikeways.

Surf City Cycles, 1211 Mission Street, Santa Cruz. (408) 426–7222. Rentals.

Dutchman Bicycles, 3961 Portola Drive at Forty-first, Santa Cruz. (408) 476–9555. Rentals.

Golf. Aptos Seascape Golf Course, 610 Clubhouse Drive, Aptos. (408) 688–3213. Eighteen holes.

DeLaveaga Golf Course, Upper Park Road at DeLaveaga Drive, Santa Cruz. (408) 423–7212. Eighteen holes.

Tennis. Cabrillo College, Aptos. Twelve courts.

Harbor High School, Santa Cruz. Six courts.

Jade Street Park, Capitola. Four courts.

Santa Cruz High School. Five courts.

Boating. Chardonnay Sailing Charters, Santa Cruz. (408) 423–1213.

Pacific Yachting, Santa Cruz. (408) 476–2370. Day tours.

Santa Cruz Marine. (408) 475–4600. Rentals.

Fishing. Shamrock Charters, Santa Cruz. (408) 476–2648. Deep-sea.

Surfing. Club Ed, Santa Cruz. (408) 462–6083. Rentals.

Special Events

June. Strawberry Festival, Watsonville. (408) 663–4166.

July–August. Shakespeare Festival, Santa Cruz. (408) 425–1234.

August. Cabrillo Music Festival, Santa Cruz. (408) 662–2701.

August. Calamari Festival, India Joze Restaurant, Santa Cruz. (408) 427–3554.

September. National Begonia Festival, Capitola. (408) 476–3566. Waterborne floats in the Santa Cruz River.

October. Pumpkin and Art Festival, Half Moon Bay. (415) 726–5202. Great Pumpkin Parade; contests—carving, pie-eating, biggest pumpkin; entertainment. The town is mobbed.

October. Brussels Sprout and Italian Heritage Festival, Santa Cruz. (408) 423–5590.

November. Christmas Craft and Gift Festival, Santa Cruz. (408) 423–5590.

Other Recommended Restaurants and Lodgings

El Granada

Harbor View Inn, P.O. Box 127, Coast Highway 1. (415) 726–2329.

A contemporary Cape Cod–style motel, large rooms with bay windows, just across the road from Pillar Point Wharf.

Half Moon Bay

San Benito House, 356 Main Street. (415) 726–3425. English-gardeny bed-and-breakfast inn; famous restaurant serving eclectic nouvelle cuisine.

Cypress Inn, 407 Mirada Road. (415) 726–6002. On 5 miles of beach, luxury rooms and suites, sumptuous breakfasts.

Capitola

Capitola Venetian Hotel, 1500 Wharf Road. (408) 476–6471. Right on the beach; a 1920s Mediterranean pink stucco apartment complex; reasonable rates, for families or groups; unassuming eclectic/eccentric decor; kitchens.

Inn at Depot Hill, 250 Monterey Avenue. (408) 462–3376. Eight luxurious rooms with fireplaces, hot tubs, private gardens, breakfast.

Shadowbrook, 1750 Wharf Road. (408) 475–1511. On the banks of Soquel Creek, reached by self-operated cable car down a flower-bedecked hillside or by a winding pathway. Romantic; fresh fish; live music. Reservations essential.

Seafood Mama's, 820 Bay Avenue, upstairs at the Crossroads Center. (408) 476–5976. Call to find out what's fresh.

Miramar

Miramar Restaurant and Bar, 131 Mirada Road. (415) 726–9053. About 2.5 miles north of Half Moon Bay. Lunch, dinner, and weekend brunch at Miramar Beach; live music; seafood.

Pescadero

Duarte's Tavern, 202 Stage Road. (415) 879–0464. Cioppino; seafood specialties with a Portuguese accent.

Santa Cruz

Casablanca, 101 Main Street. (408) 426–9063. Overlooking beach and boardwalk; elegant, candlelit; fresh seafood, notable wine list, winetasting dinners.

For More Information

MISTIX. (800) 444–7275. State campground reservations, Ano Nuevo tour reservations.

Half Moon Bay Coastside Chamber of Commerce, P.O. Box 188, Half Moon Bay, CA 94019. (415) 726–5202.

Harvest Trails, 765 Main Street, Half Moon Bay, CA 94019. Map of where to buy and pick local produce.

Santa Cruz Visitor's Bureau, 701 Front Street, Santa Cruz, CA 95060. (408) 425–1234.

Capitola Chamber of Commerce, 621B Capitola Avenue, Capitola, CA 95010. (408) 475–6522.

Monterey and Big Sur

A serene scene along the Monterey Peninsula.

Spanish History, Wild Coastline

_____ 2 NIGHTS _____

Museums, mansions, mountains · Beachcombing · A golfer's dream
Shopping, biking, hiking · Chowder and cioppino
_____

Arriving on the Monterey Peninsula in the mid-1500s, Spanish explorers saw dark cypress trees, like sentries along a rocky shoreline. Rivers and streams rushed down from a rugged mountain range. Otters, seals, and whales played in the bays. In the late 1700s the Spanish returned in force to stay for a century or so, using Monterey as headquarters for their huge Baja and Alta California domains, and Father Junípero Serra built one of his largest and most beautiful missions. Then Mexico took a turn as occupier of Monterey for more than 20 years.

This rich Hispanic heritage remains in the thick-walled adobes and Spanish Colonial haciendas of Monterey and in the gnarled old olive trees and courtyard gardens planted by the early conquistadores.

In stark contrast to the historic neighborhoods and sophisticated atmosphere of today's Monterey, Big Sur is a sparsely developed stretch of wilderness running 90 miles south to San Simeon, a series of cliffs and river valleys hemmed in by a high mountain range on one side and a largely inaccessible, spectacular seacoast on the other. A long-time resident of Big Sur, author Henry Miller, said of the area, "It is a region where extremes meet, a region where one is always conscious of weather, of space, of grandeur, and of eloquent silence."

Indeed, the weather, the sky, and the sea are constantly changing in Big Sur, from clear, bright winter days to summertime's fog rolling in through the dark redwood groves. You might see a hawk, an eagle, or an osprey circling. Owls hoot at night, coyotes howl, and mountain lions moan on the far ridges. The sea boils hundreds of feet below, stretches lazily out on a rocky beach, and swells beyond the breakers to dark kelp beds where sea creatures hide.

Day 1

Morning

From the Oakland Bay Bridge, take Highway 880 south to Highway 17, connecting with Highway 1 at Santa Cruz, heading south to Monterey; it's about two hours from the Oakland Bay Bridge to Monterey. Park downtown at one of the parking garages—you'll want to walk everywhere or take public transportation; "The Wave" shuttlebus stops at several parking garages. At the **Monterey Peninsula Visitor's and Convention Bureau,** 380 Alvarado Street (408–648–5354), pick up a walking-tour map of Old Monterey. Just up the block, **Bay Books,** 316 Alvarado (408–375–1855), has cappuccinos and croissants to get you started.

Walk 3 blocks south on Alvarado, turn right on Jefferson to Pacific, and spend a couple of hours strolling in and out of the historic buildings and garden courtyards on the "Path of History." Dominating the grassy knolls of **Friendly Plaza** is **Colton Hall,** at Pacific and Jefferson, a museum in an old school. Notice the small plastered-adobe homes in back of Colton Hall, some of the first built in California.

Part of the Monterey State Historic Park complex, **Cooper Store,** on Polk Street (408–649–2836), sells antique toys, postcards, and souvenirs. Go through the store to the museums and gardens behind; a spectacular cypress towers overhead. In the heart of the Historic District is the **Monterey Peninsula Museum of Art,** 559 Pacific Street (408–372–7591), with a fine collection of Western and Asian art and photography.

Lunch: **Abalonetti's,** 57 Fisherman's Wharf, Monterey. (408) 373–1851. Sit indoors or on the wharf; calamari, Italian antipasto, pizza, seafood pasta; for forty years one of the best fish cafes on the wharf. *Look* at the dessert tray.

Afternoon

Somehow avoiding the architectural upgrade and commercial development that destroyed an "Old Town" ambience once found on Cannery Row, **Fisherman's Wharf** still smells of salt spray and carmel corn. Fishing boats bob in the harbor, seagulls squawk and wheel overhead, and salty breezes blow between slightly seedy boardwalk cafes and tourist-trap shops.

Walk along the waterfront **Monterey Peninsula Recreational Trail** that runs from the wharf all the way along Cannery Row and around Pacific Grove, a distance of 5 miles, if you care to walk that far. It's fun to dodge brown pelicans and watch sea lions barking to get your attention. You can even rent a pedaling vehicle, powered by two adults in back, with room for two little kids in front.

Take the Wave back to your garage and drive to your lodgings at the Old Monterey Inn, reviving with a glass of wine and some cheese in the magnificent living room or the gardens. You'll get lots of restaurant recommendations, some within walking distance.

Dinner: **Fishwife,** 1996 Sunset Drive, Pacific Grove. (408) 375–7107. Casual, popular, reasonably priced cafe at Asilomar beach. Wide variety of fresh fish, Cajun blackened snapper, Salmon Alfredo, key lime pie; reservations a must.

Lodging: **Old Monterey Inn,** 500 Martin Street, Monterey 93940 (408) 375–8284. A vine-covered Tudor mansion in a forest of low-hanging gnarled oaks. Patios are abloom every month of the year: hanging baskets, hundreds of pots, wisteria, and aromatic jasmine. Monterey is famous for gardens, and this one is legendary, somehow a combination English-country and Japanese garden. Understated European countryhouse decor, fireplaces galore, many elegant extras, extraordinary service. Two honeymoon cottages—one safari-luxe, one a blue oasis with canopy bed. Warm and inviting during the Christmas holidays—green boughs throughout, candles aglow.

Day 2

Morning

Breakfast: Here at the Old Monterey Inn, join guests in the formal dining room in front of the fireplace. Artichoke soufflé, homemade pastries.

Don't miss a visit to the **Monterey Bay Aquarium,** 886 Cannery Row (408–648–4888). In the summer and on weekends and holidays, it's important to arrive here at Monterey's most popular attraction when it opens at 10:00 A.M., otherwise you'll stand in a long line (an alternative is after 3:00 P.M.). Restored smokestacks and boilers on the behemoth of a building create an architectural cross between a sardine cannery and a contemporary masterpiece. Some 6,000 sea creatures reside here in giant tanks. The three-story Kelp Forest is the world's tallest aquarium exhibit, so huge that it feels as if you're swimming around in there with the sharks and the schools of silvery fish. The Monterey Bay Habitats exhibit is 90 feet long, full of fascinating reef life. Playful sea otters and bat rays have their own watery homes, and it's fun to watch them during their feeding time. There are frequent live videos from a research submarine prowling Monterey Bay, as deep as 3,000 feet. On the aquarium's decks overlooking the harbor, you can peer down and watch the otters and seals peering back at you.

Stroll about and shop on **Cannery Row.** Once a few blocks of weathered cannery buildings with funky shops and cafes, the waterfront promenade is now rampant with elegance and élan. Steinbeck and sardines were replaced by upscale boutiques and fancy hotels. The seals, otters, swaying kelp beds, and sailing yachts of Monterey Bay remain.

At the north end of Cannery Row, near the aquarium, are the **American Tin Cannery** factory outlet stores (408–372–1442)—forty-five of them.

Drive to the Spanish Bay entrance to the **17-Mile Drive,** at Asilomar near the Fishwife restaurant; you'll pay a $6.00 per car entry fee that's well worth it, even on a foggy day. Ghostly cypress forests and red lichen-painted rocks frame the many vista points. Stop and explore the beautiful beaches and many tidepools; walk or jog on the winding waterfront path. If you're a golfer, this is a chance to see three of the most famous and most difficult courses in the world. Watch for erratic traffic; everyone slows down to ogle the mansions and seaside estates.

The 17-Mile Drive ends in the village of Carmel. Drive east on Ocean Avenue to Highway 1, then south 1 mile to the Carmel Valley

exit at Rio Road, turning in to the **Crossroads Center** (408–625–4106).
Lunch: **Rio Grill,** 101 Crossroads Boulevard, Carmel. (408)
625–5436. Imaginative Southwest dishes, mesquite-grilled specialties,
Santa Fe atmosphere, bar.

Afternoon

Drive south out of Carmel on Highway 1 to Big Sur, about 30 miles
on a two-lane, winding mountain road. The brooding mountain shoulders of the **Santa Lucia Mountains** loom to your left, and to your
right it's a sheer 1,000-foot drop to a rocky, mostly inaccessible coastline pierced by the small valleys of the **Big and Little Sur rivers.** Several river and forest parks are here in the **Los Padres National Forest**
(408–385–5434), where you'll also find good campgrounds and walking and hiking trails. Shielded by tremendous cliffs, Big Sur is a banana belt, with higher temperatures than Carmel and Monterey,
getting more inches of rain but more sunny days. In wintertime you'll
often find clear blue skies here when it's drippy just a few miles north.

You'll cross the **Bixby Creek Bridge,** also known as the Rainbow
Bridge, a 260–foot-high single-spanner constructed in 1932. Just north
of the bridge, take a short sidetrip into the National Forest; turn left
onto Old Coast Road and follow it a few miles, returning to Highway
1 at **Andrew Molera State Park** (408–667–2315). The **Big Sur River**
flows down from the Santa Lucias through this 4,700–acre park, falling
into the sea at a long sandy beach. One of many hiking trails runs
along the river, through a eucalyptus grove where monarch butterflies
spend the winter, to the rivermouth, where you can see a great variety
of sea- and shorebirds.

You'll drive through **Big Sur Valley,** not a town, really, but a handful of river resorts and campgrounds on both sides of the highway.
Pfeiffer Big Sur State Park (408–667–2171) is another place to hike,
picnic, and fish in the Big Sur River. Docent-led nature walks are
given in the summer; one trail leads to **Pfeiffer Falls**, in a fern
canyon. The restaurant of **Big Sur Lodge** (408–667–2171), just inside
the entrance to the park, overlooks the river.

Pfeiffer Beach is at the end of Sycamore Canyon Road, 1 mile
south of the entrance to Pfeiffer Big Sur Park.

Lodging and Dinner: **Ventana Big Sur Country Inn Resort,** Highway 1, Big Sur, 30 miles south of Carmel. (408) 667–2331. The architecture of this mountain aerie is rustic country-luxe, the atmosphere
private and quiet. On a hillside between the sea far below and the
mountain ridges far above, the inn is a compound of several pine
buildings, each providing canyon or sea views and high-ceilinged,
wood-paneled luxury suites with fireplaces and a feeling of isolation.

Decor is of stone, wood, soft earth-toned fabrics; natural surroundings are magnificent.

Take a sunset swim in one of two lap pools, a blissful soak in Japanese hot baths, or a sauna. Massages are available on your own completely private deck. An elaborate wine-and-cheese buffet awaits in the main lounge.

Take a ten-minute walk on a foresty path to the **Ventana Inn Restaurant;** the path is lighted after dark. This is a four-star restaurant serving lunch, dinner, and cocktails. It has a warm, woody atmosphere and a spectacular stone patio floating high above the sea.

The inn also operates a private campground here, in a forty-acre redwood grove.

Day 3

Morning

Breakfast: At the Ventana Big Sur Country Inn Resort. Big breakfast buffet in the sunny dining lounge, outside, or in your room. Fresh berries, melons, tropical fruits; homemade coffeecakes, croissants, muffins; yogurt, granola.

Explore the grounds of the inn. Artfully wild gardens bloom with native flowers and vines, oceans of clematis and jasmine pour over balconies, and tree ferns canopy shady glades. Oaks in the canyons give way to pines higher on the hillsides; the higher you go, the wider the sea view. Rustlings in the underbrush may be wild turkeys, deer, quail, or perhaps a mountain lion.

More walks, hikes, backpacking, and sightseeing in this area on the edge of the **Ventana Wilderness** can be enjoyed right here with the inn as a headquarters, You'll see ancient redwoods, mountain meadows, deep canyons, and high ridges. The Santa Lucia fir is found only here, and you may see peregrine falcons, bald eagles, and wild pigs. For trail maps and information, write in advance to the U.S. Forest Service, 406 South Mildred, King City, CA 93930 (408–385–5434). Ten miles farther down the coast is **Julia Pfeiffer Burns State Park** (408–667–2315), 2,400 beautiful acres with trails along McWay Creek, leading to a waterfall that plunges into the ocean. The **Partington Creek** trail goes through a canyon and a 100-foot rock tunnel to **Partington Cove** beach, where sea otters play in the kelp beds.

Lunch: **Nepenthe,** on Highway 1 just south of Ventana Inn. (408) 667-2345. For decades a favorite destination for daytrippers from Carmel. Perched on a magical promontory at the edge of the continent, Nepenthe's stone patios look over the sea and down the shoreline. Just offshore are natural arches and seastacks, rocky remnants of an ancient coastline.

Afternoon

Below Nepenthe is the **Phoenix** (408–667–2347), an art gallery/museum/shop.

Big Sur stretches more than 60 miles farther down the coast, with many natural sights along the way. About halfway to San Simeon is **Jade Cove,** actually a string of coves, where Monterey jade is found at low tide and following storms. The two-lane highway is crossed by thirty bridges over spectacular canyons and stream-cut valleys.

Head back to the Bay Area.

There's More

Mopeds, bikes, kayaks. Moped Adventures, 1250 Del Monte, Monterey. (408) 373–2696.

Bay Bikes, 640 Wave Street, Monterey. (408) 646–9090.

Monterey Bay Kayaks, 693 Del Monte Avenue, Monterey. (408) 373–KELP.

Point Lobos State Reserve, 2.5 miles south of Carmel on Highway 1. (408) 624–4909. A rocky point surrounded by a protected marine environment; otters, whales, harbor seals, sea lions; scuba-diving; spectacular landscape; picnicking, walking, photo snapping.

Esalen Institute, 15 miles south of Big Sur. (408) 667–3000. World-famous center for the development of human potential; workshops, seminars, hot tubs; open infrequently to the public.

Golf. Old Del Monte Golf Course, 1300 Sylvan Road, Monterey. (408) 373–2436. Eighteen holes, public, oldest course west of the Mississippi.

Laguna Seca Golf Course, end of York Road off Highway 68, Monterey. (408) 373–3701. Eighteen holes, public.

Pacific Grove Golf Course, 77 Asilomar Boulevard, Pacific Grove. (408) 648–3177. Eighteen holes, public, links-style.

The Links at Spanish Bay, 17-Mile Drive, Pebble Beach. (408) 647–7500. Eighteen holes, resort course.

Poppy Hills Golf Course, 3200 Lopez Road, 17-Mile Drive, Pebble Beach. (408) 625–2154. Eighteen holes, public.

Spyglass Hill Golf Course, Stevenson Drive and Spyglass Hill, Pebble Beach. (408) 647–7500. Semiprivate, eighteen holes.

Pebble Beach Golf Links, 17-Mile Drive, Pebble Beach. (408) 624–3811. Eighteen holes, resort course.

Monterey Peninsula Golf Packages, P.O. Box 504, Carmel Valley 93924. (408) 659-5361. During high season this may be your best bet.

Special Events

January. AT&T Pebble Beach National Pro-Am. (800) 541–9091. Formerly the Bing Crosby Clambake.

February. Hot-Air Affair, Monterey. Balloon festival. (408) 649–6544.

March. Dixieland Monterey. (408) 443–5260.

April. Adobe Tour, Monterey. (408) 372–2608. Twenty-five adobes and gardens, period costumes.

June. U.S. Open Golf Championships, Pebble Beach. (408) 626–1992.

July. Monterey Bay Blues Festival. (408) 394–2652. Big names.

July. Monterey National Horse Show. (408) 372–1000.

August. Scottish Festival and Highland Games, Monterey. (408) 899–3864.

August. Monterey County Fair. (408) 372–1000.

August. Pebble Beach Concours D'Elegance and Christie's Auction. (408) 625–8562.

August. NCGA Championship, Pebble Beach. (408) 625–4653.

September. Monterey Jazz Festival. (408) 648–5354. Big names.

October. Octoberfest, Monterey. (408) 649–6544.

Other Recommended Restaurants and Lodgings

Coastal Hotel Group. (800) 225–2902. Reservations for two upscale Monterey hotels and a bed-and-breakfast inn.

Big Sur

Ripplewood Resort, Highway 1. (408) 667–2242. Breakfast, lunch, Mexican dinners.

Pacific Grove

Asilomar Conference Center, 800 Asilomar Boulevard. (408) 372–8016. A secret: When rooms are available, individual travelers may rent hotel rooms here, some rustic, some deluxe, at very reasonable rates, including full breakfast; wonderful seaside location.

Centrella, 612 Central Avenue. (408) 372–3372. Three-story, elegant Victorian bed-and-breakfast establishment; romantic; quiet.

El Cocodrilo, 701 Lighthouse Avenue. (408) 655–3311. Tropical seafood specialties, fun, colorful; Jamaican curry crabcakes, West Indian ribs, Bahamian seafood chowder.

Fandango, 223 Seventeenth Street. (408) 373–0588. European country–style cuisine, Mediterranean setting; pasta, paella, seafood, cassoulet.

Monterey

Lone Oak Motel, 2221 North Fremont. (408) 372–4924. Best-kept secret for inexpensive lodgings.

The Clock Garden, 565 Abrego. (408) 375–6100. Glorious garden terrace; notable food for decades.

For More Information

Monterey Peninsula Visitor's and Convention Bureau, 380 Alvarado Street, Monterey, CA 93940. (408) 648–5354.

Pacific Grove Chamber of Commerce, P.O. Box 167, Pacific Grove, CA 93950. (408) 373–3304.

Big Sur Chamber of Commerce, P.O. Box 87, Big Sur, CA 93920. (408) 667–2111.

MISTIX. (800) 444–7275. State campground reservations.

Carmel Village, Carmel Valley

Hundreds of unique shops await you in Carmel.

Seagulls, Shopping, and Valley Sunshine

2 NIGHTS

Art galleries · Ranch rambles · Beach walks
Serra's mission · Boutique binge · Seagulls and seafood

An artists' colony and weekend getaway since early in this century,
Carmel is a 1-square-mile village of rustic country cottages and shin-
gled beachhouses in an idyllic coastal setting. Winding lanes are
shaded with ancient oaks and cypresses, and everyone in town, it
seems, is an avid gardener—hanging baskets and bright windowboxes

crowd the neighborhoods. You can stroll and sun on white sand beaches, restaurant-hop, and shop at literally hundreds of boutiques and art galleries. Or you can spend a rainy weekend before a fireplace in one of Carmel's quaint bed-and-breakfast inns.

Out in the Carmel Valley, the Carmel River runs along between two small mountain ranges through horse farms and rambling ranch resorts. The tawny climate is warm and dry, though just a whisper away from the foggy dew of Carmel. Except for a huge shopping and restaurant area at Highway 1 and Carmel Valley Road, the valley has little commercial development. Your choices are golf, horseback riding, hiking, tennis, or lying in the sun by the pool.

Day 1

Morning

Take Highway 880 south to Highway 17, connecting with Highway 1 at Santa Cruz, heading south to Monterey; it's a little over two hours from the Oakland Bay Bridge to Carmel. Exit at Ocean Avenue and park at the big garage on your left at Junipero and Ocean; finding a legal parking place on village streets can be difficult.

Lace up your walking shoes and plan to spend the afternoon exploring. At the corner of San Carlos and Sixth is a cluster of vintage buildings and antiques shops. Just up the block on San Carlos, between Fifth and Sixth, is the **Visitor's Bureau** (408–624–2522), upstairs in the Eastwood Building; pick up a walking-tour map and schedule of events. From the balcony look down into the **Hog's Breath** (408–625–1044), an indoor/outdoor cafe with pretty good food. It's owned and occasionally visited by a man named Clint; he also owns the Eastwood Building.

Lunch: **The General Store,** corner of Fifth and Junipero. (408) 624–2233. Dine at an umbrella table under the oaks or inside by the fireplace. Casual, rustic; fresh fish, burgers, salads; bar; open until 2:00 A.M.

Afternoon

Now it's time for some serious shopping and gallery browsing. A few notables: the **Carmel Art Association,** at Dolores between Fifth and Sixth (408–624–6276), a cooperative with a wide-ranging collection, top artists, and fair prices; **Thinker Toys,** at Seventh and San Carlos (408–624–0441), has toys for every age, including trains, puppets, games, and imports; and the **Weston Galleries,** at Sixth and Dolores between Ocean and Seventh (408–624–4453), representing three generations of famous photographers. For your beach walks pick up a kite at **Come Fly a Kite,** in Carmel Plaza (408–624–3422). **Travels,** at the corner of Ocean and Dolores (408–624–0461), has thousands of gadgets, bags, books, and gifts for travelers. The **Carmel Bay Company,** on the corner of Ocean and Lincoln (408–624–3868), will take some time to explore—two floors of goodies for the garden, kitchen, and bath, plus posters and more, more. **Scotch House,** on Ocean (408–624–0595), is a mecca for cashmere sweater collectors. Enameled jewelry designed by a local celebrity artist can be found at **Laurel Burch Galleries,** at Ocean and Monte Verde (408–626–2822). The **Carmel Doll Shop,** in the Court of the Golden Eagle (408–624–2607), is a fairyland of antique European dolls, teddy bears, and Victorian gewgaws. And **The Dovecote,** on Ocean Avenue south of Dolores (408–626–3161), is a gift boutique in a landmark Carmel cottage, complete with garden sculpture and topiaries.

Take time to get lost on the sidestreets and see the charming courtyard gardens and endearing cottages that give Carmel its unique character. Many of the inns and hotels are National Historic Landmarks, such as the **La Playa Hotel,** at Eighth and Camino Real (408–624–6476), a pink Mediterranean mansion built in 1904; it's OK to peek at the hotel gardens.

Take a late-afternoon walk on **Carmel Beach,** at the foot of Ocean Avenue: truly white, powdery sand; truly memorable sunsets.

Dinner: **Fabulous Toots Lagoon,** Dolores and Seventh, Carmel. (408) 625–1915. Everything—pasta, grilled meats, salads, seafood, bar. Lots of fun.

Lodging: **Vagabond House Inn,** Fourth and Dolores, Carmel. (408) 624–7738. Half-timbered English Tudor country inn; blooming courtyard gardens; within walking distance to everything in the village; elegant, traditional decor; continental breakfast.

Day 2

Morning

Breakfast: Perhaps continental breakfast at the Vagabond House Inn and a late breakfast at **Katy's Place,** on Mission between Fifth and Sixth (408–624–0199): French toast with strawberries and nine kinds of eggs Benedict, a million omelets, and meals served indoors or out.

Before the tour buses beat you to it, drive to the **Mission San Carlos Borromeo del Rio Carmel** (408–624–1271): take Highway 1 to the south end of Carmel, then turn right on Rio Road; the mission and grounds open at 9:30 A.M. on weekdays. Star-shaped stained-glass windows, cool colonnades, extensive courtyard gardens and fountains—

this is one of the loveliest missions in California and the burial place of Father Junípero Serra. A warren of thick-walled rooms, restored from original mission buildings, hold a magnificent museum collection of early Indian, religious, and historical California artifacts. Inside, the cathedral is sienna, burnt umber, and gold, with soaring ceilings and heavy wooden pews; it is cool and silent even on the hottest days.

Continue on Rio Road 2 blocks to Santa Lucia, turning left and following this street to the waterfront, bearing left to the north end of **Carmel River State Beach** (408–624–4909), adjacent to **Monastery Beach** and the **Carmel River Bird Sanctuary.** Frequented by a wide variety of waterfowl and shorebirds—egrets, herons, hawks—these beaches are quieter and more rugged than Carmel Beach. Wander over the dunes that form a "plug" for the Carmel River most of the year. Pick up driftwood and shells; hide in the rocks with a blanket; make a 4-mile round-trip run or walk.

Lunch: **Thunderbird Bookshop and Restaurant,** at the Barnyard, Highway 1 and Carmel Valley Road. (408) 624–1803. Indoor/outdoor dining inside a big, bountiful bookstore, a fixture in the valley for decades. Curried chicken salad, burgers, salads, soups; monster desserts. Cozy by the fireplace in wintertime and during the week, when tourists have gone and Carmelites take their valley back.

Afternoon

The Barnyard (408–624–8886) is a rambling complex of fifty shops and restaurants in contemporary barn buildings. If you're a garden fancier, this will be a highlight of your trip—a wild riot of blooming native perennials, thousands of flowers in every nook and cranny around, under, alongside, and hanging from the buildings. Make an effort to find the **Carmel CraftWorks** (408–626–8565)—representing more than seventy artisans; the **Rainbow Scent Company** (408–624–4422)—it smells wonderful in here; **Succulent Gardens** (408–624–0426)—everything decorative for the garden; and the **Total Dog** (408–624–5553)—gifts for dogs and cats.

Drive out Carmel Valley Road to **Carmel Valley Village.** Along the way take a walk or hike on some of the 2,000 acres of **Garland Ranch Regional Park** (408–659–4488), along the Carmel River and up on the ridges. Plan to arrive at your valley lodgings early enough to enjoy a swim.

Dinner: **Carmel Mission Ranch,** 26270 Dolores Street, Carmel. (408) 624–3824. Overlooking the Carmel River, with views of Carmel Bay and Point Lobos. Cowboys and cowgirls kick back and eat steak; very valley, funky, and fun.

Lodging: **Los Laureles Lodge,** 313 West Carmel Valley Road,

Carmel Valley 93924. (408) 659–2233. Behind white picket fences, a ten-acre horse ranch from the 1930s, transformed into a country inn and restaurant. Pool, gardens, bar, live music; ask for a unit away from the road. Special events include barbecues and country music.

Day 3

Morning

Breakfast: In the solarium dining room of **Los Laureles Lodge**. California ranch-style breakfasts like Mom never made. Ask lodge staff to direct you to a morning walk nearby; then jump in the pool before you pack up.

Drive north on Highway 1 for about forty minutes, to **Castroville,** the Artichoke Capital of the World. **The Giant Artichoke Restaurant,** 11261 Merritt Street near the highway (408–633–3204), has artichoke nutcake, artichoke soup, and artichoke everything else.

When you see the bright blue awnings of the **Whole Enchilada** (408–633–3038), a Mexican restaurant, turn right into **Moss Landing,** on Elkhorn Slough; you can't miss Moss Landing—just look for the second largest power plant in the world. There are twenty-five antiques shops here in Old West falsefront buildings, a marina of fishing boats, and a boat graveyard. A quiet inlet makes for good kayaking; rent kayaks at the bridge.

The **Moss Landing Marine Laboratory** (408–633–2133) is on the slough, operated by nine California state universities, and open to visit. You can also walk 4.5 miles of trails in the mudflats and saltmarshes of the **Elkhorn Slough National Estuarine Research Reserve** (408–728–2822), home to hundreds of sea- and shorebirds and animals.

Lunch: **Moss Landing Oyster Bar,** at the south end of Moss Landing Road. (408) 633–5302. An earthy, popular cafe serving fresh fish and homemade pasta.

Afternoon

Head back to the Bay Area after picking up produce at **Johnny Boy's,** at the corner of Highway 1 and Elkhorn Slough Road (408–423–5443).

There's More

Tor House and Hawk Tower, 26304 Ocean View Avenue, Carmel. (408) 624–1813. The home of poet Robinson Jeffers, a medieval stone house and tower. Tours Friday and Saturday.

Mission Trail Park, Carmel. (408) 624–2522. Thirty-five acres of native vegetation, 5 miles of trails. Enter and begin wandering at Mountain View and Crespi, at Eleventh Street and Junipero, or on Rio Road across from the mission.

Picnic supplies. Nielsen Brothers Market, corner of San Carlos and Seventh, Carmel. (408) 624–6441. Perfect produce, snacks, wine, deli.

Golf. Rancho Canada Golf Course, Carmel Valley Road, Carmel Valley. 1 mile from Highway 1. (408) 624–0111. Two beautiful eighteen-hole courses.

Golf Club at Quail Lodge, 8000 Valley Greens Drive, Carmel Valley. (408) 624–2770. Eighteen stunning holes. You must be a guest at the lodge or a member of another private club.

Carmel Valley Ranch Resort, 1 Old Ranch Road, Carmel Valley. (408) 626–2510. Eighteen holes; reciprocal play for members of private clubs.

Monterey Peninsula Golf Packages, P.O. Box 504, Carmel Valley 93924. (408) 659–5361. Accommodations and tee times.

Special Events

June. Carmel Gallery Walk. (408) 659–4000.

June–August. Outdoor Forest Theatre Season, Carmel. (408) 626–1681.

July. Carmel Bach Festival, Carmel. (408) 624–1521.

August. Scottish Highland Games, Carmel. (408) 626–3551.

August. Consours d'Elegance. (408) 659–0663.

September. Carmel Shakespeare Festival. (408) 649–0340.

September. Carmel Mission Fiesta. (408) 624–1271.

October. Carmel River Run. (408) 667–2182.

November. Carmel Homecrafters' Marketplace. (408) 659–5099.

Other Recommended
Restaurants and Lodgings

Carmel

Village Corner, Dolores and Sixth. (408) 624–3588. Inside and on the patio, locals meet here to lunch and complain about how Carmel isn't like it used to be. Good sandwiches, salads; less expensive than most.

Cactus Jacks, San Carlos and Fifth. (408) 626–0909. Best Mexican food in town; outdoor patio.

Carmel Valley Village

Wills Fargo, Carmel Valley Road and El Caminito. (408) 659–2774. Steak by the pound, western atmosphere.

Carmelo

Lincoln Green Inn, between Fifteenth and Sixteenth. (408) 624–1880. In the true spirit of Carmel-quaint, sweet cottages at the south end of Carmel near Carmel River Beach.

Carmel Valley

Carmel Valley Inn, P.O. Box 115. (408) 659–3131. Casual, reasonably priced, simple rooms and suites, tennis; nice pool area open to the public for small fee.

Carmel Valley Ranch Resort, 1 Old Ranch Road. (408) 625–9500. On a hillside with golf courses and valley views, spectacular pool and gardens, dining terrace, casually elegant public areas. Accommodations are all suites with one or more bedrooms and fireplaces; decor includes wood, leather, subtle fabrics, fine art. Twelve tennis courts, spa, sauna; pricey.

Inns by the Sea, (800) 433–4732. Reservation services for several inns.

Valley Lodge, Carmel Valley Road at Ford Road, P.O. Box 93. (800) 641–4646. Small, quiet, pretty patio rooms and cottages; reasonable.

Highlands Inn, 4 miles south of Carmel. (408) 624–3801. Since 1916, upscale accommodations at a full-service resort, glorious ocean views, renowned restaurant.

Resort Time Roomfinders. (408) 646–9250. A reservation service.

For More Information

Carmel Business Association (visitor's bureau), San Carlos between Fifth and Sixth, P.O. Box 4444, Carmel, CA 93921. (408) 624–2522.

Carmel Valley Chamber of Commerce, Oak Building, Carmel Valley Road, Carmel Valley, CA. (408) 659–4000.

Eastbound Escapes

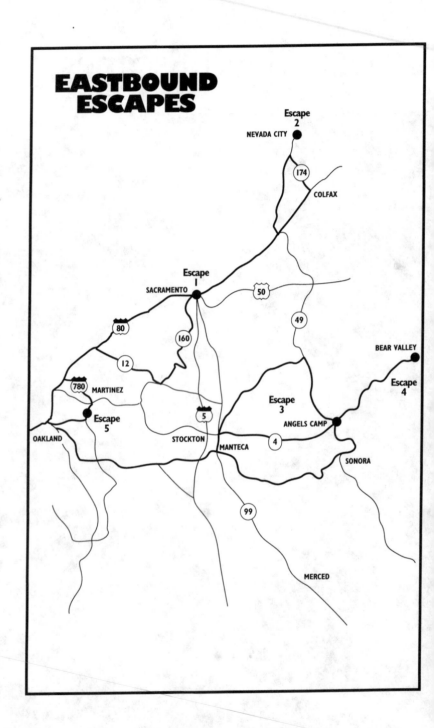

Sacramento Delta Loop

You can enjoy a riverboat cruise at Old Sacramento.

Levee Towns and Old Sacramento

———————————— 1 NIGHT ————————————

Exploring the delta · Old Town shopping · Railroad museum
The Capitol · Crawdads and California history · Cruising the river

Ambling on the levee road through ramshackle river towns, you'll find that life is slow and sweet along the Sacramento. Boats and ferries, sailboards and houseboats ply miles of meandering waterways. Blue herons silently stalk the lagoons and sloughs, home to thousands of birds and ducks, a birdwatcher's mecca. Small towns were abandoned by the Chinese workers who built the levees a hundred years ago, but crawfish cafes, scruffy saloons, and a few inns remain for weekenders seeking quiet getaways.

You'll hang out on the boardwalks of the old port of Sacramento, where ships sailed in for supplies and refreshment in the wild days of the Gold Rush—as many as 800 vessels in 1849. The look and feel of Forty-niner days has been re-created by the miraculous refurbishment and rebuilding of original hotels, saloons, restaurants, firehouses, and establishments of questionable reputation. There are upscale and down-home restaurants, paddlewheelers for river cruises, antiques shops and souvenir stands, and world-class museums highlighted by the largest and finest railroad museum in the United States.

Topping off your Sacramento delta weekend is a tour of the magnificent state capitol building and grounds.

Day 1

Morning

Drive north on Highway 80 from the Oakland Bay Bridge for about an hour. Two miles south of Fairfield, turn east on Highway 12, past the Jelly Belly factory, through the flat cattle country of Solano County, to **Rio Vista** on the Sacramento River, a 25-mile trip.

Before crossing the Rio Vista bridge, go north along the river 2 miles to the ferry to **Ryder Island**, one of the last remaining ferries in the delta; it's free. Prowl around the island a little, then return to the bridge taking Highway 160 north, the levee road.

On the east side of the river is the **Brannan Island State Recreation Area** (916–777–6671), where campers and boaters enjoy fishing and swimming in the Sacramento and a couple of sloughs. There are tent and RV camps, boat-in campsites, a public beach, and picnic sites.

Breakfast: At **Isleton** bear right at the Y to **Ernie's**, 212 Second Street (916–777–6510). Seems like Ernie's restaurant and bar has been here forever, serving crawfish for breakfast, lunch, and dinner.

Isleton consists of a down-at-the-heels collection of tinfront and falsefront western buildings. Antiques shops nearby are worth a browse.

You'll drive through **Walnut Grove**, a quiet community on both sides of the river, with a ghostly, empty Chinatown. At **Locke** turn right, leaving the highway, at Yuen Chong grocery; go 1 block down the hill and park. Just 1 block long, Locke is the only surviving rural community built and lived in by Chinese early in this century. Now it's a maze of creaky wooden buildings connected by a boardwalk. The **Dai Loy Museum**, open on the weekends, is a spooky former gambling hall and opium den. **Al the Wop's** bar and cafe is dustily atmospheric and frequented by farmhands and fishermen. **Locke Ness** buys junque and sells antiques.

Along the levee road are farmhouses and mansions from several eras, in various states of repair. If you spy tall palm trees, that's usually where the houses are located, surrounded by overgrown gardens. Slow down just north of Hood to see a particularly genteel Victorian. In the summertime keep your eyes open for **Eagle Point Orchards** (916–744–1120), where you can buy tomatoes and wonderful Bartlett pears.

Lunch: **Courtland Docks** at the Courtland Marina, Highway 160 at Courtland. (916) 775–1172. Burgers, salads, homemade soup, and apple pie.

Afternoon

At Freeport are several seafood restaurants and bars attracting daytrippers from Sacramento. It's just 9 miles farther to Sacramento, where you'll connect with I–5 north, proceeding for a few minutes to the J Street/Old Sacramento exit; there are parking garages on the east side of Old Town.

Top off the day with a late-afternoon cruise on the river. The *Spirit of Sacramento* paddlewheeler departs from the L Street landing in Old Sacramento (916–552–2933) for one-hour sightseeing trips.

Dinner: **Crawdad's River Cantina**, 1375 Garden Highway. (916) 929–2268. On the levee near I–5; Cajun popcorn, fresh fish, steaks, salads, lively atmosphere.

Lodging: **Radisson Hotel Sacramento**, 500 Leisure Lane, Sacramento. (916) 922–2020. Five minutes from Old Town. A resort hotel with pool, fitness center, par course, 35-mile biking and walking trail along the American River (bike rentals here), gardens surrounding a small lake; several restaurants. A comfortable oasis; each room or suite has a balcony or patio.

Day 2

Morning

Breakfast: At the Radisson Hotel Sacramento.

Take Sixteenth Street into **Old Town Sacramento**. Cool early mornings are the best time to prowl the boardwalks taking photos of the wooden falsefronts, climbing around on antique railcars, and sipping a cappuccino at the **Croissant Connection**, 1026 Second Street (916–446–7669).

Opening at 10:00 A.M., the **California State Railroad Museum**, on the north end of Old Town (916–448–4466), comprises 100,000 square feet housing three dozen locomotives and railcars in pristine condition. One of the engines weighs a mere million pounds. The Canadian National sleeping car rocks back and forth as if on its way down the track. Sound effects, snoozing passengers, and compartments that look as if they're occupied give you a taste of vintage train travel. Retired conductors in their dark blue uniforms are available to answer questions and pose for photos. On the second level is a dream of a toy train running through tiny towns and over bridges; to start the action, push the red button. The **Railroad Museum Gift Shop** next door has fabulous train-related toys, books, and souvenirs.

Now that you're a railroad aficionado, step over to the depot and take a short trip up the tracks along the river to the Port of Sacramento.

Nearby, the **Sacramento History Center** (916–449–2057) contains five galleries of Sacramento area history.

Explore the ***Delta King***, 1000 Front Street (916–444–KING), a huge Mississippi riverboat permanently moored here at the waterfront. Now a fourty-four-stateroom hotel and restaurant, the *Delta King* has small but comfortable cabins with windows overlooking the river; the bars and restaurant have fine river views and are popular, although somewhat touristy, for brunch, lunch, and dinner. Next to the *Delta King* is the **Visitor Information Center**, 1104 Front Street (916–442–7644).

Lunch: **California Fat's**, 1015 Front. (916) 441–7966. A New Age offshoot of the famous Victorian-style Fat City establishment next door. A contemporary jade, fushia, and royal blue cafe decor seems aquariumlike as you step downstairs into the narrow dining room; subtle sounds of a 30-foot waterfall mask everyone's conversation but your own. On the menu are *nouvelle* Chinese specialties and fresh fish, grilled crab sandwiches, Peking duck pizzas, salads, and banana cream pie; exotic drinks include a Sacramento Slammer and Electric Lemonade. Smoking is not permitted in Sacramento restaurants.

Afternoon

A hundred or so shops await your discovery in old town. The **Artists' Collaborative Gallery**, 1007 Second (916–444–3764), is a large space displaying paintings, ceramics, weavings, and jewelry by local artists, the best gallery in Old Town. Navajo rugs and Indian turquoise and silver jewelry are the specialty of **Gallery of the American West**, at 121 K Street (916–446–6662).

Mike's Puzzle Store, 1009 Second Street (916–444–0446), has hundreds, maybe thousands, of puzzles, mostly jigsaws. **Two Crows**, 1003 Second Street (916–444–3616), specializes in fascinating nature and wildlife items. **Brooks Novelty Antiques**, 1107 Front (916–443–0783), is a delightfully musty, crowded place filled with old records, juke-boxes, weird TVs, radios, vintage bikes, magazines, and posters.

Decorated to the max for every holiday and smelling like chocolate heaven, the **Rocky Mountain Chocolate Factory**, 1039 Second Street (916–448–8801), lures you in with hand-dipped ice cream bars, caramel apples, chocolate-covered strawberries, and freshly made candy. You could be in trouble here.

Fanny Ann's, 1023 Second Street (916–441–0505), is five floors of crazily antiques-crammed restaurant and bar; it's a fun place to take the kids during the day, while an adult crowd gathers here at night. **Sticky Fingers**, at 1027 Second Street (916–443–4075), holds forth on the second floor of an old building, serving up ribs, chicken, and seafood while entertaining passersby with live Dixieland and jazz from the veranda.

Walk or drive the few blocks to the **California State Capitol**, Tenth and Capitol Mall (916–324–0333), for a tour of the remarkable double-domed building and surrounding grounds. Updated and re-modeled over many decades, a hodgepodge of eras and styles, the capitol building was treated to a $70 million complete restoration in the 1970s; everything was demolished and removed except the out-side walls and the domes. Furnishings, art, ballustrades, chandeliers, and myriad bits and pieces were located or replicated and reinstalled, re-creating the original architectural masterpiece of the 1870s.

A guided tour provides background on the magnificently carved staircases, elaborate crystal chandeliers, marble parquet floors, historic artwork, and zillions of columns, cornices, and friezes decorated in gold. The "Historic Rooms" tour focuses on artifacts and interesting stories of politicos from the past. You'll learn about California lawmak-ing, and you may even be able to sit in on a legislative session.

Take a tour of the grounds, or stroll around on your own through forty acres of specimen plants and trees, many planted in the 1870s. Springtime in Capitol Park brings waves of blooming camellias, aza-leas, and dogwood, and rivers of tulips and daffodils.

It's 90 miles from Sacramento to San Francisco on Highway 80.

There's More

Train. Amtrak passenger trains from Oakland to Sacramento. (800) USA–RAIL.

Antiques. Several large shops at Del Paso Boulevard and Arden Way, and a dozen in the 800 block of Fifty-seventh Street, Sacramento. Pick up a booklet here to locate other shops in Sacramento.

Bike and Surrey Rentals of Old Sacramento, 916 Second Street. (916) 441–3836. An easy way to get around Old Town or ride 26 miles of paved bike paths on the American River Bike Trail.

California Citizen-Soldier Museum, 1119 Second Street, Old Sacramento. (916) 442–2883. Some 30,000 papers, documents, and memorabilia tracing California's rich militia and military history.

Crocker Art Museum, Third and O Streets, Sacramento. (916) 264–5423. A gigantic restored Victorian sheltering the oldest public art museum in the West, European paintings and drawings, nineteenth-century art.

Towe Ford Museum, 2200 Front Street, Sacramento. (916) 442–6802. The world 's most complete antique Ford auto collection—150 vehicles.

Victorians. A rich trove of magnificent Victorian mansions can be seen on a drive in downtown Sacramento, from Seventh to Sixteenth Street, between E and I. Outstanding examples are the Heilbron House, at 740 O Street, and the Stanford House, at 800 N Street.

Grizzly Island State Recreation Area, south of Highway 12 between Fairfield and Rio Vista. (707) 425–3828. Vast marshes inhabited by tule elk and thousands of fresh- and saltwater birds; a million birds spend the winter here. Hunting and fishing with permits in season.

Special Events

February. Mardi Gras, Sacramento. (916) 443–8653.

March. Camellia Festival, Sacramento. (916) 442–8166.

May. Sacramento County Fair, Sacramento, (916) 924–2076.

May. Sacramento Jazz Jubilee. (916) 372–5277. Many bands, lots of people, dawn-to-midnight Dixieland in Old Sacramento and other venues.

June–July. Shakespeare Festival in the Park, Sacramento. (916) 558–2228.

June. California Railroad Festival, Old Sacramento. (916) 445–7387.

June. Sacramento Renaissance Faire. (916) 966–1036.

August. Sacramento Riverfest, Old Sacramento. (916) 264–7057.

August–September. California State Fair, Sacramento. (916) 924–2032.

October. Old Sacramento Boats on the Boardwalk. (916) 366–1146.

November. Indian Arts and Crafts Fair, Sacramento. (916) 324–0971.

December. Old Sacramento Holiday Festival. (916) 443–8653.

Other Recommended
Restaurants and Lodgings

Isleton

Delta Daze Inn, 20 Main Street. (916) 777–7777. Bed-and-breakfast accommodations in a historic building, complimentary bikes, six nice rooms over a soda fountain, near the capitol.

Viera's RV Resort, 15476 State Highway 160. (916) 777–6661. Between Rio Vista and Isleton on the Sacramento River; boat-launching headquarters.

Sacramento

Aunt Abigail's Bed and Breakfast Inn, 2120 G Street. (916) 441–5007. A dream of a luxury bed-and-breakfast establishment, near the capitol.

Amber House Bed and Breakfast Inn, 1315 Twenty-second Street. (916) 444–8085. Elegant mansion with eight luxurious rooms, private baths, full breakfast.

Old Sacramento

Fat City Bar and Cafe, 1001 Front. (916) 446–6768. Hundred-year-old bar, bistro-style cafe.

For More Information

Sacramento Bed and Breakfast Association, 1403 Twenty-eighth Street, Sacramento, CA 95816. (916) 455–5312.

Sacramento Convention and Visitor's Bureau, 1421 K Street, Sacramento, CA 95814. (916) 264–7777.

Gold Rush North

Downtown Nevada City, a charming Gold Rush community.

Forty-niner Towns in the Sierra Foothills

_____ 2 NIGHTS _____

Gold mines and museums · River rambles · Victoriana
Antiques · Old West · Nuggets and gems

The foothills of the California gold country stretch more than 300 miles along the western slopes of the Sierra Nevadas all the way to the southern gate of Yosemite National Park. In several river corridors—the Yuba, the American, the Mokelumne, the Stanislaus, the Tuolumne, and the Merced—dozens of boomtowns exploded in population in the mid-1800s, when gold was discovered, only to be abandoned by the miners and adventure seekers when the lodes were exhausted.

Of the remaining communities still thriving today, Nevada City is the most completely original Gold Rush town in the state, having somehow escaped the devastating fires that plagued most of the rest of the gold country. More than a hundred Victorian mansions and Western falsefront saloons and hotels cluster cozily together here on a radiating wheel of tree-lined streets on small hills. At an elevation of about 3,000 feet, the whole place turns red and gold in the fall, when hundreds of maples, aspens, and oaks turn blazing bright.

Nearby, a historic gold-mining estate, the wild-and-woolly town of Grass Valley, and the pleasures of the South Yuba River add up to a busy weekend in the northern gold country.

Just a few miles to the east, 1.2 million acres of wilderness in the Tahoe National Forest afford endless hiking, camping, fishing, and cross-country-skiing opportunities.

Day 1

Morning

From the Oakland Bay Bridge, drive north on Highway 80 beyond Sacramento to **Auburn**—about two and a half hours—and take the Maple Street exit, parking on or near Maple. On a ridge overlooking the north fork of the **American River,** where gold was discovered in 1848, Auburn has a compact, charming Old Town of antiques shops and restaurants, worth an hour or so of investigation. For breakfast or a snack on the deck above Old Town, go to **Awful Annie's,** on Sacramento Street. (916–888–9857).

Leaving Auburn, take Lincoln Way, off Maple, north past the 1894 courthouse, a domed dazzler still in use today; continue north on Highway 49 for about thirty minutes to **Nevada City.** Approaching the lower Sierras, the pines get taller, the dirt redder, and the rivers icier; in the winter a shallow blanket of snow may dust the ground, although it seldom snows enough to require tire chains.

Take the Sacramento Street exit into town, parking in the lot at Sacramento and Broad. Put on your walking shoes and head across the bridge into town on Broad, the main street. Take a right down to the stone-and-brick **Yuba Canal Building,** at 132 Main, built in 1850 on the banks of Wolfe Creek, where you can pick up tour maps at the **Chamber of Commerce.** Since early in this century, the downtown has remained lost in time, architecturally speaking, and there is much to discover within 3 or 4 blocks.

Next door, at 214 Main, the **Firehouse Museum** has two floors of Gold Rush and Indian artifacts.

Lunch: **Posh Nosh,** 318 Broad. (916) 265–6064. Eat on the tree-shaded patio. Sandwiches, pasta, salads, homemade desserts.

Afternoon

The National Hotel, 211 Broad (916–265–4551), is the oldest continuously operating hotel west of the Rockies; take a look at the long bar, shipped around the Horn more than a hundred years ago. Rooms here are small and sweet, with Victorian furnishings and gimcracks; some have balconies overlooking the street. The old **New York Hotel,** at 408 Broad, circa 1850, now houses several gift and antiques shops.

Tanglewood Forest, 217 Broad Street (916–478–1223), is a fantasyland of wizards, fairies, and strange dolls. **Four Winds,** 310 Broad (916–265–9021), is a gallery store featuring international folk art. Next to the **Nevada Theatre,** the oldest theater in California, is the **Fisher Glass Collection** (916–478–1007), a workshop of fantastic blown glass. **Utopian-Stone,** at 212 Main (916–265–6209), specializes in gold quartz jewelry.

Mountain Pastimes Fun and Games, 320 Spring Street (916–265–6692), has toys and games for grownups. Across the street you can taste Nevada County wines made right here at the **Nevada City Winery,** 321 Spring (916–265–9463). In the past couple of decades, vineyards and wineries have popped up all over the county; they celebrate in September with a Wine Fest and Grape Stomp at the Miners Foundry Cultural Center up the street.

Dinner: **Creekside Cafe,** 101 Broad Street. (916) 265–3445. Within sight and sound of rushing Deer Creek, the terrace is the place to be on summer nights; inside are candlelit tables before a fireplace. Fresh fish, poultry, and meats in exotic sauces, good wine list.

Lodging: **Kendall House,** 534 Spring Street 95959. (916) 265–0405. In a quiet neighborhood within walking distance of downtown; large, comfortable, very private rooms with baths; two-room cottage with living/dining room, fireplace, private deck, and kitchen; beautiful gardens and pool. Sensitive to your moods, Jan Kendall will regale you with stories or diplomatically leave you alone. Many of her guests rebook a year in advance. Be sure to save time for enjoying the pool and gardens, bright with color in the fall, cool and leafy on hot summer days.

Day 2

Morning

Breakfast: At the Kendall House. Eggs Benedict in the sunny solarium or on the garden terrace. Dr. Ted Kendall is an avid runner and will direct you to walking and running trails beginning right from his front door. One scenic 10-mile route starts at Factory Street in downtown and goes out Old Downieville Highway to Newtown Road.

Drive south on Highway 49 to the south end of Grass Valley to the Empire Mine exit, going east on Empire Street for five minutes to reach **Empire Mine State Park** (916–273–8522), a 784-acre mining estate. The largest, deepest, and richest hardrock gold mine in California operated here for more than a hundred years, producing $100 million in gold from 360 miles of underground channels, some 11,000 feet deep. On a tour or on your own, see an extensive complex of buildings and equipment, including part of the main shaft. A visitor's center recounts the history of the mine in photos, exhibits, and films.

Sweeping lawns beneath 100-foot sugar pines surround the mine owner's home, **Bourne Cottage,** an outstanding example of a Willis Polk–designed English country manor with lovely gardens and a fountain pool.

Lunch: Drive back on Empire Street, across the freeway, to the first right, Mill Street, following Mill down and under the freeway to the **North Star Mining Museum** and powerhouse (916–273–4255), where a shady lawn over Wolf Creek makes a delightful picnic spot.

Afternoon

Among the many pieces of antique equipment at the North Star Museum are a working stampmill and the largest Pelton wheel in the world, a waterwheel that produced power from the creek for the North Star Mine; a large collection of photos traces mining history.

Follow Mill Street north into downtown **Grass Valley,** parking near the center of town. Inhabited during the Gold Rush by thousands of English and Irish miners who worked five major gold mines in the area, the town is honeycombed with miles of underground tunnels and shafts.

Step into **The Holbrooke Hotel,** 212 West Main (916–273–1353), the grand dame of Grass Valley since 1862. A glance in the hotel register turns up such famous guests as Presidents Cleveland and Garfield. At 114 Mill are three antiques shops, and at 108 Mill, the **Little Silver Palace** (916–477–6009) has a huge inventory of Southwest and contemporary silver jewelry. At Church and Chapel streets, the **Grass Valley Museum** (916–272–4725) is a restored school and orphanage exhibiting Gold Rush artifacts, clothing, paintings, and domestic items. The **Nevada County Chamber of Commerce,** 248 Mill (916–273–4667), is in the reconstructed home of Lola Montez, a notorious dancehall entertainer of the 1800s.

One block off Main take a stroll on Neal and Church streets to see several magnificent Victorian mansions and churches.

Take a predinner swim and enjoy wine and cheese with the

Kendalls, who will recommend their favorite dinner houses.

Dinner: **Selaya's,** 320 Broad Street, Nevada City. (916) 265–5697. Superb continental and California cuisine menu, elegant presentation.

Lodging: **Kendall House** (see day 1).

Day 3

Morning

Breakfast: Another extravaganza of a breakfast created by Jan at the Kendall House. (If you can squeeze in a piece of pie, stop in at the **Apple Fare,** 307 Broad Street, Nevada City [916–265–5458], and sit at a big round table with the denizens of Nevada City.)

For a fascinating trip along the south fork of the Yuba River, take Highway 49 north from Nevada City to Tyler Foote Crossing Road, turn right, and continue to where Tyler splits to the left to Alleghany; then turn right on Cruzon Grade Road, proceeding to **Malakoff Diggins State Historic Park** (916–265–2740), the largest hydraulic mine site in the world, a rather shocking and strangely beautiful remnant of gold mining in the 1800s, when giant waterjets, called monitors, destroyed entire mountains. A mile of hillside here was washed away, the soil and rocks clogging rivers and streams until the practice was outlawed late in the nineteenth century. Weird and colorful pinnacles, domes, and spirals, as well as a milky lake, are fringed with second- and third-growth pines.

Swimming and fishing holes on the **South Yuba River** and a 21-mile river corridor park developed by the state are accessible near Malakoff Diggins and at other points in the area (see Tahoe National Forest, opposite). Near the arched bridge where Highway 49 drops down into the South Yuba canyon, **Independence Trail** is 7 miles of paved and boardwalk forest pathway that is wheelchair accessible and great for a run or a walk.

On your way back to the Bay Area, take Highway 174 south from Grass Valley to Colfax, on the oldest, the twistiest, and one of the prettiest roads in the county, past horse ranches and small farms. Another pie emporium is on this road—the **Happy Apple Kitchen** (916–273–2822).

There's More

Golf. Alta Sierra Golf and Country Club, 11897 Tammy Way, Grass Valley. (916) 273–2010. Eighteen holes, 4 miles south of Grass Valley on Highway 49.

Hiking. The Tahoe National Forest is 5 miles west of Nevada City. Obtain maps and information on hiking and camping at the forest headquarters office at 631 Coyote Street in Nevada City. (916) 265–4531.

Special Events

February. Northern Mines Winetasting Exposition, Grass Valley. (916) 273–4667.

April. House and Garden Tour, Nevada City. (916) 265–2692.

May. Jewels to Junk Flea Market and Antique Fair, Auburn. (916) 823–3836.

June. Tour of Nevada City Bicycle Classic, Nevada City. (916) 265–2692.

June. Miners' Picnic, Empire Mine State Park. (916) 273–4667. Food, contests, gold panning, entertainment, marathon race.

July. Nevada County Airpark Fly-In, Nevada City. (916) 273–5273.

August. Nevada County Fair, Grass Valley. (916) 273–6217.

September. Nevada County Wine Fest and Grape Stomp, Nevada City. (916) 265–5040.

October. Golf Rush Jubilee Crafts Fair, Auburn. (916) 823–3836.

December. Cornish Christmas Celebration, Grass Valley. (916) 272–8315.

December. Victorian Christmas, Nevada City. (916) 265–2692.

Other Recommended Restaurants and Lodgings

Nevada City

Vlato's, 423 Broad. (916) 265–2831. Pretty garden patio setting, dinner only.

Red Castle Inn, 109 Prospect. (916) 265–5135. Four-story, spectacular Victorian Gothic mansion overlooking the town, eight rooms, gardens.

Northern Queen Inn, 400 Railroad Avenue. (916) 265–5824. On the south end of town; spacious, comfortable motel rooms, pool.

Historic Bed and Breakfast Inns of Grass Valley/Nevada City, P.O. Box 2060. (916) 477–6634.

Grass Valley

Empire House Restaurant, 535 Mill. (916) 273–8272. Swiss, German, and American cuisine; lunch and dinner.

Marshall's Pasties, 203 Mill Street. (916) 272–2844. Fresh Cornish pasties and English sausage rolls.

Holbrooke Hotel, 212 West Main. (916) 273–1353. Twenty-eight restored rooms, beautiful dining room and saloon.

For More Information

Grass Valley/Nevada County Chamber of Commerce, 248 Mill Street, Grass Valley, CA 95945. (916) 273–4667.

Nevada City Chamber of Commerce, 132 Main, Nevada City, CA 95959. (916) 265–2692.

Heart of the Mother Lode

A golden hill of California poppies.

Sutter Creek to Angels Camp

———————— 2 NIGHTS ————————

Gold in them thar hills · Antiques shopping · Historic towns
Wineries · Mining museums · Caverns and cowboys

Amador County is rolling pastures, vineyards, and orchardlands, crisscrossed by rivers that produced more gold than any other county in
the Mother Lode. Several still-alive-and-kicking Gold Rush towns and
many abandoned settlements remain. The postcard-perfect settlement
of Sutter Creek attracts weekenders who like to park for the day and

enjoy shopping, sightseeing, cafe sitting, and resting in a country inn, all within a few blocks.

Jackson is the site of a major museum, more of the antiques shops that are liberally sprinkled throughout the area, and a historic hotel saloon still frequented by the rough-and-rowdy after all these years.

Housed in buildings from the mid-1800s that are museums in themselves, restaurants and inns in the gold country are surprisingly sophisticated, reflecting the fact that big-city visitors are discovering the quiet pleasures of Amador County.

In the northern foothills a cluster of Shenandoah Valley wineries are gaining attention for their hearty Zinfandels.

Day 1

Morning

From the Oakland Bay Bridge, take Highway 580 east to 205 east, connecting with Highway 99 north to Stockton. Drive east on Highway 88 to 49, the main highway through the gold country. Turn north on 49 and proceed for ten minutes to **Sutter Creek,** cradled in a valley surrounded by oak-dotted rolling hills, a picturesque little town with white frame houses giving it a New England look. Concentrated on and around Main Street is a rich cache of nineteenth-century architecture—elaborate Victorians, Western falsefronts with overhanging balconies, and even a Greek Revival church, the United Methodist, a circa 1860 beauty whose tall steeple anchors the south end of town.

Lunch: Walking into the **Chatter Box Cafe,** at 29 Main (209-267-5935), is walking back into the 1940s. It's an old-fashioned soda fountain made nostalgic with World War II posters, Big Band records, and a long counter where town regulars meet; burgers with homemade buns, grilled cheese sandwiches, world-class onion rings, and pies, floats, sodas, and shakes.

Afternoon

A dozen antiques shops on Main include several vendors at **Sutter Creek Antiques and Central Shops,** 28 Main (209-267-5574). **Creekside Shops,** 22 Main (209-267-5520), is another group of antiques and collectibles dealers. **Old Hotel Antiques**, at 68 Main (209-267-5901), specializes in estate jewelry and old advertising signs and paraphernalia. In the **Gold Miner Candy Shoppe,** 40 Main (209-267-1525), are barrels of penny candy that no longer costs a penny.

Gold and Gems, 67 Main (209-223-1308), is anything but country-style, a large store showing fine jewelry and precious stones. Across the street the **Fine Eye Gallery,** at 71 Main (209-267-0571), has contemporary jewelry, art, and ceramics.

Some of the best shopping is at the north end of Main. **Coming Attractions,** 79 Main (209–267–0665), sells handwoven clothing. Next door is museumlike **Cobweb Collection**, 813 Main (209–267–0690), with rustic willow furniture designed by the shop owner, plus Southwest furniture, art, and antiques. A step away **Merchants Unlimited,** at 85 Main (209–267–0160), is in a garden cottage with several rooms of Victorian-motif imports, garden gifts, books, jewelry, artwork, antiques, and more.

In the **Eureka Street Courtyard** off Main is the **Glass Rush** (209–267–5097), with sand-carved and stained-glass art; **Ruby Tuesday Cafe** (209–267–0556), serving espresso, salads, and sandwiches; and the **Sutter Creek Wine and Cheese** shop (209–267–0945), where you can taste local wines, beers, and cheeses. Farther down Eureka Street, **Knight's Foundry** (209–267–5543), the only water-powered foundry still operating in the United States, is open for tours.

Duck behind a tall hedge at 75 Main for a peek at the **Sutter Creek Inn** (209–267–5606). In an overgrown country garden shaded by ancient oaks, the bed-and-breakfast inn has a long and lively history and has been completely restored to its former Greek Revival elegance, with nineteen rooms, some with fireplaces.

On **Spanish Street,** between Main and the creek that gives Sutter Creek its name, are rows of beautiful clapboard cottages and mansions.

If you're an antiques hound, make the 2-mile trip north to **Amador City** to browse in the tiny town, the state's smallest incorporated city.

North and east of here, the **Shenandoah Valley** is the heart of a grape-growing region where more than a dozen wineries are located in restored barns and stone cellars on sideroads branching off the Shenandoah Road; most are open for tasting and tours. Obtain a map from the first winery you encounter, or from the Amador Vintners Association, P.O. Box 667, Plymouth 95669.

Dinner: **Bellotti Inn,** 53 Main. (209) 267–5211. Satisfying family-style Italian dinners in a hundred-year-old hotel.

Lodging: **The Foxes,** 77 Main 95685. (209) 267–5882. Next door to the Sutter Creek Inn. Another Greek Revival beauty, with fireplaces and clawfoot tubs in almost every room, canopy beds, air-conditioning, and *muchas* foxes.

Day 2

Morning

Breakfast: At The Foxes: full breakfast in bed on a silver tray in your room or in the gazebo.

Three miles south of Sutter Creek, **Jackson** looks like a toy town as you approach from above on Highway 49. From the **Amador County Chamber of Commerce,** at the corner of Highways 49 and 88, get a walking-tour map. Sightseeing is best accomplished by wandering the boardwalks and quiet lanes on foot; parking can be a problem on the narrow streets.

Dominating Old Town on Main Street is the **National Hotel** (209–223–0500), operating for well over a hundred years as a hotel and restaurant; simple hotel rooms with private baths are reasonable. Red velvet wallpaper and brass chandeliers intact, the hotel restaurant is popular and the saloon is a rollicking place to rub elbows with cowboys and Indians on a Saturday night.

Across the street the 1862 IOOF Hall, the tallest three-story building in the county, once housed Wells Fargo offices where more than $100 million in gold dust and bullion were weighed. Check out 22,000 square feet of pine furniture at **Water Street Antiques,** 19 Water Street off Main (209–223–3833).

Above Main on Church Street is a clutch of churches and homes from the mid-1800s and the **Amador County Museum,** 255 Church (209–223–6386), in one of the oldest houses in town, sheltering a huge collection of artifacts and antiques, perhaps the premier museum in the gold country. On the hottest day it's cool and quiet in the house. Hundreds of photos re-create the Gold Rush days, and there's a fine collection of Indian baskets, vintage fashions, furniture, and many domestic items from throughout Gold Rush homes. A working scale model shows the **Kennedy Mine,** whose 5,000-foot shaft was one of the world's deepest. Ask about the Kennedy Mine Tour, given weekends and some weekdays.

Lunch: **The Balcony Restaurant,** 164 Main, Jackson. (209) 223–2855. Quiche, sandwiches, salads, and pasta in a ferny, art-filled environment.

Afternoon

It's ten minutes south to **Mokelumne Hill,** through the wooded canyon of the Mokelumne River, which separates Amador and Calaveras counties. Drop down off the highway into little "Mok Hill," a ghost of its former rowdy self. Once the most lawless town in the Mother Lode, Mokelumne Hill is now a quiet burg of winding streets shaded by magnificent old locust and oak trees. The **Hotel Leger,** 8304 Main Street (209–286–1401), rocked and rolled in the 1860s, and it's still a good place to stop in and have a cold beer under the slow ceiling fans of the saloon. Rooms here are charming, with antiques, comforters, and fireplaces; there's a great veranda for Main Street watching, as well as gardens and a swimming pool. Ask about the murder mystery weekends.

Across the street from the hotel, the **Adams and Company Genuine Old West Saloon and Museum and Less** (209–286–1331) should not be missed.

Drive ten minutes south on the highway through farmlands and cattle ranches to **San Andreas,** following the signs to the Historic District.

In the **Calaveras County Museum and Archives,** 30 North Main (209–754–6513), take your time perusing the extensive displays of Indian and mining artifacts, interesting old documents and papers, re-created miner's cabins and stores, and a Miwok tepee. The jail out back is where Black Bart, the notorious stagecoach robber and poet, languished for a time.

Seek out the **Thorn Mansion**, at 87 East St. Charles (209–754–1027), the restored home of Sheriff Ben Thorn, who captured Black Bart. On three acres of gardens with ponds, creeks, waterfalls, and a putting green, it's now a bed-and-breakfast inn.

Eleven miles east of San Andreas, off Railroad Flat Road, is **California Caverns** (209–736–2708), where you can take a tour through narrow passageways and huge limestone chambers to see colorful stalagtite and stalagmite formations.

It's fifteen minutes south to **Angels Camp.** On the way make a short stop at Altaville to see some colorful historic buildings and to prowl about three marvelous, circa 1850 cemeteries west of the highway.

Dinner: **La Hacienda,** 5 South Main, Angels Camp near the junction of Highway 4. (209) 736–6711. Best Mexican food in the county. Or, for a continental menu, try **Piaggi's,** 1262 South Main, Angels Camp (209–736–4862), serving fresh pasta, cioppino, steaks, and burgers.

Lodging: **Cooper House,** 1184 Church Street, off south Main, Angels Camp 95222. (209) 736–2145. A 1911 Craftsman-style beauty on a shady street; spacious suites with baths; air-conditioned.

Day 3

Morning

Breakfast: At Cooper House. Full breakfast in the elegant dining room or in the garden gazebo.

The Jumping Frog Jubilee brings thousands of spectators to Angels Camp every May to watch the jumpers do their thing. You can even rent a frog and try your own version of the wild gyrations necessary to make the frogs win the jumping contests.

On the north end of town, the **City of Angels Museum,** 753 Main (209–736–2181), is chock-full of displays relating to pioneer and Gold Rush days, with carriages, antique mining and farm equipment, and a steam locomotive on the grounds. On Main Street are a plethora of historic buildings, shops, hotels, and museums to fill your afternoon. In midtown a grassy park has remnants of five mines that pulled in more than $20 million in gold between 1886 and 1920.

Just south of Angels Camp, Highway 49 crosses the upper fingers of **New Melones Lake** (209–536–9094), created from the second largest earth-filled dam in the United States. On more than 100 miles of tree-lined shoreline are campgrounds and marinas, headquarters for fishing, sailing, waterskiing, and houseboating expeditions.

Take Highway 4 east to Stockton, then retrace your route to the Bay Area.

There's More

Volcano. A few miles east of Jackson and Sutter Creek is **Daffodil Hill,** where a spectacular display of spring color occurs between mid-March and the end of April; wildflowers, 50,000 daffodils, and tulips bloom in a farmer's field. The St. George Hotel, on Main Street in Volcano (209–296–4458), serves good lunches and dinners, with a menu dependent on the chef's whim of the day.

Lake Amador, 33 miles east of Stockton off Highway 88. (209) 274–4739. Some 425 acres of warmwater fishing, boating, sailing, swimming, camping.

Pardee Lake, near Jackson. (209) 772–1472. About 2,200 acres of warmwater fishing, boating, sailing; pool; camping; no water skis, jet skis, or swimming in the lake.

Lake Camanche, near the junction of Highways 88 and 12, between Jackson and Stockton. (209) 772–1472. Some 7,700 acres of warmwater fishing, boating, sailing; camping.

Special Events

April. Antique Show and Sale, Sutter Creek. (209) 267–0773.

April. Mother Lode Dixieland Jazz, Jackson. (209) 223–0350.

May. Calaveras County Jumping Frog Jubilee, Angels Camp. (800) 225–3754.

June. Amador County Wine Festival, Angels Camp. (209) 223–0350.

July. Christmas in July Jazz Festival, Sutter Creek. (209) 223–0350.

August. Gold Country Bluegrass Festival, Plymouth. (209) 223–0350.

September. Black Bart Day, San Andreas. (800) 225–3754.

Other Recommended
Restaurants and Lodgings

San Andreas

Black Bart Inn, 55 St. Charles. (209) 754–3808. A coffeeshop patronized by everyone in town.

Nonno's Cucina Italiana, in the Hotel Leger, Mokelumne Hill. (209) 286–1401. Sumptuous, elegant Italian food served family-style; rosemary garlic chicken, calamari, polenta, pasta; reasonable prices; saloon.

Razzle Dazzle, Central Sierra Plaza. (209) 754–1108. Bagel sandwiches, quiche, gourmet burgers.

The Robin's Nest, P.O. Box 1408. (209) 754–1076. Bed-and-breakfast accommodations in an 1895 mansion; nine rooms with bath; full breakfast.

Jackson

Broadway Hotel, 225 Broadway. (209) 223–3503. A white-with-blue-trim, three-story clapboard with verandas and beautiful gardens; rooms with private baths; large breakfast buffet.

Amador Inn, 200 Highway 49. (209) 223–0211. Nice motel, pool, coffeeshop.

Amador County Bed and Breakfast Referral. (209) 296–7778.

Plymouth

Forty-niner Trailer Village, P.O. Box 191. (209) 245–6981. Recreation halls, pool, playground, store, laundry, beauty shop.

For More Information

Amador County Chamber of Commerce, 125 Peak Street, Corner of Highways 49 and 88, Jackson, CA. (209) 223–0350.

Calaveras Lodging and Visitor's Association, 1301 South Main, Angels Camp, CA 95222. (209) 736–0049.

Stockton Visitor's Bureau, 46 West Fremont, Stockton, CA 95202. (209) 943–1987.

Gold Country South

A trip to Columbia takes you back in time.

Columbia, Bear Valley, Jamestown

_____ 2 NIGHTS _____

Big trees, big valley • Wineries • Railtown
Historic park • Caverns • Gold Rush village

From the charming village of Murphys to the wide-open meadows of
Bear Valley, then to old Columbia and rough-and-ready Jamestown,
you get a lot of gold country in this quick escape.

The most perfectly re-created Gold Rush town in the United States,
Columbia is a living museum, with costumed performers, horse-drawn

vehicles, and sights and sounds of the past that make you feel as if you've traveled back in time. Pines and maples shade the boardwalks in the hot summer months, when the place is packed with families; spring and fall are the best times to visit.

This brief warm weather introduction to Bear Valley may encourage a return visit when the snow flies. The ski resort appeals to Bay Area residents who prefer a casual country atmosphere for their cross-country and downhill skiing.

On the way home you'll spend a morning in the rowdy little burg of Jamestown, with perhaps a ride on a steamtrain.

Day 1

Morning

Drive from the Oakland Bay Bridge east on Highway 580, connecting with 99 north to Manteca, then 120 east to Highway 49, turning north to the Highway 4 junction, stopping in the town of **Murphys**— all told, about two and a half hours from the Bay Area.

Ulysses S. Grant and Mark Twain sat a spell on the veranda of the **Murphys Hotel,** before the locust trees became the tall umbrellas we see today. More than a dozen centuries-old buildings line the main drag, while narrow sidestreets are a kaleidoscope of wild country gardens, white picket fences, and ancient walnut trees shading turn-of-the-century cottages and mansions.

Murphys Creek runs cheerily through town, a small park on its banks, perfect for a picnic.

Lunch: **The Peppermint Stick,** 454 Main, Murphys. (209) 728-3570. Soup, salad; Miner's Bread Bowl filled with soup, chili, or beef stew; espresso, ice cream sodas, sundaes.

Afternoon

Main Street strolling will turn up **L'Atelier** (209–728–2139), featuring the works of local artists, and **Murphys Cheap Cash Store** (209–728–2700), where you can get a western outfit or a Victorian dress.

Bullet holes in the front door of Murphys Hotel, 457 Main (209–728–3444), remain from the good old days when Black Bart trod the floorboards; step in for a look at the great old long bar, where Saturday nights can be quite lively. Rooms and suites here are reasonable and include a substantial continental breakfast.

One mile north of Murphys, on Sheepranch Road, **Mercer Caverns** (209–728–2101) are irresistibly spooky, cool, and fascinating limestone chambers of crystalline formations.

Seven small wineries are located within 5 miles of Murphys, including ivy-covered **Black Sheep Winery** (209–728–2157), on the west end of town. In an old carriage house on Main Street beside Murphys Creek, **Millaire Winery** (209–728–1658) is a tourist attraction in the fall, when crushing and pressing take place for all to see.

Just off Sheepranch Road is the **Stevenot Winery** (209–728–3436), in a lovely valley at 1,900 feet. In the sod-roofed miner's cabin that is the tasting room, try medal-winning Zinfandel, Chardonnay, and Cabernet. A map and information on Calaveras wines are available by calling (800) 695–3737.

Take Highway 4 for about forty-five minutes through the Stanislaus National Forest to **Bear Valley Lodge,** in a spectacular, high mountain meadow at 7,200 feet, surrounded by dramatic granite peaks, snow-capped in wintertime and early spring. What can you do here? Just mountain-bike, float in the pool, walk in the pines, get a massage, fish in seven nearby lakes, climb a rock, play tennis, or hike to scenic ridgetops in the **Calaveras National Forest** (209–795–1381).

Winter fun includes skiing on one of the most extensive networks of cross-country trails in the country, 65 miles of groomed trails and endless acres of unmarked meadows. Or you can ski downhill from 8,500 feet on **Mount Reba** or skate on an acre of ice.

In front of a fireplace constructed of king-size boulders, relax with a refreshment in the cathedral lounge before dinner.

Dinner and Lodging: **Bear Valley Lodge,** P.O. Box 5038, Bear Valley 95223. (209) 753–2327. Rooms in the five-story lodge are simple and comfortable, or you can camp or rent a house or cabin nearby.

Day 2

Morning

Breakfast: European breakfast buffet and cappuccinos at Bear Valley Lodge.

Heading back on Highway 4, if you've a mind to see some *big* sequoias and take a walk or a hike, stop at **Calaveras Big Trees State Park** (209–795–2334). Short nature trails are accessible near the visitor's center, but the biggest trees—1,300 of them—are found in the South Grove, 1 mile from the parking lot up the **Big Trees Creek Trail.** You can swim here, too, in the Stanislaus River.

Continue on Highway 4, connecting with 49 to **Columbia State Historic Park** (209–532–0150). When gold was discovered here in 1850, the population boomed within a month from fewer than 100 to 6,000 people, and 150 saloons, gambling halls, and stores opened up. Many western falsefronts and two-story brick buildings with iron shutters remain, inhabited by costumed proprietors who contribute to the living history atmosphere. The state began accumulating artifacts and restoring the buildings in the 1940s. Musicians and performers are encountered on the streetcorners and in the restaurants and the theater; horse-drawn stages clip-clop up and down the streets; artisans demonstrate horseshoeing, woodcarving, and other vintage crafts; and you can pan for gold or take a horseback ride.

A few of the many shops and restaurants: **Fallon Ice Cream Parlor** (209–533–2355), for floats, shakes, and sodas at an authentic soda fountain counter; **Dreamwest Trading Company** (209–533–3300) has gold nuggets, rocks, guidebooks, and history books; **Columbia Candy Kitchen** (209–532–7886), where a four-generation family makes fresh taffy, brittles, fudge, and penny candy; **De Cosmos Daguerrean** (209–532–0815), to get your tintype taken; and **Bearcloud Gallery** (209–533–8660), specializing in American Indian art.

Lunch: **Columbia House Restaurant,** Main Street. (209) 532–5134. Traditional American fare.

Afternoon

The Columbia experience is enriched by "talking buttons" outside several storefronts; push these buttons to hear about the museum displays in the windows. Trodding the creaky floorboards of the **William Cavalier Museum,** at Main and State streets, you'll see photos of the people who lived here during the Gold Rush, as well as huge chunks of ore, quartz, and semiprecious stones. More than $1.5 billion in gold was weighed on the Wells Fargo Express scales in this town.

On the north end of town, the **Columbia Grammar School,** in use from 1860 to 1937, is outfitted with an endearing collection of antique desks, inkwells, old books, and kids' stuff.

Snacks, sodas, and sarsaparillas are easy to find in one of the several saloons (kids OK). Take a ride through the woods nearby on the **Columbia Stage** (209–532–0663).

Farther along on Parrot's Ferry Road is **Natural Bridges,** where Coyote Creek has created a colorful limestone cave. Walk on the streamside nature trail and consider swimming or rafting through the cave—not as scary as it looks.

Dinner: **City Hotel,** Washington Street, Columbia. (209) 532–1479. Big-city cuisine in elegant Gold Rush–era surroundings; superb continental menu and good wine list; dinner daily, weekend lunch and brunch. You'll be surprised to find out who the chefs and waitpersons are.

Lodging: **Fallon Hotel**, on Washington Street on the south end of town 95310 (209) 532–1470. A Victorian extravaganza of rococo wallpaper, antique furniture, and Oriental rugs.

Day 3

Morning

Breakfast: Expanded Continental breakfast at the Fallon Hotel.

Continue on Highway 49 through Sonora to Jamestown. (**Sonora** is the county seat and a highway junction; traffic spoils somewhat the Old Town atmosphere here, although sidestreets, antiques shops, and historic buildings make this worth a stop if you have the time.)

Boomed and busted several times in the past 150 years, **Jamestown** retains an anything-can-happen, Wild West atmosphere, from the days when it was just a bawdy cluster of tents on a dusty road. When the golddiggers began to rush, saloons and dancehalls were erected, then hotels and homes.

Attractions include the **Railtown 1897 State Historic Park,** on Fifth Avenue (209–984–3953), a twenty-six-acre exhibit of vintage steam locomotives and passenger cars, a roundhouse, and a grassy picnic area in an oak grove. You can take a one-hour train ride through the foothills or a two-hour "Twilight Limited," a sort of sunset cruise with refreshments, entertainment, and a barbecue dinner at the end.

A stroll up and down Main Street will turn up the **Saunders Gallery of Fine Art,** at 18190 Main, in the historic 1877 **Carboni House** (209–984–4421), showing carvings, photos, and paintings by local artists, and **Jamestown Mercantile I** and **II** (209–984–6550), two large antiques co-ops. Behind the Jamestown Hotel in the Marengo Courtyard, taste local wines at **Chestnut Wine and Gifts** (209–984–3366), and check out Native American art, jewelry, and baskets at the **Bear n' Coyote Art Gallery** (209–984–4562).

The **Jamestown Hotel,** circa 1920, at 18153 Main (209–984–3902), is an old beauty restored to its former elegance—long bar, restaurant, and nice rooms.

Lunch: **Country Kitchen Gourmet Cafe,** 18231 Main. (209) 984–3326. Homemade American food in an old-fashioned ice cream parlor; save room for pie.

Afternoon

Retrace your route back to the Bay Area.

There's More

Gold mining and panning. Tours of an operating open-pit gold mine, Wednesdays only, Jamestown. (209) 984–4641.

Gold prospecting trips, one to three hours, Vallecito near Angels Camp. (209) 736–0287.

Biking. Bear Valley Mountain Bike Center, Bear Valley. (209) 753–2834. Rentals, trail maps, guides.

Golf. Forest Meadows Golf Course, 14 miles east of Angels Camp on Highway 4, Murphys. (209) 728–3439. Eighteen holes in a pine forest.

Phoenix Lake Golf Course, 21448 Paseo De Los Portales, Sonora. (209) 532–0111. Ten minutes from Sonora; nine beautiful holes under oak trees beside a lake.

Rafting. Outdoor Adventure River Specialists, P.O. Box 67, Angels Camp. (209) 736–4677. American, Stanislaus, Merced, Kern, and other rivers.

Special Events

April. Gunfighter Rendezvous, Jamestown. (209) 984–4616.

June. Dixieland Jamboree, Jamestown. (209) 984–4616.

July–August. Music from Bear Valley. (209) 753–BEAR. Big-name classical, operatic, jazz, and theatrical performers.

October. Harvest Festival, Columbia State Historic Park. (209) 532–0150.

October. Fiddle and Banjo Contest, Columbia State Historic Park. (209) 532–0150.

December. Christmas Lamplight Tour, Miner's Christmas, and Las Posadas, Columbia State Historic Park. (209) 532–0150.

Other Recommended Restaurants and Lodgings

Jamestown

Lulu's Saloon and Grill, 18201 Main. (209) 984–3678. Fun and food in an antiquey atmosphere; dozens of vintage lamps and chandeliers.

Michelangelo's, 18228 Main. (209) 984–4830. Contemporary cafe and bar; nouvelle Italian menu, pizza, pasta.

Sonora

Serenity, 15305 Bear Cub Drive. (209) 533–1441. Five miles from Sonora off Highway 108 east. The Hoovers' big, beautiful country house is surrounded by porches and six acres of live oaks and pines, completely quiet; spacious, pretty rooms with private baths; sumptuous breakfasts.

Gold Country Inns of Tuolumne County, P.O. Box 462. (209) 533–1845.

La Casa Inglesa B and B, 18047 Lime Kiln Road. (209) 532–5822. About 2.5 miles from town. English country elegance.

Columbia

Harlan House, 22890 School House. (209) 533–4862. Victorian mansion renovated in 1992; three rooms with baths; full breakfast.

Trails End RV Park, 21770 Parrotts Ferry Road. (209) 533–2395. Shady spots near the state park.

Bear Valley condominiums and cabin rentals, P.O. Box 5038. Bear Valley, 95223. (800) 794–3866.

Murphys

Dunbar House, 271 Jones Street. (209) 728–2897. Luxurious, historic bed-and-breakfast inn near Main Street; private baths; gardens; bountiful breakfast and wine buffet.

San Andreas

Gold Strike Village, 1925 Gold Strike Road. (209) 754–3180. Mobile home and RV park; pool, clubhouse, laundry, hiking trails, camping.

Arnold

Lodge at Manuel Mill, White Pines Road. (209) 795–2622. Bed-and-breakfast inn, totally secluded on forty-three acres of woods; five rooms with private baths and wood stoves; full breakfast.

For More Information

Jamestown Visitor's Information Center, P.O. Box 699, Jamestown, CA 95327. (209) 984–4616.

Calaveras Lodging and Visitor's Association, 1301 South Main, Angels Camp, CA 95222. (209) 736–0049.

Bear Valley Ski Company, P.O. Box 5038, Bear Valley, CA 95223. (209) 753–2301; snow phone, (209) 753–2308.

East Bay Getaway

The Union Hotel, built in 1882, is a downtown landmark.

Benicia, Mount Diablo

1 NIGHT

Top of the mountain · Antiques shopping · Muir's home
Art galleries and studios · California history · Seaside walks

Many people live here all their lives and never take a look at the Bay Area from the high vantage point of Mount Diablo. On a clear winter day after a storm, you can see Half Dome in Yosemite and Mount Lassen, 163 miles away. Camping and picnic sites on the mountain are spectacular, to say the least.

After a ride up the mountain and a short sojourn to John Muir's home, it's on to Benicia, a breezy waterfront town on the north shore of Carquinez Straits, where the Sacramento Delta meets the sea.

Benicia is an artisans', craftspersons', and antiques dealers' community. The California state capital for a brief period in the 1850s, this was a lively port, providing barracks for the U.S. Army. Dozens of restored homes, military buildings, churches, hotels, and saloons are still in use today, grandly residing on the tree-lined streets of Benicia, as they have for more than a hundred years.

Day 1

Morning

From the Oakland Bay Bridge, take Highway 24 east to Walnut Creek, going north on 680 to the Ignacio Valley Road exit. It's 2 miles to a right on Bancroft/Walnut Avenue; then follow the signs to Gate Road, leading into **Mount Diablo State Park** (510–837–2525). You'll pass horse and cattle ranches on your winding ascent to the summit, at 3,849 feet; there's a visitor's center about 3 miles from the top. Oaks and madrone give way to pines and juniper as you rise above the clouds. In the 1800s horse-drawn stages brought visitors up this steep road to a sixteen-room hotel! Except for hazy days in the summertime, you can usually see the entire Bay Area and much of Northern California from here. If you're up for a morning hike, get a trail map from the rangers and explore on your own, or take a guided interpretive hike.

Take Highway 680 north to Highway 4 west, to the Alhambra/Martinez exit, stopping at the **John Muir National Historical Site,** 4202 Alhambra Avenue (510–228–8860), to see John Muir's grand, seventeen-room Victorian home. The famous Yosemite naturalist and founder of the Sierra Club lived here for many years, and his letters and papers are on display, as are rooms full of fabulous antique furnishings. Stroll about on eight acres of lovely grounds.

Take Highway 4 to 680 north, across Suisun Bay to the Central Benicia exit, cruising into town and down First Street, past a pretty green park with an old-fashioned gazebo and weeping willows.

Lunch: **First Street Cafe,** 440 First Street, Benicia. (707) 745–1400. Soups, salads, deli sandwiches, espresso; homemade pastries and desserts.

Afternoon

Walk up to the **Benecia Chamber of Commerce,** at 601 First (707–745–2120) for a map, then set the scene for your historical tour of town by visiting the **Benicia State Capitol and Historical Park,** at West G and First streets (707–745–3385); built in 1852, it's been completely restored. Next door the **Fischer-Hanlon House** was a Gold Rush–era hotel that ended up a Victorian mansion lived in by a wealthy family; docents lead tours of the home and gardens.

On the streets west of First are oodles of glorious homes from the Victorian and later eras. Notice the **Captain Walsh House Bed and Breakfast Inn,** at 235 East L, an 1850 beauty shipped around the Horn from Boston.

Take a walk or a bike ride on the **Waterfront Pathway** system of trails, accessible in several places on the waterfront between the **Benecia Pier** at the foot of First Street and West Fourteenth at the west end of town; you'll see signs pointing to the trails. Along the pathway are boat-launching and fishing sites, benches, small parks, and a par course. A bike trail continues west into the **Benicia State Recreation Area,** where you can picnic and fish.

Dinner: **The Restaurant at the Union Hotel,** 401 First Street, Benicia. (707) 746–0100. Continental cuisine much lauded by restaurant reviewers, in a dining room warmed with antiques and stained glass. Some of the best entertainers in the Bay Area perform in the lounge on weekends.

Lodging: **Union Hotel,** a three-story landmark built in 1882, with a checkered history that includes some years as a brothel. A dozen spacious rooms, some with huge spa tubs, each decorated in a different era—art deco, Louis XVI, early American, Victorian, and more. For the fun of choosing, you may wish to obtain a brochure in advance with photos of each room.

Day 2

Morning

Breakfast: Continental breakfast at the Union Hotel and/or espresso and pastries at the **First Street Cafe,** 440 First Street. (707) 745–1400.

Walk down one side of First Street and up the other for a shopping, sightseeing, and gallery-hopping tour of Benicia; it's 1 mile from one end to the other. One of more than twenty antiques shops, **Hagen's House of Clocks,** at 513 First (707–745–2643), has one of the largest collections of old clocks in the state. The **Country Florist,** at 700 First (707–746–6028), has a vast inventory of country and Victorian ornaments and collectibles. Look at the fine handcrafted ceramics at the **Pot Factory,** at 426 First (707–745–1223).

If the First Street shops don't quench your thirst for wonderful old things, go to **The Dial Antiques,** at 190 West J Street (707–745–2552);

on this street is a magnificent corridor of centuries-old palm trees.

Lunch: **Waterfront Cafe and Bistro,** 127 First Street, Benicia. (707) 745–4635. Freshly roasted coffees, deli sandwiches, salads, books, newspapers.

Afternoon

Drive a few blocks east on H Street to an industrial area where artisans' studios and galleries will keep you wandering. Some of the glassblowers are world-famous: **Zellique,** at 701 H (707–745–5710), and **Nourot Glass** and **Smyers Glass,** at 675 H (707–745–1463).

Drive north on East 5 a few blocks, turning right on Military East to more studios and galleries, such as **Studio 41,** at 949 Grant (707–745–0254), where contemporary crafts and wearable art are produced and sold. Stop in at the **Arts Benicia** office, 1063 Jefferson (707–747–0131), for information on where to find the studios. On Tyler street are several sculptors and painters, plus a wallpaper designer and a neon artist.

Also in this neighborhood are three historical buildings, a twenty-room neoclassical mansion from the 1860s, the **Commandant's Home;** the **Guard House,** circa 1870; and the **Clocktower Fortress,** with 2-foot-thick stone walls, once an arsenal.

To get a good look at the "Mothball Fleet" of eighty-five decommissioned American warships, take Highway 780 east to 680 north to the Lake Herman Road exit and the vista point.

Return to 780 west, cross the Carquinez Bridge south on Highway 80, and duck under the bridge into Crockett.

Lunch: **Nantucket Fish Company,** foot of Port Street, Crockett. (510) 787–2233. Steamed clams, fresh fish, salads, pastas. Near the industrial behemoth C and H Sugar refinery, under the giant concrete legs of the bridge.

Head back to the East Bay or San Francisco.

There's More

Camel Barn Museum, 2024 Camel Road, Benicia. (707) 745–5435. Built in 1853 to house the animals of the U.S. Camel Corps, a bright idea of Secretary of War Jefferson Davis; now a community museum.

Sandoval's Back Stage, 2032 Columbus Parkway, Benicia. (707) 746–7830. Live comedy and music. Also Sandoval's California Mexican cuisine.

Wind Enchantments, 113 West I Street, Benicia. (707) 745–9185. Sailboarding rentals and lessons.

Special Events

April–May. Glassblowers Open House, Benicia. (707) 745–1463.
June. Historic Home Tour, Benicia. (707) 745–8817.
August. Glassblowers Open House, Benicia. (707) 745–1463.
September. Benicia First Street Jazz Festival. (707) 745–2120. Dixieland, Big Band, blues, more.
September. Benicia Waterfront Celebration. (707) 745–9791.
September. Benicia Handicraft Fair. (707) 745–2120.
October. California Maritime Academy Whaleboat Regatta. (707) 745–2120. Some 15,000 people come out to watch seventy boats in rowing competitions.
October. Mountain Bike Race on Mount Diablo. (510) 933–5289. A tough climb.
November. Christmas Parade, Benicia. (707) 745–9791.
December. Glassblowers Open House, Benicia. (707) 745–1463.
December. Christmas Home Tour, Benicia. (707) 745–3186.

Other Recommended Restaurants and Lodgings

Point Richmond

East Brother Light Station Bed and Breakfast, 117 Park Place. (510) 233–2385. On a tiny island in San Pablo Bay, just north of the Richmond–San Rafael Bridge, a unique and elegant inn; a parade of ships and boats glide by all day and night. You're ferried the short distance from the mainland in a small boat; accommodations include full breakfast and candlelit gourmet dinner.

Benicia

Captain Dillingham's Inn, 145 East D Street. (707) 746–7164. Ten rooms in an 1850, bright yellow Cape Cod–style inn 1 block off Main. Jacuzzi tubs, private baths, full breakfast, English country gardens.

Captain Walsh House Bed and Breakfast Inn, 235 East L. (707) 747–5653. An elegant Victorian Gothic, one of the most famous houses in Northern California.

For More Information

Benicia Chamber of Commerce, 601 First Street, Benicia, CA 94510. (707) 745–2120.

Escapes Farther Afield

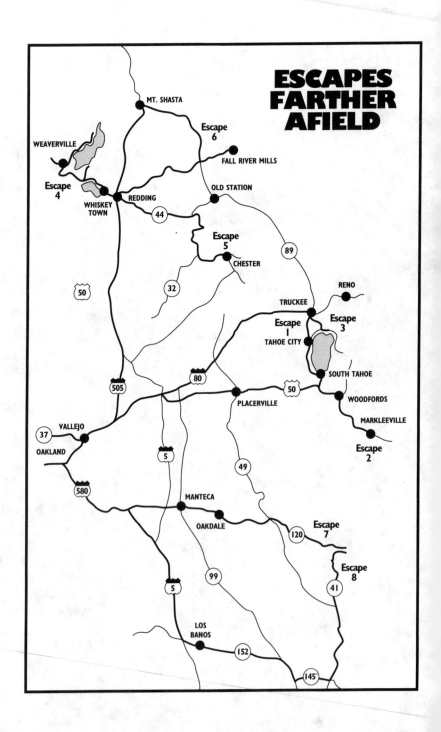

ESCAPES
FARTHER
AFIELD

MT. SHASTA

Escape
6

WEAVERVILLE

FALL RIVER MILLS

Escape
4

OLD STATION

WHISKEY
TOWN

REDDING

44

Escape
5

CHESTER

89

32

50

RENO

TRUCKEE

Escape
1

Escape
3

TAHOE CITY

80

SOUTH TAHOE

505

50

WOODFORDS

PLACERVILLE

MARKLEEVILLE

VALLEJO

Escape
2

37

OAKLAND

5

49

580

MANTECA

OAKDALE

Escape
7

120

99

Escape
8

5

41

LOS
BANOS

152

145

Old Tahoe on the West Shore

Emerald Bay is one of the most photographed spots in California.

Mansions in the Mountains

—————————————— 2 NIGHTS ——————————————

Vintage mansions · River rambling · Mountain hikes
Beaches, bikes, hikes · Boating on quiet bays · Winter fun

The 1920s were the halcyon days of Lake Tahoe's west shore, when wealthy nabobs from San Francisco built mansions and zipped about in sleek varnished speedboats, and when wooden steamers still cruised the lake, revelers aboard. Much of this area is still privately owned; restaurants and beaches are frequented by people who've spent their vacations here for decades. The pace is slow, except in the nightspots and shops of Tahoe City. Even in the high summer season, you can doze on a quiet beach, walk and bike on silent forest trails, and poke around contentedly in a rented boat. And the rowdy, rushing Truckee River is always there for fishing, rafting, and strolling along beside.

The sun shines an average of 274 days a year at Tahoe. Soft spring days are clear and wildflowery; fall is brisk, with aspen color glittering through the pines. Winter is lively at several small, inexpensive down-hill and cross-country resorts, and positively posh at the big ski resorts: Squaw Valley, Northstar, and Alpine Meadows.

Day 1

Morning

To start your four-hour drive to Lake Tahoe from the Oakland Bay Bridge, drive north on Highway 80 for ninety minutes, to the Nut Tree Road exit, near Vacaville.

Breakfast: At an annex of the big **Nut Tree** complex across the freeway, the **Coffee Tree.** (707) 448–8435. Fresh and colorful, with big booths and a counter. The strawberry waffles and dollar-size pancakes are dynamite. Pick up some apricot nutbread and peanut brittle to keep you going on the road. (On one of your Highway 80 trips, you may wish to browse in the ninety-two discount store outlets located here.)

Now turn on the cruise control for your drive through the **Sacramento Valley** and up into the mountains. When you see Sacramento's skyline, watch for the Reno Highway 80 exit; you will skirt the city on the west side. Before long, the valley floor gives way to the foothills of the High Sierras and spreading oaks begin to share the hillsides with pines and firs. There's a highway reststop at Donner Summit, at 7,227 feet, and a few miles farther you'll turn right onto Highway 89, driving 13 miles south to Tahoe City, past Squaw Valley, through the **Truckee River Canyon**. The paved **Truckee River Bike Path** starts at Alpine Meadows, winds along the Truckee 4 miles to Tahoe City, then takes a 9-mile route south along the lake. At some point during your west shore sojourn, you'll want to rent bikes at Tahoe City, or just walk, jog, or push a baby carriage on the path. In the low-water days of the late summer and fall, the river slides quietly along. In winter and spring it boils and crashes past ice-decorated trees and snowy islands.

Arriving in Tahoe City, turn right at the junction with Highway 89, which turns sharply south along the western lakeshore. Cross **Fanny Bridge**—where people are always lined up, leaning over to see the trout ladder where the Truckee joins the lake—and stop at the **Gate-keeper's Museum** and lakeside park, 130 West Lake Boulevard, Tahoe City (916–583–1762), to see an exceptional collection of Washoe and Paiute Indian baskets, artifacts, and historical memorabilia. Here you get a first view of Tahoe, North America's largest Alpine lake, 22 miles long and 12 miles wide.

Lunch: Just up the road from Fanny Bridge, at the **Swiss Beer Garden** at **Swiss Lakewood Lodge,** 5055 West Lake Boulevard (916) 583–7200. Bratwurst, sandwiches, salads, German beer, apple tarts—all in a blooming garden under the pines. (At night, classical French cuisine with a Swiss accent in the main restaurant; extensive wine list.)

Afternoon

Drive 9.5 miles south on Highway 89 to **Sugar Pine Point State Park** (916–525–7982) to visit one of the grand dames of Tahoe, a spectacular three-story, 12,000-square-foot Queen Anne–style summer home, the **Ehrman Mansion.** Built at the turn of the century by a San Francisco banker, the mansion still looks like the privately owned lakeside estate it once was, surrounded by sweeping lawns shaded by tall pines. Rangers give daily tours of the mansion and boathouse, imparting stories of old days on the lake. After the tour wander around the grounds, spread a blanket on the beach, or take a walk on trails along the lakeshore. A longer hike is accessible from the large campground across the road; rangers have maps for you.

In the late afternoon drive north on 89 to **Sunnyside Restaurant and Lodge,** 1850 West Lake Boulevard, 2 miles south of the Tahoe City Y (916–583–7200). Sunnyside has one of the best blue water and high mountain views on the lake. People-viewing is excellent here, too. Boats of every description come and go in the marina; French-fried zucchini and onion rings are tops; and once you get settled outside on the deck or inside by a lakeside window, you'll find it hard to move from the spot. Here you can rent jet skis, sail- and powerboats, and take a sailing lesson. Winter evenings are warm and friendly in the lounge in front of a giant river-rock fireplace. Old canoes are suspended from the high beamed ceiling; paintings of antique lake cruisers line the walls.

Dinner: **Chambers Landing,** 1 mile south of Homewood. (916) 525–7672. Overlooking the lake on a glass-enclosed and heated terrace. Try the Moroccan lamb or fresh fish, and you owe it to yourself to have a Chambers Punch. A small bar on the Chambers pier is popular with locals. On one side of the pier is a private beach for people staying in the Chambers Landing condos (see page 172), and on the other side is a public beach, one of the nicest on the west shore.

Lodging: **The Rockwood Lodge,** 5295 West Lake, P.O. Box 226,

Homewood 96141. (916) 525–5273. A stone mansion, circa 1930, with a knotty-pine interior emboldened by hand-hewn beams, the Rockwood is only 100 feet from the lake but seems a million miles away. The four rooms are cozy and comfortable, with European-style down beds, in-suite basins, robes, and views of the trees or the lake. The main lounge has a huge stone fireplace and a bottle of wine waiting for you.

Day 2

Morning

Breakfast: Here at the Rockwood Lodge. Belgian waffles and fruit crepes are part of a robust selection of goodies. The dining room looks onto a grassy meadow shaded by tall pines. An expert on local wildlife, proprietor Connie Stevens runs a wildlife reserve on the property, taking in injured animals and birds until they are well enough to be returned to the wild.

Go out the back door of the inn and stroll or bike up the road to the **Homewood Ski Area** (916–525–2922); Connie can suggest an easy or a challenging route. (Adjacent to the lodge, the ski area is small and friendly, less expensive and less intimidating than the big glitzy resorts.)

With Rockwood beach chairs and towels, step across the road to the public beach at **Obexer's Marina** (916–525–7962) and swim, if you dare; at 6,229 feet, the miraculous sapphire-blue, clear water of the lake is always chilly. Surface temperatures in August allegedly reach the low seventies. Get a few rays on the beach, or rent a boat here and motor along the shoreline.

Now pick up picnic supplies in Homewood and head south toward Emerald Bay. On the way check out **Meeks Bay Resort and Marina** (916–525–7242), owned by the U.S. Forest Service, a popular jet- and water-ski beach with an unparalleled view of the lake. This is a good place for beachy activities like rowing, canoeing, and paddleboating (all rentable) or just hanging out in the sun, though all the motors create plenty of noise during the summer. A little cafe serves snacks and burgers, and there are a 150-unit campground and a few cottages.

About 5.5 miles from Meeks Bay, **Emerald Bay** appears in its glittering blue-green glory far below. One of the most photographed pieces of scenery in California, the bay can be seen from several vista points along Highway 89, but you must trundle down a steep 1-mile trail (or take a tour boat) to reach the real treasure of the bay—the Scandinavian castle of **Vikingsholm** (916–525–7232), built in 1928. A cross between an eleventh-century castle and an ancient church, the mansion is considered the finest example of Scandinavian architecture

in North America. Take a ranger's tour to see the extensively decorated and furnished estate home.

Lunch: Have your picnic here at Vikingsholm.

Afternoon

From Highway 89 at Emerald Bay, there is an easy 2-mile loop hike
to **Eagle Falls** and beautiful **Eagle Lake,** surrounded by the sheer
walls of Desolation Wilderness, where many trailheads lead into the
southern Tahoe National forestlands.

One of the most accessible but least known wilderness areas at
Tahoe is **Blackwood Canyon,** off Highway 89 just north of Tahoe
Pines. Perfect for easy walks, rollerblading, and biking, the paved road
is the only development and has almost no traffic; this road is a good
add-on to the shoreline bike path. Forests, meadows, and the banks of
Blackwood Creek make good picnic spots. You can hike on the flat
valley floor or drive up the road to the steep trails of 8,000-foot
Barker Pass, hooking up with the **Pacific Crest Trail.** There are also
an off-road-vehicle camp and a trails area here in the canyon.

Dinner: **Gar Woods Grill and Pier,** 5000 North Lake Boulevard,
Carnelian Bay. (916) 546–3366. About fifteen minutes north of Tahoe
City, on the lake, with a zinger of a view. The glassed-in deck with
heaters is a place to take your time enjoying pasta, fresh seafood, or
the restaurant's famous "Hot Rock" specialties, wherein you grill your
own dinner. The bar is popular and lively, a good place to have an
appetizer and people-watch. Sunday brunches are legendary. Try the
White Chocolate Snickers Cheesecake. Uh-huh.

Lodging: Rockwood Lodge.

Day 3

Morning

Breakfast: Rockwood's.

Explore the small town of **Tahoe City,** the action and shopping
headquarters of the west shore. Boutiques are found in the **Cobble-
stone, Boatworks,** and **Roundhouse** malls; pine-scented breezes
and lake views make shopping at the Boatworks particularly pleasant.
The **Heritage Gallery** (916–581–2208) features vintage Tahoe photos
and original paintings of the area. **Sports Tahoe** (916–583–1990) is
jammed with fabulous clothes for every season at the lake.

Just north of Tahoe City is the **Watson Cabin Living Museum,** 560
North Lake Boulevard (916–583–8717), one of the oldest structures on
the lake. Docent guides in period costumes will point out the interesting original furnishings.

Lunch: **River Ranch,** Highway 89 and Alpine Meadows Road. (916) 583–4264. On your way out of Tahoe City to head home, stop here for lunch and a last look at the Truckee. A small, charming hotel on the river, River Ranch offers a popular indoor/outdoor restaurant and bar, located at the south end of the Truckee bike path.

Highway 89 takes you to Highway 80 south and the Bay Area.

A secret: At Bowman, 5 miles north of Auburn, is **Ikeda's,** 13500 Lincoln Avenue (916–885–4243), visible from the freeway. Only you and I know that this is a terrific little place for burgers and fresh veggies and fruit to take home. For another good place to purchase fresh valley produce, nuts, olives, and juices, take the Pedrick Road just north of the Nut Tree, stopping at the Quonset hut building on the west side of the highway.

There's More

Squaw Valley USA, P.O. Box 2007, Olympic Valley 96146. (800) 545–4350. The 1960 Winter Olympics were held in this huge resort area, one of the world's largest and best ski mountains, actually five peaks. The valley is spectacular in every season. You can stay here in a luxury hotel, a reasonable lodge, a bed-and-breakfast inn, a rented condo, or a house. A 150-passenger aerial cable car accesses the High Camp complex, where you can ice-skate, hike, mountain-bike, swim, picnic, play volleyball and tennis, bungee-jump, or just blink in amazement at the mountain surroundings.

Alpine Meadows Ski Area, P.O. Box 5279, Tahoe City, CA 96145. (916) 583–6914. A major ski area for all abilities, priding itself on having the longest season; more laid-back atmosphere than Squaw. Ski runs have scary names like Chute That Seldom Slides, Promised Land, and Our Father. Trailhead to Granite Chief Wilderness.

Tour boat. Departing from Round House Mall in Tahoe City, the only tour boat on this side of the lake is the *Sunrunner* (916–583–0141), a 65-foot motorized catamaran that goes to Emerald Bay and along the shoreline past Fleur du Lac and other magnificent old Tahoe estates.

B. L. Bliss State Park, 3.6 miles south of Meeks Bay. MISTIX reservations: (800) 444–7275. Has 168 campground sites, beautiful white sand beach, picnics, good swimming, and a lovely 4-mile trail leading to Emerald Bay.

Granlibakken Ski Area, P.O. Box 165, Tahoe City, CA 96141. (916) 583–9896. Nordic skiing.

Homewood Ski Area, Homewood, CA 95718. (916) 525–2992. Five lifts; a good choice for kids and beginners.

Public beaches. Chambers Landing, Obexer's, Sugar Pine Point, Meeks Bay, Homewood.

Just north of Tahoe City is the uncrowded beach and pier at Lake Forest; boats can be launched and camping is available.

Note: It's legal and perfectly acceptable to access any beach from the water, even if adjacent to private property.

Hiking. Mount Tallac. (916) 573–2600. A four-hour loop to the 9,700-foot summit; trailheads at Baldwin Beach and Fallen Leaf Lake.

Donner Lake to the Pacific Crest Trail. Drive 4 miles west on Old Highway 40 from the lake's west end; watch for the trailhead on the left. A 15-mile, strenuous hike along the ridge of the Sierra crest, descending down Squaw Valley's Shirley Canyon. You'll need to park your car at Squaw Valley's Olympic Village Inn.

Camp Richardson Pack Station, P.O. Box 8335, South Lake Tahoe 96158. (916) 541–3113. Horseback riding and packing into Desolation Wilderness.

Shirley Lakes trail starts behind the Olympic Village Inn. A nice 4-mile hike from the Squaw Valley; do all or part of a four-hour round-trip, stopping to wade or swim in the creek or the lake, gambol in wildflower-strewn meadows, and nap under the pines.

Golf. Tahoe City Golf Course. (916) 583–1516. Nine holes.

Resort at Squaw Creek, Squaw Valley. (916) 581–6637. Eighteen-hole, Robert Trent Jones course, surrounded by the glory of the valley.

Northstar, Basque Drive, Truckee. (916) 562–2490. Eighteen holes; one of the prettiest and most challenging courses at Tahoe.

River rafting. Truckee River Rafting Center, 205 River Road, Tahoe City 96145. (916) 583–RAFT.

Fanny Bridge Raft Rentals, Tahoe City. (916) 583–3021.

Ballooning. Mountain High Balloons. (916) 587–6922.

Special Events

July. Squaw Valley Community of Writers Poetry Session. (916) 583–6985.

August. Tahoe Yacht Club Concours D'Elegance, Boatworks Mall, Tahoe City. (916) 583–8022. Classic wooden boats.

August. Squaw Valley Community of Writers Fiction and Screen Session. (916) 583–6985.

August. Squaw Valley Festival of Fine Arts and Crafts. (916) 583–6985.

August. Truckee Championship Rodeo. (916) 587–6462.

September. Splendor of the Sierra Fine Art Show, Northstar-at-Tahoe. (916) 587–0288.

September. Antique and Classic Car Show, Tahoe City. (916) 525–4429.

October. Octoberfest, Alpine Meadows Ski Resort. (916) 583–2371. Dining, dancing, and Bavarian festivities.

Other Recommended
Restaurants and Lodgings

Tahoe City

Wolfdale's, 640 North Lake Boulevard. (916) 583-5700. California cuisine with a unique Japanese flair; reservations essential.

Jake's on the Lake, 780 North Lake Boulevard, Boatworks Mall. (916) 583–0188. Groovy, popular, lots of fun, right on the lake. Seafood bar and backgammon in the lounge; continental cuisine and hearty mountain food.

Sunnyside Restaurant and Lodge, 1850 West Lake Boulevard. (916) 583–7200. Casually elegant lakefront rooms and suites, each with tiny balcony, some with fireplaces, wetbars, sundecks. Tahoe mountain–style decor, down comforters, pine armoires. Ask for a quiet room, away from the dining room and the road. Breakfast buffet and afternoon tea are served in a cozy lounge.

Cottage Inn, 1690 West Lake Boulevard. (916) 581–4073. Two miles south of Tahoe City on Highway 89. Fifteen mountain-style cottages with Scandinavian decor, fireplaces, hearty breakfasts, sauna, private beach. Ask for a unit away from the road.

Tahoe Taverns, 300 West Lake Boulevard. (916) 583–3704. Near Fanny Bridge. Large complex of casual condos in a pine grove, right on the water; pool, lawns; quiet, pretty location on the edge of town.

Tahoe Vista

Captain Jon's, 7220 North Lake Boulevard. (916) 546–4819. French country cuisine, fresh seafood, casual elegance, one of the best restaurants at Tahoe. Cocktail lounge and lunch cafe on the lake; the dinner house has a partial view.

Homewood

West Shore Cafe, 5180 West Lake Boulevard. (916) 525–5200. A terrace on the beach, heaters, umbrellas, nouvelle cuisine, fresh fish, grilled meats, excellent wines, lunch, dinner; accessible by boat.

Chambers Landing, P.O. Box 537, Homewood. (916) 525–7202. Some 43 privately owned condos; a quiet, private hideaway in an aspen grove; lawns, views; private beach and pool. One of the nicest condo complexes at Tahoe, offering three- and four- bedroom luxury.

Tahoma

Alpenhaus Country Inn, P.O. Box 262. (916) 525–5000. Swiss Alpine lodge run by a retired navy captain and his kids; across from the lake, on the bike route. Several upstairs rooms have old-fashioned, rather feminine decor, with rocking chairs and quilts, private baths; ask for a room at the back. Rustic, remodeled cottages have two bedrooms and kitchens. Pretty pool area and hot tub. Rates include hefty breakfasts of mountain omelets and home fries. Hearty lunches and dinners: bratwurst, fresh fish, steak, pasta. Family-style Basque dinners one day a week are popular and noisy, with live music and sing-alongs; the kids will love this.

Soda Springs

Rainbow Tavern Lodge, P.O. Box 1100. (916) 426–3871. Old Tahoe–style lodge, circa 1925; small, comfortable hotel rooms; good restaurant and bar. On the Yuba River near cross-country and downhill skiing, hiking, fishing.

Sugar Pine Point State Park Campground, Meeks Bay. MISTIX reservations: (800) 444–7275. Offers 175 sites.

Olympic Valley

Resort at Squaw Creek, P.O. Box 3333. (800) 3CREEK3. A 405-room, luxury destination resort with golf course, ice rink, shops, tennis, and a chairlift to ski runs and High Camp.

Squaw Valley Inn, 1920 Squaw Valley Road. (800) 323–7666. Charming shingle-and-stone complex near the ski tram; hotel rooms, swimming pools, neato lounge with big stone fireplace.

For More Information

Tahoe North Visitors and Convention Bureau, P.O. Box 5578, Tahoe City, CA 96145. (800) TAHOE–4–U.

Cal Trans Road Conditions. San Francisco: (415) 557–3755. Sacramento: (916) 653–7623.

Nevada Road Conditions. (702) 793–1313.

Advice: In the summer and on snowy weekends, avoid driving to Tahoe on Friday afternoons or returning on Sunday afternoons, unless you've got hours to waste. Every month of the year, check the weather and road conditions. Snow can fall even in June.

The drought: Water levels have dropped steadily in the lake for several years, and many boat launches are out of commission. Check before you arrive with your boat.

Tahoe South and the Hope Valley

Sorenson's Resort is one of the many places you can relax in the Hope Valley.

Aspens and Silver Dollars

_____ 2 NIGHTS _____

Peaceful valley · Cozy cabins · Apple pie · Hot springs
Casino night · Old Tahoe estates · Beachtime

A triple-header: quiet hours in the aspen meadows and along the trout streams of Hope Valley; historical sights and lakeside fun; and casino-hopping under the neon lights of South Lake Tahoe. You'll get your first glimpse of Lake Tahoe, the largest alpine lake on the continent, at Echo Summit on Highway 50.

Day 1

Morning

Take Highway 80 to Sacramento, then Highway 50 to Kyburz, a three-and-one-half-hour trip from San Francisco or the East Bay.

Lunch: **Strawberry Lodge**, Highway 50, Kyburz, CA 95920. (916) 659–7200. Good American food and soda fountain specialties in a restored 1940s lodge; walking trails nearby.

Afternoon

Continue a half hour to Meyers, just south of South Lake Tahoe, and turn right onto Highway 89 for the half-hour drive over Luther Pass, sliding down into the aspen-studded, stream-freshened high mountain meadows of **Hope Valley,** at 7,180 feet. Sparsely developed, green, and gorgeous, the 1-mile-wide valley is crisscrossed by the **Carson River,** a trout angler's dream. Cross-country skiing is superb on dozens of flat meadows; downhill skiing can be had at Kirkwood, at the southwest end of the valley, over Carson Pass.

Turn left at the Highways 89 and 88 intersection, then immediately right into **Sorensen's Resort,** 14255 Highway 88, Hope Valley, CA 96120 (800–423–9949), where you will spend the night. About Hope Valley, John Muir said, "You wade out into the grassy sun-lake, feeling yourself contained in one of nature's most sacred chambers, withdrawn from the sterner influences of the mountains."

A clutch of log cabins in a pine and aspen grove, Sorensen's is romantic and family-oriented at same time. Some old and some new rustic cabins have homespun country decor, brass beds, wood stoves, and some kitchens, all in forested, creekside settings. Cozy with a wood-burning stove, **Sorensen's Country Cafe** serves hearty breakfasts, lunches, and dinners, indoors and outside under the trees. Buy guidebooks and fishing licenses here. The west fork of the Carson is just across the road.

Owners John and Patty Brissenden will direct you to fishing holes and wildflower walks and will arrange river-rafting or cross-country skiing expeditions. Located in the **Toiyabe National Forest,** Sorensen's provides flyfishing and cross-country-skiing instruction and rentals.

Ask about the guided hike on the Emigrant Trail. Worn smooth by pioneers on their way west, it's a fascinating route, with evidence of how wagons and animals were winched and hauled up and down steep grades and cliffsides.

Once a reststop for emigrants of the 1800s, Sorensen's idyllic piece of the High Sierras is thick with wildflowers until the snow flies; in the fall the aspens look like streams of fire across the valley floor. At night lights twinkle around the cabin doors, wood smoke is in the air, and if you've a cabin away from the road, all you can hear is the sound of a rushing stream.

Dinner: Here in Sorenson's Country Cafe. Sit at a big wooden table with other guests, and tuck into beef stew or fresh fish, homemade bread, and fruit cobbler. Everyone seems to turn in early to enjoy the cabins and rest up for early-morning outings. But if you can't stand the quiet, make the forty-five-minute drive into the **Carson Valley** and pay your dues at the **Carson Valley Inn Casino,** 1627 Highway 395, Minden (702–782–9711).

Day 2

Morning

Breakfast: At Sorensen's. Fall out from under your comforter into the cafe for all-you-can-eat waffles with fruit or an old-fashioned bacon-and-eggs breakfast. There are a little stocked trout pond and a small play area to keep kids busy.

An old logging road adjacent to the resort leads up a pine forest, past huge boulders and views of the rugged mountains. It's 7 moderately strenuous miles to the top of the mountain, an 11-mile loop. Looking out over the valley, you'll see that it's greener than the bark beetle-stricken Tahoe Basin. Say a silent thank-you to the tireless Friends of Hope Valley, who continue valiantly to hold off developers.

In the late morning drive ten minutes east on Highway 89, to the **Woodford Stage Stop,** 92 Old Pony Express Road (916–694–2930). There are many roadside pullouts where you can stop and fish in the Carson or play along the banks.

A hundred-year-old stop on the Pony Express route, Woodford's is now a great old general store with groceries and fishing gear. The famous "Snowshoe" Thompson stopped here regularly on his Placerville-to-Genoa mail crossing in the mid-1800s.

Lunch: At the Woodford Stage Shop. Eat at the counter, have a sandwich or some chili, followed by the sour cream apple pie that people drive hours to get.

Afternoon

Proceed 6 miles southeast on Highway 89 to **Markleeville,** population one hundred, circa 1875, the seat of Alpine County. A stroll around town will turn up the **Cutthroat Saloon** (916–694–2150), **Gunslinger's Pizza** (916–694–2483), and the **Alpine County Historical Museum Complex** (916–694–2317). Bikers in leathers and tourists hobnob in the gloom of the saloon, shooting pool, playing pinball, pretending to be regulars. Some 10,000 rough-and-tumble silver miners once lived here, but now this is a sleepy two-block-long burg of clapboard buildings, where travelers alight briefly on their way to campgrounds and fishing.

In the middle of Markleeville, you'll see the sign for **Grover's Hot Springs** (916–694–2248), a state park 4 miles west of town. Here 148-degree water flows out of underground springs into swimming and soaking pools—wonderful any day of the year, and delightfully steamy when snow is on the ground. There are campgrounds here and walking trails, although the hot pools are the main attraction.

Between Grover's and Markleeville, trout fishing and cool wading are good in **Markleeville Creek.** Several nearby creeks, lakes, and the upper **East Carson River** are planted with rainbows; information can be obtained at **Monty Wolf's Trading Post,** in Markleeville (916–694–2201).

(*Note:* The route from here to Bear Valley on Highway 4 is 39 miles over 8,700-foot Ebbets Pass on a treacherous two-lane road. If you've got extra vacation days and you're not driving a large RV, consider taking this route. The scenery is incredible, and there are many lakes, streams, trails, and campgrounds.)

It's about an hour from Markleeville back to Meyers. Turn right (north) on Highway 50, then right again on the **Pioneer Trail,** proceeding 5.5 miles to make a left on Tahoe Boulevard and drive into the town of South Lake Tahoe.

Check in at **Lakeland Village,** Highway 50 near the base of Ski Run Boulevard, in **South Lake Tahoe** (916–541–7711). Here are 260 condo and lodge units on the lake, set back from the road in nineteen acres of pines and featuring a private sandy beach, two swimming pools, tennis courts, saunas, and some fireplaces and kitchens.

This is your night to hit the casinos, so get into your sequins and silver-tipped cowboy boots. Several multistory casinos are within a hop of one another, some connected by an underground walkway. Big names put on big shows at **Harrah's** (702–588–6611), **Caesars** (702–588–3515), **Harvey's** (702–588–2411), and the **Horizon** (702–588–6211). Up-and-coming stars play in the lounges and smaller clubs. Casino restaurants are a bargain; views are dizzying from rooftop restaurants. South Lake Tahoe is 8 miles of hotels, motels, restaurants, tourist traps, and neon lights. A blazing tunnel of excitement at night, the town's charm wears a bit thin in the light of day, especially if your wallet is lighter than when you blew into town.

Dinner: **The Summit,** on top of the world at Harrah's at the north end of South Lake Tahoe, P.O. Box 8, Stateline, NV. (702) 588–6611. Continental dining, tables on terraced levels, breathtaking views.

Do it.

Day 3

Morning

Breakfast: **Ernie's,** near the Y, 1146 Emerald Bay Road. (916) 541–2161. Down-home American breakfasts; only Tahoe locals and you know about Ernie's.

Toss your last few quarters away and head south, following Highway 89, also called **Emerald Bay Road,** out of town to the south end of the lake. At 9,735 feet **Mount Tallac** towers over a plethora of sights and things to do on the south shore. Relive the 1920s heydey of the rich and famous at the **Tallac Historic Site** (916–573–2600). Restored and open to tour are several formerly private estates, an old casino, and a hotel. Many musical and art events are held at Tallac, from jazz to bluegrass, from craft demonstrations to photo exhibits. In August the **Great Gatsby Festival** looks like the good old days, with antique boats and merrymakers in period costume. The 5-mile, 3,500-foot hike to the top of Mount Tallac rewards the hiker with magnificent views; trailheads are across the road from Baldwin Beach.

Also at Baldwin Beach is the **U.S. Forest Service Lake Tahoe Visitor's Center** (916–573–2600), offering exhibits of geology, natural environment, and history; nature trails; and interpretive programs.

Baldwin, Pope, and **Kiva beaches** are accessible by bus (916–573–2080) from South Lake Tahoe; a network of hiking trails connects the beaches, the visitor's center, and the Tallac Historic Site. Near Baldwin Beach is the only virgin forest remaining in the entire Tahoe Basin, which was logged out completely in the 1800s. The beautiful, green forests you see around the lake are second- and third-growth. The ancient Sugar pines and Douglas fir of the primary forests were cut for railroad construction and for the building of San Francisco and other boomtowns. Shorter in height, sparser and lacking in the rich biodiversity that sustained earlier timberlands, today's trees are vulnerable to erosion, disease, and the vagaries of weather; a long-term drought and a bark beetle infestation in the 1980s and early 1990s devastated much of what remains of Tahoe's precious woods.

Lunch: **Fresh Ketch Lakeside Restaurant,** 2433 Venice Drive (watch for the left turn, just north of the Highway 50-89 Y at the south end of town). (916) 541–5683. Indoor or outdoor dining, overlooking busy Tahoe Keys Marina; salads, sandwiches, fresh fish; bar.

Afternoon

Head home on Highway 50, or head for the beach, the Heavenly Valley aerial tram, a golf course, or out on the lake on a paddlewheeling cruise boat.

There's More

Beaches. Three public beaches in South Lake Tahoe, each with extensive recreational facilities, including pools: El Dorado Beach, Regan Beach, and Connelly Beach (behind Timber Cove Lodge, between El Dorado Beach and Ski Run Boulevard).

Beaches not as overrun in the summertime are Nevada Beach, 1.5 miles north of town at Elk Point Road, and Zephyr Cove, 4 miles north of the stateline on Highway 50.

Tours on the lake. *Tahoe Queen,* South Lake Tahoe. (916) 541-3364. A huge paddlewheeler, day and evening trips to Emerald Bay, departs from Ski Run Marina.

The MS *Dixie.* (702) 588-3508. A smaller paddlewheeler, departing from Zephyr Cove. A cotton barge on the Mississippi in 1927, the *Dixie* was a floating casino at Tahoe; then it sank and was raised and converted to a tour boat.

Heavenly Valley Ski Area, P.O. Box 2180, Stateline, NV 89449. (916) 541-SKII. One of the biggest ski resorts in the world; dozens of runs for every ability. With one of the highest skiable summits in the United States, Heavenly's mountain overlooks Tahoe on one side and the Carson Valley on the other.

Heavenly's Aerial Tram, at the east end of Ski Run Boulevard, South Lake Tahoe. (916) 541-1330. Open all summer for a five-minute, 1-mile ride up into the sky overlooking the lake and mountains. An easy 2-mile trail loops the mountaintop; a restaurant serves pretty good lunches, brunches, and dinners—romantic, with lights twinkling below.

Kirkwood Meadows, P.O. Box 1, Kirkwood, CA 95646. (209) 258-7000. Major cross-country and downhill skiing area and summer resort; condo rentals. Highest base elevation at Tahoe: 7,800 feet. Hundreds of acres of wildflower-strewn meadows, hiking trails.

Golf. Edgewood Tahoe Golf Course, Highway 50 at Stateline. (702) 588-3566. Eighteen holes; the site of major tournaments; the most challenging course at the lake. Located behind the Horizon Casino.

Glenbrook Golf Course, Highway 50 at Glenbrook. (702) 749-5201. Nine holes; no reservations taken.

Tahoe Paradise Golf Course, on Highway 50 in Meyers. (916) 577-2121. Eighteen-hole course.

Hiking. Desolation Wilderness. Hundreds of lakes, thousands of acres of outback, many trails. Easy accessibility makes it extremely popular; best off-season. For an 11.4-mile loop daytrip, take the Glen Alpine trailhead at the end of Fallen Leaf Lake Road, hiking to Lake Aloha. (At Glen Alpine Springs is a covey of Bernard Maybeck–designed cabins at streamside.) ·

Round Lake, 6.4-mile loop to a neato swimming hole. Take Highway 89 south out of Meyers; 3.6 miles before Luther Pass is roadside parking on the north, trailhead on the south.

Showers Lake, 10.2-mile easy loop to the highest lake in the Upper Truckee River basin. From the intersection of Highways 88 and 89 in Hope Valley, take 88 to Carson Pass; continue to a bend with a parking area.

Tahoe Rim Trail. Trailhead information: (916) 577–0676. A 150-mile trail.

Kayaking. Kayak Tahoe at Camp Richardson, P.O. Box 11129, Tahoe Paradise, CA 96155. (916) 544–2011. Day tours, camping, lessons, rentals.

Lake Tahoe Historical Society Museum, 3458 Lake Tahoe Boulevard, South Lake Tahoe. (916) 541–4975.

Shopping. Factory stores at the Y of Highways 50 and 89.

Tahoe Factory Stores, 2501 Highway 50.

Round Hill Mall, north of South Lake Tahoe at Zephyr Cove. Unique, nontouristy shops and a good Mexican restaurant.

Boating. Tahoe Keys Marina, South Lake Tahoe. (916) 541–2155. Boat launch, sail- and powerboat rentals, *Tahoe Paradise* tour boat, restaurant.

Woodwind Sailing Cruises. (702) 588–3000. Thirty-passenger, 41-foot trimaran with a glass bottom; peaceful way to cruise the lake; departs from Zephyr Cove.

Special Events

March. Echo to Kirkwood Cross Country Race, Kirkwood. (209) 258–7248.

June. Reno Rodeo, Reno. (702) 329–3877.

June–September. Valhalla Summer Festival of Art and Music, South Lake Tahoe. (916) 542–4166. Concerts and exhibits in and around historical mansions.

June–July. Lake Tahoe Sailweek, Tahoe Keys Marina. (800) AT–TAHOE. Sailboats from across the country converge for a weeklong series of races.

July–August. Music and Shakespeare at Sand Harbor. (916) 583–9048.

August. Hot August Nights in Reno. (702) 829–1955. Fifties and sixties cars, rock-and-roll.

August. Great Gatsby Festival, Tahoe Keys Marina, Tallac Historic Site. (916) 546–2768. Antique and classic wooden boat show, Roaring Twenties living history.

September. Reno National Championship Air Races, Reno. (702) 972–6663.

Other Recommended Restaurants and Lodgings

Kyburz

Strawberry Lodge, Highway 50. (916) 659–7200. Twenty miles west of the town of South Lake Tahoe. Quiet, comfortable, restored 1940s lodge surrounded by the pines of a National Forest. Good restaurant, ice cream parlor; cross-country skiing, mountain-biking, tennis, swimming; nearby fishing, hiking, downhill skiing.

Hope Valley

Hope Valley Resort, 14655 Highway 88. (916) 694–2292. Store, restaurant, RV park.

South Lake Tahoe

Christiania Inn, P.O. Box 18298. (916) 544–7337. Eclectic Swiss chalet design; five rooms with private baths upstairs; restaurant downstairs; five-minute walk to ski.

Camp Richardson, P.O. Box 9028. (916) 541–1801. Just east of Emerald Bay on Highway 89. A big resort with marina, beach, riding stables, lodge, restaurant, cottages, 230-unit campground, and a general store. A favorite family summer-vacation venue for decades.

Accommodation Station, 2520 Lake Tahoe Boulevard, #3. (916) 542-5850. Rental of homes, condos, and cabins.

Cantina los Tres Hombres, Highway 89, .25 mile north of Highway 50. (916) 544–1233. Good Mexican food in a lively cantina atmosphere.

Hot Gossip, Highway 50 at Ski Run Boulevard. (916) 541–4823. Espresso, pastries, magazines and books, light breakfast, lunch, a locals' spot.

Embassy Suites Resort, 4130 Lake Tahoe Boulevard. (800) 362–2779. Luxury suites; Old Tahoe–style architecture; full breakfast and cocktail hour free.

Emerald Bay

State park campgrounds at Emerald Bay. MISTIX reservations: (800) 444–7275. Drive-in and boat-in sites.

Kirkwood

Caples Lake Resort in the Hope Valley, P.O. Box 88 (209)

258–8888. Launch; rent powerboats, canoes, sailboats, paddleboats. Lodge and cabins, restaurant, store.

For More Information

Lake Tahoe Visitor's Authority, 1156 Ski Run Boulevard, South Lake Tahoe, CA 96151. (800) AT–TAHOE.

Alpine County Chamber of Commerce, P.O. Box 265, Markleeville, CA 96120. (916) 694–2475.

Cal Trans Road Conditions. South Lake Tahoe: (916) 577–3550. San Francisco: (415) 557–3755. Sacramento: (916) 653–7623.

Nevada Road Conditions. (702) 793–1313.

Advice: In the summer and on snowy weekends, avoid driving to Tahoe on Friday afternoons or returning on Sunday afternoons, unless you've got hours to waste. Every month of the year, check the weather and road conditions. Snow can fall even in June.

The drought: Water levels have dropped steadily in the lake for years, and many boat-launching locations are out of commission. Check before you arrive with your boat.

Tahoe North

The 39 trillion gallons of water in Lake Tahoe provide for great sailing.

Peaceful Pines and a Western Town

_____ 2 NIGHTS _____

Mountain meadows · Lakeside walks
Old railroad town · Beachtime · Winter resorts

_____

The Washoe Indians called it *Tahoe*, or "Big Water." Twenty-six miles
long and 12 miles wide, Lake Tahoe is 1,600 feet deep and "clear
enough to see the scales on a cutthroat trout at 80 feet," according to
Mark Twain. Surrounded by snow-frosted mountains and dense evergreen forests, the translucent blue water is hypnotic and cold, very

cold. Legends tell of Indian chiefs in full regalia and women in Victorian garb floating motionless and frozen at the bottom of the lake.

On the north shore are little traffic, no neon, and few people. Fewer beaches and restaurants, too, but some of the best. A handful of small casinos add spice. The high life at south Tahoe and the action in Tahoe City are both within a half-hour or so, but on this short trip you'll want to stay put.

The old miners' and loggers' town of Truckee, still rough-and-tumble after all these years, makes a fun stop on your way to the lake.

Day 1

Morning

From the Golden Gate Bridge, drive north on Highway 101, turning east on Highway 37 to Vallejo, where you'll catch Highway 80 north to Sacramento; it's a four-hour drive to the north shore.

Breakfast: At Sacramento take the J Street/Old Sacramento exit, stopping for breakfast at the **Whistle Stop Cafe,** on Front Street between K and L, in Old Town (916–446–4445). Open at 6:30 A.M. for Belgian waffles, homemade cinnamon rolls, and steak and eggs.

From here it's an uphill pull, two hours from the valley floor to Donner Summit, at 7,135 feet. Just past Baxter stop at the **Emigrant Gap Viewpoint,** on the west side of the road. Looking out over hundreds of miles of high country, you see the tremendous tilted block of the Sierras, sloping shallowly toward the west. Glacial canyons are gouged out of the granite, and the Yuba and Bear rivers have cut their own valleys. Pioneers winched their wagons down into the Bear Valley from here at 4,000 feet, then dragged themselves back up to Washington Ridge on the opposite side of the valley, the most difficult section of their journey to a new life in the West. In the Tahoe area you can find worn pioneer trails and grooves cut into cliffs and tree trunks by the winching ropes.

Beyond the summit of Donner Pass, take a reststop at **Donner Memorial State Park** (916–587–3841), a camping and picnic area at 5,950 feet, with a short, pleasant walking trail. The **Emigrant Trail Museum,** located within the park, depicts stories of the Donner party tragedy and the building of the railroad through the Sierras in the 1800s. You'll see traintracks, mostly covered with snow buildings, running along rugged mountainsides above Donner Lake. Taking the Amtrak train from Oakland to Truckee is a relaxing way to get to Tahoe; parties of skiers have fun doing this in the wintertime, and the scenery—wow!

Donner Lake, 3 miles long with a shoreline of 7.5 miles, is a smaller, quieter, less developed version of Tahoe, and many vacationers prefer it. You can camp, launch a boat, rent a cabin, fish, hike, ski, and enjoy the crystal blue waters.

Continuing on Highway 80, take the Central Truckee exit into **Truckee,** where 2 blocks of restored brick-and-stone falsefront buildings face the railroad tracks. It looks and feels like the rollicking old railroading and logging town it's been since the mid-1800s. In 1873 at least one prisoner a day was hauled out of a Truckee saloon to the Nevada County jail. The jail is now a charming museum of the old days. Amtrak blasts into town a couple of times a day.

There's good shopping on Truckee's Commercial Row, a string of boutique, western wear, and ski equipment stores. Here you can purchase a sheepskin coat, moccasins, a fringed vest, or a stocking cap.

Lunch: **O.B.'s Pub and Restaurant,** on the main street of Truckee. (916) 587-4164. In a hundred-year-old building; a cacophony of antiques, stained glass, wooden booths, Old Town ambience. California cuisine; soup, chili, salads, sandwiches; Watney's on tap.

Afternoon

Proceed east out of Truckee on Highway 267 through the **Martis Valley,** passing Northstar (see page 190) as you climb up Brockway Summit—a short but icy ascent in the winter—on your way to the stoplight at Kings Beach. Stop here and jump in the lake, then take a left on Highway 89, crossing into Nevada at Crystal Bay; it's five minutes to Incline Village.

If there is a secret hideaway at Tahoe, it's **Incline Village,** a small community of gorgeous homes and condos sprinkled on the shores of the lake and across steep mountainsides, with breathtaking views. Quiet and traffic-free, Incline has many virtues, such as the small, excellent ski resort of Diamond Peak; two Robert Trent Jones golf courses; two of Tahoe's loveliest beaches; and one elegant casino hotel.

Some people spend their entire vacation at Incline, using only their feet or bikes for transportation. A small, exquisite beach park, **Burnt Cedar Beach,** is available only to those who rent or own (renting a condo or house is the way to go here); the park has a big heated pool, a lifeguard, a snackbar, a kids' playground, shady lawns for lounging, picnic tables, barbecues, shallow water for wading, deep water for swimming, and a killer view. **Ski Beach,** in front of the Hyatt Regency Lake Tahoe, has all of that except the pool, and it's long enough for a morning walk.

Park at the east end of Lakeshore Drive at the Hyatt and walk back along the lake on the paved walking/biking/jogging path, stopping to snap photos, take in the view, fill your lungs, and pick up pinecones.

Have a sundown cocktail at **Hugo's** (702–832–1234), a romantic beachfront bar across from the Hyatt, while the lights start to twinkle on around the lake. Appetizers and softly delivered live music make for a well-earned happy hour after a day on the road.

Dinner: **Azzara's,** 930 Tahoe Boulevard, in the Raley's Center. (702) 831–0346. Comfortable, very popular place serving Italian everything. Especially good are the Sicilian artichokes, turkey with mozzarella and tomatoes, the saltimbocca, and the pizza; reservations necessary.

Lodging: **Coeur du Lac Condominiums,** c/o Brat Realty, P.O. Box 7197, Incline Village, NV 89452. (800) 869–8308. Contemporary mountain-style condos tucked into a pine forest, with walking paths, a heated pool, saunas, fireplaces, one to four bedrooms, lots of privacy; within walking distance to shopping, beaches, and ski shuttles.

This evening lurk around the **Hyatt,** even if you're not a gambler. The "Fantasy Forest" in the casino is something to see: full-size pine trees studded with a zillion tiny lights and huge chandeliers reflected in a mirrored ceiling—even lights in the carpet. You can lounge in front of the big fireplace and people-watch, or you can plunge in and throw some money away. *Tip:* Play the slot machines at the ends of the aisles, near the center of the room; payoffs occur on the most visible machines.

Day 2

Morning

Breakfast: **Wildflower Cafe,** 769 Tahoe Boulevard. (702) 831–8072. Rubbing shoulders with skiers (snow or water) and construction workers at the counter or at a wooden table, have a Paul Bunyan–size breakfast of waffles or eggs and potatoes.

You'll find every kind of clothing and equipment for outdoor recreation at the **Outdoorsman** (702–831–0446); pick up picnic supplies at **Raley's** (702–831–3400; both stores are near Azzara's). Now head east on Tahoe Boulevard to Country Club Drive and turn left, then right at the top of the hill onto Highway 431, also known as the Mount Rose Highway.

Dominating the mountain skyline on the north shore is **Mount Rose,** above Incline. From the scenic overlook on 431, almost the entire 22-mile-long lake gleams below, rimmed by the Sierras on the west and the Carson Range on the east. Seven miles beyond the lookout point is **Tahoe Meadows,** at 8,600 feet, a series of huge meadows where you can enjoy miles of cross-country skiing and summertime hiking, easy or strenuous. Sometimes a little soggy, the meadows are crisscrossed with small streams and crowded with wildflowers most of the year—buttercups, purple penstemons, marsh marigolds, Alpine shooting stars. Chickadees and jays flit through the willows and the pines.

The 12-mile loop hike to the summit of Mount Rose, at 10,776 feet, is a half-day trip that starts on an old jeep road near the cinderblock building. Even if you can't make it to the top for the view that awaits, you may wish to start up this trail; there are a pond with a frog chorus in residence and wildflowers galore. At the top you'll see the whole lake basin and the Carson Valley sweeping away into the distance, and even Lassen Peak on a very clear day.

Afternoon

Have your picnic here or take it back down the mountain to Tahoe Boulevard, going east out of Incline—actually Highway 28—a few miles to **Sand Harbor State Park** (702–831–0494), picturesque, with two white sand beaches, tree-shaded picnic spots, and lake and mountain views—the most beautiful beach park at the lake. The annual **Music and Shakespeare Festivals** (916–583–9048) are held here on July and August evenings. On a clear summer night, you'll watch the sun go down over the lake while you sit on a blanket sipping wine and the kids play on the sand nearby. The lights go down, the stars come out, and magic begins on stage. Many people come back every year.

After an afternoon dip in the lake or a dip in the Burnt Cedar pool, or perhaps a nap, drive to **Crystal Bay,** at Stateline (five minutes west of Incline on Highway 89), and go into **Cal-Neva Lodge** (800–225–6382), the high-rise hotel casino at Stateline. It's one of the oldest casinos on the lake, made famous by a former owner, Frank Sinatra. Off the lobby the Indian Room is a vast, beam-ceilinged lounge with a big boulder fireplace and a fascinating collection of early Tahoe artifacts, bearskins, and bobcats. If you're in the mood to tie the knot, step into one of three wedding chapels on the grounds.

Just down the road at **Kings Beach**, if it's a summer weekend, there's probably an arts and crafts fair going on.

As the sun starts to set, continue on Highway 89 to **Gar Woods,** 5000 North Lake Boulevard, Carnelian Bay (916–546–3366), for cocktails or tea; this is one of a handful of restaurants located right on the lake.

Dinner: At **Colonel Clair's,** 6873 North Lake Boulevard. (916) 546–7358. Cajun specialties and fresh fish; knotty-pine booths; noisy, popular, elbow-to-elbow friendliness; amazing food.

Lodging: **Coeur du Lac Condominiums,** c/o Brat Realty, P.O. Box 7197, Incline Village, NV 89452. (800) 869–8308. Contemporary mountain-style condos tucked into a pine forest, with walking paths, a heated pool, saunas, fireplaces, one to four bedrooms, lots of privacy; within walking distance to shopping, beaches, and ski shuttles.

Day 3

Morning

Breakfast: At **The Original Old Post Office,** 5245 North Lake Boulevard, Carnelian Bay. (916) 546–3205. Only the locals knew about this place, until now. Down-home cooking, monster-size breakfasts starting at 6:00 A.M. every day. You may wait on weekends, but not long.

Before heading back to the Bay Area, play a round of golf on one of Incline's falling-off-the-mountain golf courses; play tennis on one of the town's twenty-six courts; or take the kids to the **Ponderosa Ranch** (see below).

Heading back toward Truckee, you may wish to stop at **Northstar** (see page 190) and take the chairlift—anytime of year—to walking trails on the mountaintop.

There's More

Ponderosa Ranch, on the east end of Incline Village on Highway 28. (702) 831–0691. The original set used to film the TV show "Bonanza." An elaborate western town and theme park, haywagon breakfasts, shooting gallery, museum, gold panning, Hossburgers, ice cream parlor. If the kids are under twelve or so, this is a must.

Golf. Incline Championship and Executive Courses, Incline Village. (702) 832–1144. Two beautiful mountainside courses; also good cross-country skiing on the lower course.

Old Brockway Golf Course, North Lake Boulevard at Kings Beach. (916) 546–9909. Nine holes; inexpensive and easy.

Tahoe Donner Golf Course, Truckee. (916) 587–9440. Eighteen holes.

Skiing. Diamond Peak at Ski Incline, P.O. Box AL, Incline Village. (702) 832–1177. Dazzling views, best for intermediates and beginners.

Mount Rose Ski Area, 2222 Mount Rose Highway. (702) 849–0706. Two sides of a big mountain; plenty of runs for all abilities; check wind conditions before purchasing a lift ticket.

Tahoe Donner Ski Area. (916) 587–9494. For beginners and families.

Hiking. Marlette Lake. Trailhead at Spooner Lake, near the junction of Highways 28 and 50. A 10-mile, moderately strenuous loop with a lake and killer views at the top; aspens make this a stunner in the fall.

Also at Spooner Lake (702–831–0494): trout fishing, hiking, picnicking, mountain-biking, equestrian trails, cross-country skiing, rentals.

Mountain-biking. The famous Flume Trail starts at Spooner Lake, rides up to Marlette Lake, across the mountainside, then downhill at a 60 percent slope to Incline Village, 14 miles. For information on biking on Brockway Summit and other areas, call the Tahoe Area Mountain Bicyling Association at (916) 541–7505.

Fishing. Giant Kokanee salmon, released into the lake by accident in 1940, lurk below rocky ledges on the north shore, along with several species of trout. Crystal Bay is the best spot to catch them.

Casinos. Cal-Neva Lodge, the Tahoe Biltmore, and the Crystal Bay Club at Crystal Bay Stateline, five minutes west of Incline Village on Highway 28.

Tennis. Twenty-six courts in Incline Village, at the Lakeside Tennis Resort (702–831–5300), and at public courts.

Special Events

June. Gigantic Arts and Crafts Fair at Kings Beach. (916) 546–2935.

June. Truckee Tahoe Air Show. (916) 587–1119.

July–August. Music and Shakespeare at Sand Harbor. (916) 583–9048. Beautiful outdoor amphitheater.

July. North Lake Tahoe Symphony Association Summer Music Series. (702) 832–1606. Sunday-afternoon concerts.

Other Recommended Restaurants and Lodgings

Incline Village

Spatz, 341 Ski Way. (702) 831–8999. Dramatic lake view from 7,000 feet, nouvelle cuisine, bar, lunch on the deck, elegant ambience.

Vacation Station, P.O. Box 7180. (702) 831–3664. Homes and condos to rent.

Hyatt Regency Lake Tahoe, 111 Country Club Drive at Lakeshore. (702) 832–1234. A 460-unit, full-service hotel and casino with several restaurants: Hugo's Rotisserie, on the beach, upscale, fresh seafood, steaks, lunch, dinner, and elaborate Sunday brunch; Ciao Mein, classy Italian/Oriental cafe, great name; Sierra Cafe, open twenty-four hours, a fancy coffeeshop with good food and keno. Shuttle service to major ski resorts. European-mountain-lodge interior; hotel rooms and lakeside cottages; state-of-the-art health club; outdoor pool; tennis.

Tahoe Vista

Le Petit Pier, 7238 North Lake Boulevard. (916) 546–4464. In the French country tradition, a small, elegant place with a world-class wine list and a nouvelle cuisine menu; on the lake, pricey, for *very* special occasions. Sundown cocktails in the lakeside bar.

Soda Springs

Royal Gorge's Rainbow Lodge, P.O. Box 1100. (916) 426–3661. Historic 30-room hotel, restaurant, bar. Royal Gorge is one of the largest cross-country skiing resorts in the world. Rainbow Lodge is at the Royal Gorge trailhead. There is also a European-style wilderness lodge, circa 1930, to which you can ski or be ferried by horse-drawn sleigh, wrapped in a fur robe—yes! Moonlight cross-country tours are unforgettable.

Northstar, Truckee. (916) 587–0248. Five minutes east of Truckee on Highway 267. A complete resort village, with lodge rooms, condos, and houses to rent; a major ski resort; golf course; equestrian trails; shops, cafes, and restaurants. In the summer chairlifts take hikers and mountain-bikers up to wonderful mountain trails.

For More Information

Tahoe North Visitor's and Convention Bureau, P.O. Box 5578, Tahoe City, CA 96145. (916) 583–3494.

Truckee Donner Visitor's Center, P.O. Box 2757, Truckee, CA 96160. (800) 548–8388.

Incline Village Visitor's Bureau, 969 Tahoe Boulevard, Incline Village, NV 89451. (702) 832–1606.

Cal Trans Road Conditions. San Francisco: (415) 557–3755. Sacramento: (916) 653–7623.

Nevada Road Conditions. (702) 793–1313.

Advice: In the summer and on snowy weekends, avoid driving to Tahoe on Friday afternoons or returning on Sunday afternoons, unless you've got hours to waste. Every month of the year, check the weather and road conditions. Snow can fall even in June.

The drought: Water levels have dropped steadily in the lake for several years, and many boat launches are out of commission. Check before you arrive with your boat.

Trinity Loop

Discover the wonders of nature at Eagle Creek Falls.

The Lakes, the Alps, Weaverville

——————————— 2 NIGHTS ———————————

Gold Rush towns • Lakes, rivers, forests • Historical sites
Trout fishing • Exploring the alps • Antiques and junque

Freshened with fifty-five sparkling Alpine lakes, the dark, brooding forests of the Trinity Alps loom 9,000 feet above Trinity Lake, which snakes several miles through a rugged valley. This is one of the wildest regions of the United States, sparsely populated and little known, even to Californians. You'll see no stoplights and no parking meters in Trinity County. Black bears, mountain lions, Roosevelt elk, mink, river otters, eagles, and spotted owls still inhabit the 500,000 acres of the Shasta-Trinity National Forest.

The Trinity River leaps with salmon and steelhead, yielding fish of ten pounds or more. In the many lakes and streams, trout and bass keep fisherpersons happy in every season.

When you tire of the lakes, rivers, and forests of the Trinity outback, explore the charming little towns once inhabited by Gold Rush forty-niners, pioneers, and Chinese immigrants from a hundred years ago.

Day 1

Morning

Drive north from the Golden Gate Bridge on Highway 101, connecting with Highway 5 north to Redding, 246 miles all told. Drive through Redding on Highway 299 (see Escape Farther Afield Six).

Lunch: **Westside Deli Redding French Bakery,** 1561 West Cypress, downtown Redding, (916) 222–0787. Luscious deli sandwiches, pastries.

Afternoon

Drive west out of Redding on Highway 299 for 8 miles, to Whiskeytown Lake. It's a winding two-lane mountain road, but passing lanes and pullovers make it comfortable. Turn left to **Whiskeytown Lake Visitor Information Center** and overlook, P.O. Box 188, Whiskeytown 96095–0188. (916) 241–6584. **Whiskeytown Lake** is a cool blue jewel with 36 miles of primarily undeveloped shoreline. About 3 miles from the visitor's center, park at **Brandy Creek** and take a walk along the lake's edge on **Davis Gulch Trail,** about 2 miles long. This is a great family lake, where kids catch catfish, bluegill, and crappie. Their moms and dads go for the bass, trout, and kokanee—up to five-pounders. There are three boat ramps, and the Oak Bottom and Brandy Creek resorts rent boats. The **Whiskeytown General Store** (916–246–3444) started supplying groceries and fishing tackle fifty years ago and never stopped. At the **Oak Bottom Marina** (916–359–2269), you can camp in a tent or an RV and can rent a canoe, fishing boat, or small sailboat and have a picnic; this is the best swimming spot.

Turning back onto Highway 299 at the north end of the lake, drive forty minutes to **Weaverville,** a nineteenth-century town beneath a dramatic **Trinity Alps** backdrop. Most of the town's original structures were destroyed by fire and replaced in the mid-1800s by brick buildings with wooden overhangs and spiral wooden staircases. A circa 1900 bandstand and the second oldest courthouse in California contribute to an Old West atmosphere.

A must-see here in the center of town is the **Joss House State Historic Park** (916–623–5284), where the "Temple amongst the Forest beneath the Clouds" has been restored to its ornate glory. In the 1850s thousands of Chinese sought gold along the Trinity, and this Chinese temple, with its carved altars, tapestries, and colorful artifacts, was built for their Taoist worship. Continuously used as a temple since then, the Joss House is now part of a state park, shady and cool with a creek running through.

Next door the Gold Rush and pioneer days are alive and kicking at the **Jake Jackson Museum and Trinity County Historical Park** on Main Street (916–623–5211); stampmill, miner's cabin, blacksmith shop, and other displays are here. Across the street in a hundred-year-old building is the **Highland Art Center** (916–623–5111), where local artists show their works.

At the **Western Shop,** 226 Main Street in Old Town (916–623–6494), outfit yourself with cowboy boots or moccasins and a western shirt. Go to **Brady's Sport Shop,** 201 Main (916–623–3121), for hunting and fishing equipment and information. Brady's is on the ground floor of the **Weaverville Hotel,** 201 Main (916–623–3121), which has been operating continuously since 1861; rooms upstairs are inexpensive and comfortable.

Dinner: **Historic Pacific Brewery,** 401 South Main, across from the Joss House. (916) 623–3000. Hearty American food in a circa 1850 brick building.

Lodging: **Weaverville Victorian Inn,** 1709 Main Street, Weaverville 96093. (916) 623–4432. Sixty nice rooms, contemporary Victorian decor; some rooms with spas and views of a woodsy setting. Ask about the inn's meals-and-lodging specials.

Day 2

Morning

Breakfast: **The Mustard Seed,** 210 Main Street. (916) 623–2922. In Old Town, surrounded by wonderful elm trees; sit indoors or out. Belgian waffles, quiche, bacon-and-eggs; try the homemade apple pie—yes, for breakfast!

Head northeast out of town on Highway 3, beginning your exploration of the **Trinity Lake** area and the **Shasta-Trinity National Forest.** The jagged teeth of **Trinity Alps** loom to the west over the entire lake basin, covered on lower slopes with dense forestlands. Long and skinny, Trinity Lake has 157 miles of rugged shoreline and hundreds of coves that seem to absorb and hide houseboats, water-skiers, jet skis, and fishing boats; the lake always seems quiet and uncrowded, even in the summertime. The west side of the lake is dotted with campgrounds, resorts, and boat launches, while the east side, with somewhat restricted auto access, is largely undeveloped; campers and backpackers love it. Try your luck at fishing for trophy-size large-mouth bass, trout, kokanee salmon, and catfish.

About 20 miles out of Weaverville, there is an interesting sidetrip on Rainier Road (a dirt road across the highway from the Mule Creek Guard Station). If you've an interest in forest management, this is an opportunity to see areas of clear-cutting, replantings, and selective cutting, as well as one of the tallest sugar pines alive, the 247-foot-tall **Sandam Tree.**

Three miles farther is another sidetrip—a 2-mile round-trip on a paved road to **Bowerman Barn.** On the National Register of Historic Places, it's one of the last of its unique type of structure. Docents will point out the stone foundation, whipsawn siding, and hand-forged square nails.

Lunch: **The Trinity Alps Resort,** at Stuart Fork Road. (916) 286–2205. The resort has one of the area's best restaurants, with a deck overlooking a stream. The forty private, rustic housekeeping cabins are right on **Stuart's Fork River,** which rushes clear and cold down from the alps. There are also a bar, general store, trail horses, and sports equipment.

Afternoon

Proceed 6 miles to **Trinity Center,** a small town that was entirely relocated to this spot when the giant **Trinity Dam,** one of the highest earth-filled dams in the world, was constructed in 1961. At the **Scott Museum,** on Airport Road (916–266–3367), you can see Indian artifacts, covered wagons, stagecoaches, and tons of artifacts reminiscent of old pioneer and Gold Rush days.

Highway 3 continues north along the shore of Trinity Lake to the **North Shore Vista;** stop to wade and play in the lake and take a walk. Arrive at your lodging destination early enough to stroll about and enjoy the farm animals and peace and quiet of the ranch.

About 10 miles above Trinity Center is **Coffee Creek,** where several resorts are located. Turn left onto Coffee Creek Road and meander along to see zowie views of the alps and access traiheads into the Trinity Alps wilderness.

Dinner: **Ycatapom Inn Restaurant,** in a historic building on Mary

Road in Trinity Center. (916) 266–3321. Steak, fish, world-class salad bar, casual.

Lodging: **Carrville Bed and Breakfast Inn,** P.O. Box 3536, Trinity Center 96091. (916) 266–3511. Six miles north of Trinity Center. A turn-of-the-century stage stop, now a country ranch resort, circa 1920, with spreading lawns, pool, llamas, and miniature horses. Gracefully decorated Victorian-era bedrooms open to long verandas; a massive rock fireplace warms the main lounge.

Day 3

Morning

Breakfast: At the Carrville Inn. Big breakfasts of homegrown fruit and farm eggs, plus homemade sausage and muffins.

Drive south on Highway 3 to the junction with Highway 105, turning east toward the **Trinity Vista;** from here you get a spectacular view of mountain peaks and a number of managed forest units in various states of harvest. Some 25 million board feet of timber are removed annually from this section of the National Forest; new timber crops are scheduled for harvest in 80 to 120 years.

It's another 8 miles or so to **Lewiston,** a flower-bedecked burg dating from the 1860s. The town is so tiny that you can see all of it in one glance, strung out prettily along the rushing **Trinity River.** A 1903 landmark is the **Old Lewiston Bridge,** one of the last one-lane bridges still in use. Below the bridge and in nearby **Lewiston Lake,** fisherpersons flycast for rainbows, brooks, and browns.

The Country Peddler, TNT Antiques, and the **Old Lewiston Mercantile,** all on Main Street, sell antique bottles, folk art, and collectibles of every description—literally thousands of square feet of good browsing, something to think about if your companion is fishing and you're not. Also on Main Street, **The Hitchin' Post** (916–778–3486) is a general store and deli.

Lunch: **Lewiston Hotel,** on Deadwood Road. (916) 778–3823. Built in the 1860s as a stagecoach stop, authentically funky historic ambience; burgers, sandwiches, salads, bar. Grizzle-bearded denizens of Lewiston sit on the hotel porch—or are they stockbrokers from the city who vowed not to shave or change clothes while on a fishing trip?

Afternoon

Between Lewiston and the Trinity Dam, you can picnic by the river, wade, swim, and fish in calm waters from the side of the road or from a small boat. Across from **Pine Cove Trailer Park,** P.O. Box 255,

Lewiston (916–778–3838), are a fishing pier, swimming beach, boat ramp, and marina, a nice place for an evening swim.

It's 36 miles from Lewiston back to Redding and the Highway 299 junction with Highway 5, where you turn south to the Bay Area.

There's More

The Laag's Place and Big Ben's Doll Museum, P.O. Box 783, Weaverville. (916) 623–6383. Across from the Victorian Inn on Main Street; 3,000 dolls from 1840 to the present; old bottles; gift shop (in midwinter, call first).

Trinity River Gorge/Burnt Ranch Falls, Highway 299 West. One mile past Burnt Ranch, turn right into the U.S. Forest Service campground. Take the trail at the end of the campground road to the most spectacular and scariest part of the Trinity River, where kayakers and rafters shoot the rapids. A fifteen-minute hike down the sheer walls of Burnt Ranch Gorge. Do it.

Special Events

June. Peddlers' Fair, Lewiston. (916) 778–3486. Antiques, art, and crafts dealers from all over California display and sell; music; food.

June. Whiskeytown Lake Regatta. (916) 628–5223. Held Memorial Day.

August. Trinity County Fair, Hayfork. (916) 628–5223.

July–August. Ruth Rodeo, in Ruth. (800) 421–7259.

Other Recommended Restaurants and Lodgings

Trinity Center

Wyntoon Resort, P.O. Box 70. (916) 266–3337. Just north of Trinity Center, ninety wooded acres; RV, trailer, and tent camping; marina; store; boat, jet-ski, and bike rentals; picnic and barbecue areas.

Ripple Creek Cabins, Star Route 2, Box 3899. (916) 266–3505. Four miles north of Coffee Creek, on Trinity Lake. Several nicely decorated housekeeping cabins located in a pine grove on Coffee Creek; wonderful views.

Weaverville

Granny House Bed and Breakfast, 313 Taylor. (916) 623–2756.

Two-story Queen Anne Victorian whose former owner, much beloved in Weaverville, recently died at age 102; *mucho* breakfast.

Indian Creek Bar and Grill, 7 miles west of Weaverville on Highway 299. (916) 623–4775. Built early in this century and still chock-full of strange old memorabilia. Mexican food, steaks, ribs, great pies.

Lewiston

Old Lewiston Bed and Breakfast Inn, P.O. Box 688. (916) 778–3385. Small, comfortable rooms; back porch overlooking the Trinity River.

Trinity River Lodge, P.O. Box 137. (916) 778–3791. Camper, trailer, and fishing resort; trees, lawns, boat launch, store.

Old Lewiston Bridge RV Resort, near Lewiston Bridge on Rush Creek Road, P.O. Box 148. (916) 778–3894. Twenty-six acres on the river; shady and green; tent sites.

For More Information

Trinity County Chamber of Commerce, P.O. Box 517, Weaverville, CA 96093. (800) 421–7259.

Lewiston Chamber of Commerce, P.O. Box 105, Lewiston, CA 96052. (916) 778–3730.

MISTIX, state park camping and RV site reservations. (800) 444–7275.

Backpacking permits: Trinity Alps Wilderness, P.O. Box 1190, Weaverville, CA 96093. (916) 623–2121.

Mount Lassen, Lake Almanor

Majestic Mount Lassen rises above Lake Helen.

Mountain Magic, Lake Country

_____ 2 NIGHTS _____

Volcano vibrations · Lakeside walks · Fishing · Forest trails
Picnic on top of the world · Summer and winter sports

The largest "plug dome" volcano in the world, 10,457-foot Lassen Peak last blew its top in 1921. Hot springs, boiling mudpots, and sulfury steam vents remind us that sometime in the next few hundred years, a drive through Lassen Volcanic National Park may not be a good idea. For now, though, it's one of the wonders of the world, and a great deal of the giant park can be seen on a 35-mile drive up and over the 8,000-foot summit and on 150 miles of interconnecting wilderness trails. Beneath a dramatic skyline of craggy volcanic peaks lie fifty mountain lakes surrounded by cedar, fir, pine, and aspen forests. And this is one of the only parts of the world where peregrine falcons and bald eagles can be seen.

Anglers from all over the world come to the Lassen area for wild-trout fishing in the cold, clear waters of Hat Creek and the Fall and McCloud rivers on the north side of the National Park. In the winter-time cross-country skiers, snowshoers, and snow campers take off into the spectacular backcountry; snow may fly as early as September and as late as May. South of Lassen, 13-mile-long Lake Almanor is a laid-back fishing and camping destination.

Day 1

Morning

From the East Bay take Highway 80 to Highway 505 near Vacaville, connecting with Highway 5 to Red Bluff, a four-hour drive.

Lunch: **Golden Corral,** 250 Antelope Boulevard, Red Bluff. (916) 527-3950. Bountiful buffet and salad bar, Philly steak, burgers.

Afternoon

Continue for a half-hour to Redding, then take Highway 44 east through Shingletown, passing grassy meadows, and llama and horse farms on the way to **Lassen Volcanic National Park,** P.O. Box 100, Mineral, CA 96063 (916–595–4444). At the north park entrance, stop at the visitor's center (916–335–7575) for the *Lassen Park Road Guide* and a schedule of naturalist-led tours, interpretive programs, and kids' story hours that may fit in with your plans.

Very near the entrance is **Manzanita Lake,** a postcard-perfect, ev-ergreen-surrounded lake with dazzling views of the mountain. Take the easy one-hour-long, 1.5-mile hike around the lake by yourself or on a ranger's tour. Nonmotorized boating and camping are permitted at Manzanita, a lake favored by trout anglers; camping sites are pretty and private. In the fall Canada geese and wood duck can be seen in great numbers, resting on their way south.

Leaving the park, continue on Highway 44 about 14 miles to **Old Station,** where you will spend the night. A stagecoach stop in the 1850s, it was abandoned due to Indian troubles, then became an army outpost and a reststop for loggers. Now Old Station is a tiny, rustic community at the headwaters of upper **Hat Creek,** one of the most challenging and most rewarding wild-trout streams in the United States. The water is easy to access here in the village and from several campgrounds on Highways 44 and 89, which meet at Old Station.

The Fall River is a true spring creek, one of the few in the state. Averaging 3,000 fish per mile, many exceeding 20 inches in length and eight pounds in weight, the Fall is a "catch and release only" river, a gently flowing ribbon of water meandering through lush green farmland meadows in the wide Fall River Valley.

About .5 mile west of Old Station, across from Hat Creek Campground, is the **Spattercone Crest Trail,** a 2-mile self-guided trail winding past volcanic spattercones, lava tubes, domes, and blowholes, a two-hour walk, best in early morning.

Dinner and Lodging: **Mount Lassen Inn,** P.O. Box 86, Old Station 96071. (916) 335–7006. Hat Creek rushes right by the back door of this circa 1930 clapboard bed-and-breakfast inn. Suites with private baths have brass beds and dormer windows. Innkeeper Gene Nixon will serve a memorable dinner to you in an antiques-filled dining room— game hens with fruit and nut dressing, perhaps. Or try **Uncle Runt's Place,** across the road (916–335–7177), for plainer fare.

Day 2

Morning

Breakfast: At Mount Lassen Inn. Smoked salmon and cream cheese omelets or heart-shaped waffles, either in a little dining area in your room or downstairs with other guests.

Ask Gene to put together a picnic lunch for you to take on your trek through Lassen National Park. Or pick up supplies at the little store at Manzanita Lake.

Head back to the National Park for your day-long explorations by car and on foot. **Lassen Park Road** winds for 35 miles around three sides of the park, past woodlands, meadows, and clear streams and lakes. Miles of trails, including 17 miles of the **Pacific Crest Trail,** twist through aromatic conifer forests, magnificent stands of aspens and cottonwoods, and wildflower-strewn meadows. You'll see old lava flows, natural sulfurworks, hot steam, and boiling mud. Several lakes allow fishing, canoeing, and nonpowered boating. In the *Lassen Park Road Guide,* more than sixty points of interest and trails are specified, numbered to correspond with road signs. Lassen can get snow any day of the year, and you may wish to carry chains from October through April.

Lily Pond Nature Trail, starting at the **Loomis Museum** parking lot near Manzanita Lake, is a 1-mile, hour-long, easy walk around a small lake and through a shady forest to **Chaos Jumbles,** an interesting avalanche area.

The **Bumpass Hell Trail** is a 3-mile, easy walk into the park's most active thermal area, where you'll walk on boardwalks over hot springs, steam vents, mudpots, and other eerie manifestations of the earth's hot insides. An easy 3-mile walk on the **Trail to Paradise** brings you to a beautiful glacier-carved meadow for spectacular displays of wildflowers most of the year.

The .25-mile **Devastated Area Interpretive Trail,** at road marker #44, is one of several trails that are handicapped accessible. Lodgepole pines and aspens are particularly lush here, breathtaking in the fall.

It's a 700-foot descent, 1.5 miles one way, to **Kings Creek Falls,** a 30-foot cascade, with streams, meadows, and lots of trees along the way.

Lunch: A picnic in a mountain meadow.

Afternoon

In the 8,000-foot summit area, views of mountains 1,000 feet above and plunging valleys and canyons are distracting, to say the least. Crystal-clear, blue-green **Emerald Lake** and **Lake Helen** lie beside the road. A less-than-delicate scent of rotten eggs from the misty **Sulfur Works** vents gradually become a memory on the last 6 miles in the park, a downhill drop of 1,400 feet.

Near the southwest entrance of the park is the **Lassen Park Ski Area** (916–595–3376). Equipment can be rented for sledding, snowshoeing, snowboarding, and cross-country and downhill skiing; the downhill skiing is challenging only for beginners. The entire main road through the park is available for cross-country skiing, with unending views of snowbound mountains, valleys, and lakes.

Dinner: Continue out of the park on Highway 89 to the **Black Forest Lodge,** 10 miles west of Chester at Mill Creek. (916) 258–2941. German and American food; fresh trout; bar; friendly and fun.

Lodging: **Stover's St. Bernard Lodge,** P.O. Box 5000, Mill Creek 96061. (916) 258–3382. Next door to the Black Forest. A 1912 hotel with knotty-pine walls and country-fresh decor, shared baths; good restaurant and fabulous bar with stained-glass and antiques. Cross-country ski out the back door.

Day 3

Morning

Breakfast: At St. Bernard Lodge. Blueberry pancakes; steak and eggs.

Drive 10 miles to the resort town of **Chester,** at **Lake Almanor,** a pine-fringed lake at 4,500 feet, the snowy peak of Lassen and surrounding mountains mirrored in its clear, calm waters. Almanor is popular for trout, bass, catfish, and perch fishing, plus king salmon, not usually found in landlocked lakes. Swimmers, boaters, and waterskiers like the sandy beaches, small lodges, and campgrounds on the western shore.

Lunch: **Timber House Lodge,** Highway 89 at First Street. (916) 258–2729. This place you've got to see. Massive stone-and-tree-trunk construction, including the furniture; good basic American food, bar.

Afternoon

From the south end of the lake, take Highway 89 south, connecting with Highway 70 west though the **Plumas National Forest,** along the north fork of the Feather River. Turn south on Highway 101 for a three-hour drive back to the Bay Area.

There's More

Fishing. Boat-launching access on the Fall River and Hat Creek is limited; it's best to get advice at local fishing shops like The Fly Shop, 4140 Churn Creek Road, Redding 96002. (916) 222–3555. Take the Churn Creek Drive exit off Highway 5; go east over the highway to Bechelli Lane to a weathered gray building with a big fish on the side, visible from the highway. Advice on what's biting and where to catch 'em; top-quality equipment and clothing; guides, tours, and maps—a fisherperson's mecca. Call ahead for fishing conditions.

Fishing tours. Clearwater Trout Tours, 274 Star Route, Muir Beach, CA 94965. (415) 381–1173. Flyfishing schools, public and private outings, guides, lodge on the Fall River.

Sidetrip. For the intrepid backpacker, RVer, or four-wheel driver, 11 miles from Old Station on Highway 44 East is the 7-mile rough road to Butte Lake, at 6,000 feet. A beautiful campground sits at lakeside, surrounded by ponderosa pines and rugged volcanic outcroppings. Motorized boats are not allowed, and the fishing is phenomenal. Interesting cindercones and other volcanic formations, plus two more lakes and backcountry trails, make this a great way to go.

Golf. Fall River Valley Golf Course, west of Fall River Mills on Highway 299. (916) 336–5555. Eighteen holes; clubhouse, restaurant, pro shop.

Fort Crook Museum, in Fall River Mills. (916) 336–5110. Open May–October. Pioneer history, Indian artifacts; pioneer cabin, schoolhouse, jailhouse, blacksmith shop, and more.

Special Events

May. Airport Day at Fall River Airport. (916) 243–2643. Air show, jet fly-bys, parachute jumping.
July. Burney Basin Days. (916) 336–5840. Parade, barbecue, dances, fireworks, entertainment.
July. CCA Rodeo, McArthur. (916) 243–2643.
September. Intermountain Fair of Shasta County. (916) 243–2643.

Other Recommended Restaurants and Lodgings

Cassel

Clearwater House on Hat Creek. 274 Star Route. (415) 381–1173. Located between Lassen and Shasta (Clearwater Trout Tours). Flyfishers' delight. A turn-of-the-century farmhouse, seven rooms with baths, all meals.

Fall River Mills

Rick's Lodge, Glenburn Star Route. (916) 336–5300. Restaurant/bar, three meals, pool, boat and motor rentals, guide service, flyfishing school. Beautiful location on the Fall River; store selling flyfishing gear, snacks; free airport service from Fall River Mills.

Paynes Creek

Oasis Springs Ranch, P.O. Box 454. (800) 339–9887. A first-class flyfishing lodge; horseback riding available as well. The crystal-clear, rushing waters of Battle Creek run by the door. Situated 25 miles east of Red Bluff off Highway 36; guests are transported from Payne's Creek by jeep.

Old Station

Hat Creek Resort, P.O. Box 15. (916) 335–7121. Motel, cabins, RV park.

For More Information

Fall River Valley Chamber of Commerce, P.O. Box 475, Fall River Mills, CA 96056. (916) 336–5840.
Shasta Cascade Wonderland Association, P.O. Box 1988, 1250 Parkview Avenue, Redding, CA 96099. (916) 243–2643.

Lassen Volcanic National Park, P.O. Box 100, Mineral, CA 96963. (916) 595–4444.

MISTIX, state park camping and RV site reservations. (800) 444–7275.

Lassen County Chamber of Commerce, P.O. Box 338, Susanville, CA 96130. (916) 257–4323.

Snowfone ski reports. (916) 595–4464.

Road conditions. (916) 244–1500.

Shasta Cascade

White rivers of ice cap beautiful Mount Shasta.

Mountain Majesty, Rivers, Lakes, Timberlands

2 NIGHTS

Lakeside walks · High country views · Waterfowl, waterfalls, wilderness
Boating and fishing · Cavernous pursuits

One in a chain of Cascade Range volcanoes stretching from Northern California to southwestern Canada, Mount Shasta is a frosty, 14,162-foot presence that seems to take up half the sky in Siskiyou County.

Mist-shrouded glacial peaks and white rivers of ice are visible for hundreds of miles.

The second tallest mountain in the lower forty-eight states, Mount Shasta presides over vast timberlands and wilderness areas freshened with lakes, rivers, and streams, offering a paradise for hikers, anglers, summer and winter sports enthusiasts, and just plain lovers of high country scenery.

On a weekend in the Shasta area, you may fall under the magic spell of the mountain and return again to see it streaked with lightning in a summer thunderstorm or transformed into a frozen white wave in winter.

Your route along Highway 5 follows the mighty Sacramento River— wide, cool, and green; fringed with overhanging trees; plied by fishing boats and water-skiers; and nourishing a valley that feeds the world.

Day 1

Morning

From the Oakland Bay Bridge, it's 325 miles to Redding. Take Highway 80, connecting with Highway 505 above Vacaville; then take Highway 5 north to Redding through miles of farmlands, lush and green in the winter and spring, golden dry in summer. Bordering the valley are the crumpled eastern foothills of the Coast Range and the distant peaks of the Sierra Nevada. Defunct volcanoes called the **Sutter Buttes** rise dramatically above the valley floor.

Two hours from the Bay Area, it's fun to make a pit stop at Corning, the "Olive City." Right off the freeway at the Central Corning exit, on Main Street, is the **Olive Pit** (916–824–4667), since 1967 the place to taste and buy dozens of kinds of olives, plus almonds and nut butters. The cafe serves olive burgers, sandwiches, and frozen yogurt. Back on the highway just beyond the Olive Pit is a pretty, shaded rest-stop with lawns and trees.

Between **Redding** and **Red Bluff** is most of the mature riparian woodland left in the state, home to an incredible concentration of wildlife, including 20 species of fish and 200 species of birds. Overhanging the banks of the salmon-spawning riffles are sycamores, cottonwoods, oaks, and willows. (See page 211 for information on fishing and boating access.)

Near Redding the valley begins to roll, and the peaks of the Klamath Mountains and the Cascades emerge in the distant north and east. The Sierra Nevada ends; the Cascades begin.

Lunch: Take the Central Redding/Highway 99 exit into town, turning left on Market for ½ block to **Cheesecakes Unlimited,** 1334 Market Street, Redding (916–244–6670). Super sandwiches, pita bread concoctions, and that *cheesecake.*

Afternoon

Follow Market south to the **Shasta Cascade Wonderland Association,** at Market and Parkview Avenue (916–243–2643), for maps, brochures, and guidebooks. Ask for directions to Park Marina Drive, a riverside boulevard circling back to Highway 99 and Highway 5 north.

It's 23 miles to **Lake Shasta,** one of the best fishing lakes in California, fed by the Sacramento, McCloud, Pit, and Squaw rivers. At an elevation of 1,000 feet, surface water reaches eighty degrees in the summer, perfect for houseboating and waterskiing.

Take the Shasta Caverns Road exit, driving 2 miles to **Lake Shasta Caverns** (916–238–2341), a dramatic natural wonder. The tour includes a fifteen-minute boat ride across the lake to a wooded island, where a bus takes you 800 feet up a steep road through aromatic bay, oak, and manzanita, past exciting dropoffs and views of the lake that you'll see from no other spot. Groups of about twenty people are guided into a series of giant chambers, up and down hundreds of stone steps. The atmosphere is delightfully spooky, damp, and drippy—a constant fifty-eight degrees, refreshing in the summer when outside temperatures can reach over a hundred degrees. Multicolored columns, 20-foot-high stone draperies, stalactites and stalagmites, brilliant crystals, and unusual limestone and marble formations are subtly lighted and fascinating. After the cavern tour you can explore the walking paths, have a picnic overlooking the lake, or try panning for gold.

It's 38 miles from the caverns to the town of **Mount Shasta**, in the shadow of the mountain and almost completely surrounded by the **Shasta National Forest.** Motels line the road into the town, a flower-bedecked overnight stopping point for travelers on their way to the Northwest.

Dinner: **Avalanche,** at the south end of town, 412 South Mount Shasta Boulevard. (916) 926–5496. A small, friendly cafe and fish market; mountain views; giant shrimp cocktail, chowder, a wide variety of fresh fish every day.

Lodging: **Ward's Big Foot Ranch,** 1530 Hill Road, Mount Shasta 96057. (916) 926–5170. A country estate located 2 miles northwest of downtown. Spectacular mountain views; redwoods, pines, lawns, and gardens; llamas; a rushing stream; walking and biking trails. Two bedrooms in the house; a cottage with fireplace sleeps six.

Day 2

Morning

Breakfast: At Ward's Big Foot Ranch. On the deck or in the family dining room; Barbara Ward's Scandinavian *abelskivers* and hearty egg dishes.

Just up the road from Ward's are the **Sisson Museum** and **Mount Shasta Fish Hatchery,** 1 North Old Stage Road (916–926–5508), with displays of the history, geology, and climate of the mountain. Walk around to see the hatching and rearing ponds. Trail maps and guidebooks of the area are sold here.

Drive 3 miles south on Stage Road to **Lake Siskiyou,** surrounded by dazzling mountainscapes and a tree-lined shore. Fresh, clean, pine-scented **Lake Siskiyou Camp-Resort**, 4239 West Barr Road, Mount Shasta 96067 (916–926–2618), is one of the prettiest multiuse camping and RV facilities in California. You can even rent a fully equipped trailer for use on-site. Walk around the lake, lounge on the beach and swim, launch a boat, or rent water toys, kayaks, canoes, pedalboats, sailboats, and fishing equipment. A store, snackbar, outdoor movies, and playground are also found here.

For a more challenging hike, take the **Sisson-Callahan National Recreation Trail.** Start by driving southwest out of Mount Shasta along West Barr Road to North Shore Road to the north fork of the Sacramento River. You wade through a shallow stream, then go .5 mile on an old logging road alongside the river to hook up with the trail. The route has spectacular views of the Trinity Alps, Mount Eddy, Castle Crags, and Mount Shasta. At the 9-mile point you'll meet up with the **Pacific Crest Trail**. For maps and information on area trails and hiking Mount Shasta, go to **Fifth Season**, North Mount Shasta Boulevard (916–926–3606), or **Shasta Mountain Guides,** 1938 Hill Road (916–926–3117).

Lunch: **Michael's,** 313 North Mount Shasta Boulevard. (916) 926–5288. Homemade pasta, soup, burgers.

Afternoon

From Mount Shasta take Highway 89 east around the base of the mountain into the **Shasta National Forest** and **McCloud River Valley.** Two miles south at the first exit is **Mount Shasta Ski Park** (916–926–8600), with ski runs at 5,000 feet. Here you'll find downhill and cross-country skiing; two triple chairlifts; a day lodge, restaurant, and ski school; and equipment rental and night skiing. In the summer try the excellent mountain-bike trails, and ride up the chairlift for the view of a lifetime, a forty-minute round-trip. For more cross-country ski trails, watch for **Bunny Flat, Sand Flat,** and **Panther Meadows** off Highway 89.

Ten miles farther is the logging town of **McCloud.** To reach the Nature Conservancy's **McCloud River Preserve,** go 9.2 miles south on Squaw Valley Road in McCloud; at the McCloud Reservoir bear right, go 2.2 miles, then turn right onto a dirt road to the preserve. Rushing down from the mountain, the river has cut a steep, narrow canyon teeming with wildlife and densely forested with old-growth Douglas fir and ponderosa pine. The Nature Conservancy's precious piece of wilderness includes several miles of protected wild trout waters, open to the public on a restricted basis. Beautiful nature trails are yours for the walking. For complete information and maps, call the conservancy at (415) 777–0487.

Seven miles from McCloud on Highway 89, at Fowlers Campground, the **McCloud River Falls** are a sidetrip well worth taking. Accessible by car, the three falls on a 2-mile stretch of river plunge into deep pools perfect for swimming. The third cascade has picnic tables above and a ladder that divers use to jump into the pool.

Along Highway 89 the bare spaces on the forested hillsides are examples of clear-cut logging.

It's about an hour's drive, over 4,000-foot Dead Horse Summit, to **McArthur-Burney Falls State Park** and **Lake Britton** (916–335–2777). The big attraction here is two million gallons of water a day tumbling over a misty, fern-draped 129-foot cliff. Take the 1.5-mile hike down into a forest fairyland gorge where wild tiger lilies, maples, dogwood, black oak, and pines decorate the streamside; the loud rush of the falls and the stream intensifies the experience. It takes about a half-hour for the fit and fast, an hour for amblers and photographers, and two hours for waders, fisherpersons, and walkers who take offshoot trails. Good trout fishing can be had in the deep pool at the foot of the falls and in the 2-mile stream above and below.

Hikes in and near the park include a 1.5-mile flat route to **Lake Britton Dam,** then 3 miles farther to **Rock Creek,** and an 8-mile route to **Baum Lake** and the **Crystal Lake Hatchery.**

Around 9-mile-long Lake Britton are camping and RV sites, not too private. Accessible by boat (rentals here), with a terrific swimming hole at its foot, **Clark Creek Falls** is a jet of frigid water crashing into the lake. Crappie, bass, and catfish bite all season; some of the best fishing is downstream from the lake at the outlet of Pit River #3 Powerhouse, a piece of water designated as a wild-trout stream where only artificial lures with barbless hooks can be used.

It's fifteen minutes from here to Highway 299, where you turn north to Fall River Mills.

Dinner: **Rick's Lodge,** Glenburn Star Route, Fall River Mills 96028.

(916) 336–5300. Have a steak and listen to anglers spinning tales of big trout on the Fall River and Hat Creek, believed to be the finest fly-fishing waters in the state; the Fall averages 3,000 fish per mile, rainbows up to 24 inches long. Restaurant/bar; three meals.

Lodging: Simple rooms at **Rick's Lodge.** Beautiful location on the Fall River. Pool; boat and motor rental; guide service; flyfishing school; store selling flyfishing gear and snacks.

Day 3

Morning

Breakfast: At Rick's Lodge. All-American bacon-and-eggs, biscuits and gravy.

Fall River Mills is headquarters for fishing and hiking in the northern Lassen river valleys. There is golf to be had at the **Fall River Valley Golf Course,** west of town on Highway 299 (916–336–5555). Open May through October, the **Fort Crook Museum**, in town (916–336–5110), has exhibits of pioneer history, Indian artifacts, and several historical buildings. A unique state park, **Ahjumawi Lava Springs,** 3.5 miles north of Highway 299E (916–335–2777), is 6,000 acres of wetlands and wilderness encompassing Big Lake, Ja-She Creek, and portions of the Tule, Fall, and Pit rivers, a sanctuary for thousands of birds, including bald eagles. The park is accessible only by boat; rentals can be arranged at Rick's Lodge.

Take Highway 299 west at Redding (or proceed on to Mount Lassen; see Escapes Farther Afield Five). Children will enjoy **Waterworks Park,** 151 North Boulder Drive, Redding (916–246–9550), where three giant waterslides and a 400-foot "Raging River" are great summer coolers. Take a walk in Redding: there's a 6-mile round-trip on the banks of the Sacramento. Drive north on Market Street and take a left on Riverside. You'll see a sign for parking near the trail.

Lunch: **Westside Deli French Bakery,** 1600 California Street. (916) 222–0787. Sandwiches for here or for the road.

Afternoon

On the way south on Highway 5, 400-acre **Anderson River Park,** on the Sacramento River, has hiking, biking, and jogging trails. This is the destination for rafters floating down from Redding; raft rental companies pick you up here and shuttle back to Redding.

Just north of Red Bluff is a lovely spot on the river, **Ide Adobe State Park,** 3040 Adobe Road (916–527–5927), cool and shady, with giant oaks, lawns, picnic tables, and historical displays. You can fish here, but swimming in the fast current is not advisable.

Head south to the Bay Area.

There's More

Castle Crags State Park, 6 miles south of Dunsmuir off I–5. (916) 235–2684. A 6,000-foot granite fortress of giant pillars and monster boulders; good trout fishing in several streams; 2 miles of the Sacramento River; swimming, hiking, rock climbing. Get maps at the park office and amble up the sun-dappled Indian Creek Nature Trail, a 1-mile loop. The Vista Point loop is 5 view-filled miles. The Crags Trail to Castle Dome is 5.5 strenuous miles up and into the Castle Crags Wilderness; the Pacific Crest Trail is accessible from here. People often stop here just to fill up jugs with natural soda water.

Shasta Dam, fifteen minutes off Highway 5 above Redding (a thirty-minute trip in the summer, longer on the weekends). Walk out on the dam; see old photos and a film.

Houseboats. With a shoreline of 365 miles, Shasta is very popular for houseboating. Boats range from 15 to 56 feet long, sleeping four to twelve people; they're easy to navigate and may include air-conditioning, TV, and washers and dryers. Rentals at twelve houseboat marinas cost $1,000 per week and up.

Fishing. Best in fall, not in August when it's hot.

Ice fishing at Castle Lake; road plowed all winter.

River fishing on the McCloud, Sacramento, Klamath, Salmon, and Scott.

One of the state's best-kept trout fishery secrets is the 12 miles of the lower Sacramento River between Redding and Anderson, fishable every month of the year. You'll need a driftboat and a guide, at least the first time; call Bob's Guide Service at (916) 222–8058. For more fishing information, see Escapes Farther Afield Five.

Golf. Lake Shastina Golf Resort, 5925 Country Club Drive, Weed. (916) 938–3201.

Railroading. The Blue Goose, P.O. Box 660, Yreka 96097. (916) 842–4146. A circa 1910 train hauling lumber and freight daily between Yreka and Montague, a 7-mile trip. Climbing on board the steamer at 10:00 A.M., you'll cruise past cattle ranches, sawmills, and lovely landscape. The train may be attacked by bandits as it approaches the historic town of Montague. There's an hour or so to picnic on the village green or take a horse-drawn tour; then it's back to Yreka.

Wild Horse Sanctuary, P.O. Box 30, Shingletown 96088. (916) 474–5770. Stay in frontier-style cabins at the base camp; track wild horses through the foothills of Mount Lassen; observe and photograph wild horses and burros in their protected habitat. Wild West adventure, campfires, hearty meals.

Llama packing. Rainbow Ridge Range Llama Backpacking of Mount Shasta, P.O. Box 1079, Mount Shasta. (916) 926–5794. Marble Mountains, Trinity Alps, Scott and Salmon river areas.

Special Events

June. Heritage Days at McArthur Burney Falls State Park. (916) 335–2777. Large crowds turn out for Native American dancers, musicians, pioneer crafts, square dancing, fiddlers.

June. Dunsmuir Railroad Days. (916) 235–2177. Since 1940, a celebration of historic railroad days, parade, barbecue, jazz festival.

June. Sacramento River Jazz Festival, Dunsmuir. (916) 235–2721. Great day on the green in Dunsmuir City Park.

July. McCloud Lumberjack Fiesta. (916) 964–2520. Fishing tournaments, parade, barbecue, entertainment, lumberjack show.

Other Recommended Restaurants and Lodgings

Fairfield

Fusilli Ristorante, 620 Jackson. (707) 428–4211. A favorite upscale dinner spot for skiers and vacationers on their way south to the Bay Area. Take the Travis Boulevard exit, going East on West Texas to Jackson in downtown Fairfield.

Tail of the Whale restaurant and bar at Bridge Bay Resort, Redding, under the bridge at the south end of Lake Shasta. (916) 275–3021. Views of the lake, dependable American food, bar.

Mount Shasta

Mount Shasta KOA Campground, 900 North Mount Shasta Boulevard. (916) 926–4029. A grassy, gardeny place for RVs and tents; animal corrals, camping cabins, store; on-site recreation; area tours.

Mount Shasta Ranch, 1008 W. A. Barr Road. (916) 926–3870. Bed-and-breakfast inn in a circa 1920s ranchhouse; cottages; country breakfast; spa; mountain views. Just a few minutes from Lake Siskiyou.

Dunsmuir

Railroad Park Resort, 100 Railroad Park Road. (916) 235–4440. Restaurant and motel in antique railroad cars; pool; spa. Good jumping-off point for exploring and hiking in Castle Crags. Also, RV park, campground, cabins.

Redding

Tiffany House Bed and Breakfast, 1510 Barbara Road. (916) 244–3225. Pretty rooms with bath; huge, beautiful yard; pool and spa.

River Inn, 1835 Park Marina Drive. (916) 241–9500. Edge of town on a small lake with mountain views, nice motel rooms, pool, barbecue, boat launch into Sacramento River.

Lakehead

Lakeshore Villa RV Park, 20672 Lakeshore Drive. (916) 238–8688. Twenty-five miles north of Redding; boat launch; waterskiing, swimming, fishing.

Antlers Resort and Marina, P.O. Box 140. (916) 238–2553. Overlooking the lake for forty years; houseboats, cabins, marina, jet skis, and ski boats.

O'Brien

Holiday Harbor, P.O. Box 112. (800) 776–BOAT. Eighteen miles north of Redding on Shasta Caverns Road. RV hookups, boat launch, houseboats, waterskiing, fishing, boat rental, restaurant.

For More Information

Mount Shasta, U.S. Forest Service, 204 West Alma, Mount Shasta, CA 96057. (916) 926–4511.

Shasta Cascade Wonderland Association, P.O. Box 1988, 1250 Parkview Avenue, Redding, CA 96099. (916) 243–2643.

McArthur-Burney Falls State Park, Route 1, Box 1260, Burney, CA 96013. (916) 335–2777.

MISTIX, state park camping and RV site reservations. (800) 444–7275.

Yosemite

A view of Bridalveil Fall from Wawona Tunnel.

The Big Valley

_____ 2 NIGHTS _____

Waterfalls and wildflowers · Historic hotels · Hetch Hetchy
Trailside picnics · Mountaintops, monoliths · Sequoia groves

The Indians called it *Ahwahnee,* or "Deep, Grassy Valley." John Muir
saw it as a "great temple lit from above." You'll wax poetic in
Yosemite Valley when a setting sun paints a shining 4,000-foot curtain
across the face of Half Dome and glitters like a crown on snowcapped
peaks high above the lush river valley where you stand.

Americans have camped and hiked below the granite monoliths of Yosemite Valley since before Abraham Lincoln dedicated the valley and the Mariposa Big Trees to the state in 1864; sixteen years later the national park was created. Automobiles were officially admitted in 1913, and in the 1930s victims of the Great Depression lived here in their cars, eating fish from the streams.

Today Yosemite Valley is an international tourist attraction, jam-packed with visitors in the summertime, when miles of cars line up at dawn, each heading for one of 2,700 campsites. Fall is a good time to come. Kids are back in school and the Merced River becomes a stream of molten gold, bright maples reflecting in its chilly waters. Crunchy carpets of rust-colored pine needles are rimmed with fernrows turned yellow. Crisp breezes rustle hauntingly through the aspen groves.

In spring the wildflowers are a riot of color, and the valley's famous waterfalls are at their booming best. Nowhere in the world are so many high falls concentrated in so small an area as the 7 square miles of Yosemite Valley. And a winter weekend at Yosemite can be unforgettable, whether you cross-country ski on silent forest trails or view a white wonderland through the tall windows of the old Ahwahnee Hotel.

Bay Area residents are lucky to be close enough to visit Yosemite in every season.

Day 1

Morning

Drive from the Oakland Bay Bridge east on Highway 580, connecting with 99 north to Manteca, then 120 east to the Big Oak Flat entrance to **Yosemite National Park,** a four-hour drive. The highway narrows here, ducking under huge overhanging boulders before emerging above the boiling Merced River into the valley, at an elevation of 4,000 feet. At the **visitor's center** in the Yosemite Village Mall at midvalley (209–372–0299), outfit yourself with a map and a guidebook. Depending on the weather and the season, plan explorations on foot and by shuttle.

Lunch: **Degnan's Deli,** in Yosemite Village, near the visitor's center. Sandwiches and salads for a picnic. Or, for a sit-down lunch, **The Loft,** in the same building: steak, chicken, sandwiches, homemade soups.

Afternoon

Jump on the shuttlebus and tour the valley. At stop #7, walk a short path to the base of **Yosemite Falls,** three cascades dropping 2,425 feet, the third highest waterfall in the world. (At stop #8 is the trail-head for a six-hour, strenuous hike to the top of the falls.)

For an hour's easy walk in the meadows around **Mirror Lake,** with wonderful views of Half Dome and Mount Watkins, get off at stop #17. The **Tenaya Zig Zags/Snow Creek Trail** is a little-used, 3.5-mile route to the rim of the valley, beginning east of Mirror Lake—not an easy hike but views are eye-popping.

Now that you're warmed up to Yosemite, go into the **Ansel Adams Gallery** (209–372–4413), near the visitor's center; since 1902 the place has been a camera store and gallery of signed Adams photos, prints, and posters of the valley in its seasonal raiments.

Dinner: **Ahwahnee Hotel Dining Room,** Mid Valley. (209) 372–1489. Twenty-four-foot trestle-beamed ceiling and two-story windows with views of **Royal Arches,** spectacular when frosted with snow and ice; Continental cuisine in a restaurant that's been called America's most beautiful. Dress is casual at breakfast and lunch. At dinner men must wear coats and ties; women, dresses or nice pantsuits.

Lodging: **Ahwahnee Hotel.** (209) 252–4848. Standing gloriously aloof in a woodland setting, with granite cliffs rising up startlingly all around, the art deco hotel is in perfect shape, with painted beams, decorated floors, and stained-glass windows faded into subtle Indian colors. Sofas, armchairs, and fabulous old Oriental rugs are arranged by a huge fireplace in the Great Lounge. Built in 1927, the place still has a halcyon-days atmosphere and is museumlike, enriched with paintings, photos, and priceless Native American baskets. When fall leaves blow along the footpaths and wood smoke curls silently into a twilight glow, the spirit of summers past come alive at the Ahwahnee.

Day 2

Morning

Breakfast: An American breakfast in the Ahwahnee Hotel Dining Room.

Purchase picnic goodies and set off on the 32-mile drive on Glacier Point Road to **Glacier Point,** atop the sheer southern wall of the valley. Several waterfalls, as well as **Half Dome, El Capitan,** and other famous pinnacles, surround the valley. Looking 3,200 feet down, you can spot the river snaking along, and you're likely to see climbers making a several days' ascent to the dizzying 2,850-foot summit of El Capitan. A vertical wall of granite four times as large as Gibraltar, "El Cap" is a memento of glaciers that tore off and ground into little pieces great sections of mountain. The Ice Age created Yosemite's domes, spires, stacks, and split mountainfaces. Rivers and streams deepened the canyons and ravines, watering a natural garden on the flat valley floor and filling the Merced River. Mesmerizing, the view from Glacier Point puts hundreds of millions of years of geologic history on display. The faint thundering sound you hear in the springtime is **Nevada Falls,** 2 miles away.

In the summer it's possible to take a hikers' bus to Glacier Point and walk all the way down to the valley, 4.8 miles, a three- to four-hour hike.

Along Glacier Point Road are several memorable stops to make. **Dewey Point,** at 7,385 feet and overlooking **Bridalveil Fall** and El Capitan, is accessible by a beautiful 7-mile round-trip trail just west of Bridalveil Campground. To reach **Mono Meadow** and **Mount Starr King View,** park 2.5 miles beyond Bridalveil Campground and take the trail east, dropping for .5 mile to the meadow, continuing to a spectacular view 1 mile farther on: 3 miles round-trip.

Six miles past Bridalveil Campground, park on the left and take the 2-mile round-trip trail past deep rock fissures to **Taft Point,** overhanging the valley.

Lunch: Have a picnic on top of the world at Glacier Point or on a nearby nature trail.

Afternoon

Explore some of the 800 miles of hiking trails in the Yosemite backcountry or amble along the banks of the Merced River, trying your luck at trout fishing. Lie about on a sunny beach or take a swim in the river or at the Ahwahnee. If you've become fascinated by the history and geologic wonders of the park, you may wish to get in on one of the many seminars, lectures, theater presentations, and tours offered throughout the year.

Dinner and Lodging: At the Ahwahnee Hotel.

Day 3

Morning

Breakfast: At the Ahwahnee Hotel Dining Room.

Take Big Oak Flat Road to the **Merced Grove** of giant sequoias. It's a 2-mile walk into the grove from the road; few people take this hike, thus giving you the opportunity to be alone with the big beauties.

If you'd rather drive, take the 6-mile steep, narrow road to **Tuolumne Grove,** a magnificent stand of sequoias that includes the famous "Dead Giant" drive-through tree.

Lunch: A picnic amid the sequoia groves.

Afternoon

Proceed to the Big Oak Flat entrance to Yosemite (trail maps here), then north on Evergreen Road to the **Hetch Hetchy Valley and Reservoir,** where there is much to see. The drowning of the spectacular valley in the 1930s was vigorously opposed by John Muir and the Sierra Club, but the dam was built; today the reservoir continues to supply San Francisco with water and power.

A sun catcher, the valley is quite hot in the summer, but delightful for hiking October through May. Hetch Hetchy Reservoir is 8 miles long, ringed with granite domes and dramatic cliff faces, a habitat for a great variety of wildlife; fishing is good, although swimming and boating are not allowed. From the top of the dam, take the flat trail through the tunnel and along the north edge of the reservoir; about 2 miles beyond, **Tueeulala Fall** and **Wapama Falls** thunder down, the latter so enthusiastic that it sometimes washes out the trail. And at 6.5 miles out, **Rancheria Falls** are misty and refreshing.

Return to the Big Oak Flat entrance and take Highway 120 east through Oakdale to 99, crossing Highway 5 to 205, connecting with 580 to the East Bay.

There's More

Winter fun in Yosemite. Ice skating at Curry Village, with spectacular views of Half Dome. Downhill skiing at Badger Pass, with 6 lifts to the 8,000 foot summit. Nordic skiing on 350 miles of trails and roads; 23 miles of machine-groomed track and skating lanes. Snowcat and snowshoe tours. For more information call (209) 372–1244.

Rafting. Ahwahnee Whitewater Expeditions, P.O. Box 1161, Columbia, 95310. (209) 533–1401. Rafting on the Merced, Tuolumne, Stanislaus, and Carson rivers.

Hershey Chocolate Company, 1400 South Yosemite Avenue, Oakdale. (209) 848–8126. Free tours of the chocolate factory during the week; located 20 miles east of Manteca on Highway 120.

Special Events

November–December. Yosemite Vintners' Holidays. (209) 454–2020. Banquets and seminars with prominent vintners.

December–January. The Bracebridge Dinners, in the Ahwahnee Hotel Dining Room. (209) 372–1489. The Renaissance is re-created at elaborate performances and monumental banquets; reservations by lottery.

Other Recommended
Restaurants and Lodgings

Accommodations in the National Park at the Ahwahnee Hotel, Yosemite Lodge, Wawona Hotel, and White Wolf Lodge and in tent cabins, cabins without baths, and campgrounds can be arranged by calling (209) 252–4848 or writing to P.O. Box 577, Yosemite 95389.

Yosemite Cedar Lodge, 8 miles from Yosemite, El Portal. (800) 321–5261. Featuring 200 deluxe and moderate rooms, some family units and suites, a restaurant, swimming pools, access to the Merced River.

Coulterville

Hotel Jeffery, 1 Main Street. (209) 878–3471. Gloriously restored, circa 1850, twenty-room hotel; garden patio, saloon, restaurant.

For More Information

Yosemite National Park, P.O. Box 577, Yosemite, CA 95389. General information: (209) 372–0265. Reservations: (209) 252–4848.

MISTIX, campground reservations. (800) 365–2267.

Tuolumne County Visitor's Bureau, P.O. Box 4020, Sonora, CA 95370. (209) 533–4420.

Advice: Hikers and campers should keep in mind that sudden storms are not uncommon in Yosemite, any month of the year. Weather changes rapidly in the Sierras, and snow can fall as early as September.

Southern Sierras

Clark's Cabin is dwarfed by a giant sequoia tree.

Wawona and the Lake Country

_____ 2 NIGHTS _____

Walks in the woods · Sequoia giants · Fireside chats
Yosemite history · Railroad ride · Lunch at the lake

The southern part of Yosemite National Park, called Wawona, is the place to go in midsummer, when Yosemite Valley is crowded with cars and people. Wilderness trails are silent, except for the crunch of your own footsteps and the prattle of squirrels and Stellar's jays.

The historical heart of the park, Wawona is anchored by the gracious old Wawona Hotel, riding the edge of magnificent Wawona Meadow like an aging but still glistening white oceanliner.

Between Yosemite and Kings Canyon National Park, the lake country of the central Sierras remains relatively undiscovered by Californians. Some 700 miles of trout streams and numerous lakes, reservoirs, and campgrounds make this an area you'll want to explore on many weekends. Just off Highway 41, at an elevation of 3,400 feet and situated on the 1,000-acre blue sparkler of Bass Lake, are a luxury resort; cabins, condos, and campgrounds; marinas for sailing, fishing, and waterskiing boats; and endless hiking trails in the surrounding Sierra National Forest.

Day 1

Morning

It's 200 miles from the Bay Area to Yosemite. From the East Bay take Highway 580 east to I–5 south. Then take Highway 152 through Los Banos to 99 south and 145 east in Madera to 41 north to **Oakhurst,** an antiques center and busy gateway to Yosemite and the recreational lakes country. Take Highway 41 north from Oakhurst for twenty minutes, to the right turn on Highway 222; it's now 4 miles to **Bass Lake.**

A warmwater lake reaching seventy-eight degrees in the summer, Bass Lake is good for fishing in the spring and fall for trout, bass, catfish, and bluegill; it's also popular for all types of water sports and camping.

Lunch: **Ducey's on the Lake,** at Pine Lake. (209) 642-3131. Dine on a sunny deck overlooking Bass Lake. Grilled chicken, salads, burgers, fresh fish, pasta.

Afternoon

It's 14 miles on Highway 41 to **Marriott's Tenaya Lodge at Yosemite,** 1122 Highway 41, Fish Camp (800–635–5807)—a destination resort overlooking forested mountains and valleys and located five minutes from Yosemite Park. The two-story atrium lobby and the restaurants, lounge, and public areas have a casual but luxurious feel and are decorated with Indian artifacts and western-style furnishings. Tours from the hotel get you into the park and to the Badger Pass ski area. There are a fully staffed children's daycamp program here and, nearby, many trailheads for walks, hikes, and mountain-bike rides through pine forests and along streamsides. Bikes are available at the hotel. Five minutes away is a stable for guided horseback rides.

At the end of an afternoon in the great outdoors, take a dip in the indoor or outdoor pools.

Dinner: At the **Sierra Restaurant,** in the lodge. Fresh fish, local produce, California and Northern Italian cuisines, fireplace, mountain views.

Lodging: At **Marriott's Tenaya Lodge.** A 242-room resort hotel with two pools, a fitness salon, a sauna, steam baths, and spas.

Day 2

Morning

Breakfast: At the **Parkside Restaurant,** in the lodge. All-American breakfasts. If you decide to picnic today, the Parkside Deli will put together sandwiches, salads, and giganto brownies.

Drive or bike 7 miles on Highway 41 into the park to **Mariposa Grove** and take the tram through the grove to see the 209-foot, 300-ton **Grizzly Giant;** the **Columbia** (290 feet); and hundreds more 2,000-year-old giant sequoias. This is the largest and most impressive of three sequoia groves in the park. At several tram stops you can hop off and wander along nature trails, the best way to enjoy these magnificent beings, the largest living things on earth. A vista point, accessible by a short walk from the top of the grove, overlooks the entire Wawona basin. In the **Mariposa Grove Museum** are displays about the big trees and the flora and fauna of Yosemite. Continue to drive the main road for a few minutes until you reach the Wawona Hotel, which is located across the street from the golf course.

Lunch: At the **Wawona Hotel.** (209) 252–4848. Good American food in a Victorian-era dining room, with charming Old Yosemite touches.

Afternoon

With long verandas looking over sweeping lawns and meadows and the **Wawona Golf Course,** the **Wawona Hotel** is a National Historic Landmark and the oldest resort hotel in the state. Rooms are simple and nicely maintained. Barbecues are held outdoors on summer weekends.

Just down the road is the **Yosemite Pioneer History Center**, a compound of historic buildings and vintage vehicles. Here costumed docents play the parts of residents from bygone days.

Stroll around **Wawona Meadow,** beginning across from the hotel, a flat route through the pines around the huge wildflower-strewn meadow, ending behind the hotel, a 3-mile round-trip. This is one of several meadows making Wawona a popular area for cross-country skiing.

A more challenging hike is to **Chilnualna Falls,** a steep, 8-mile round-trip through pines, cedars, and manzanita to a jetting avalanche of water, refreshing when you jump in the icy pool at the base of the upper falls. The trailhead is located 1.7 miles east of the main road, on Chilnaulna Falls Road.

Beaches and swimming spots are easily accessible on the south fork of the **Merced River** as it runs through Wawona.

Dinner: At Marriott's Tenaya Lodge. Or, if an extraspecial dinner is called for, take the twenty-minute drive to Oakhurst to **Erna's Elderberry House** (see page 224).

Lodging: Marriott's Tenaya Lodge.

Day 3

Morning

Breakfast: At Marriott's Tenaya Lodge.

Five minutes from the lodge, on Highway 41, is the **Yosemite Mountain Sugar Pine Railroad** (209–683–7273), set in a lovely wooded glade. An eighty-four-ton vintage locomotive, the largest ever built for a narrow-gauge track, pulls open cars 4 miles through forest-lands into **Lewis Creek Canyon**. Steam rolls out from under the great engine, black smoke belches up into the sky, and a conductor spins tales of when the railroad hauled millions of board feet of lumber out of the Sierras. From here rough-sawn boards floated in a wooden flume through a steep canyon all the way to Madera, more than 40 miles away. From June through September, a "Moonlight Special" evening train excursion ends with a steak barbecue and live music around a campfire. There's a beautiful picnic spot here, and cross-country skiing is excellent throughout the Sugar Pine area.

Lunch: **Narrow Gauge Inn,** next to the railroad station. (209) 683–7720. The Victorian era and the Old West are combined in the dining hall and Bull Moose saloon; cozy in cool weather, when logs burn in the big stone fireplaces.

Afternoon

Retrace your route back to the Bay Area.

There's More

Nelder Grove. Ten miles north of Oakhurst on Highway 41, take Sky Ranch Road 6 miles; also accessible by vehicle from Tenaya Lodge via several miles of dirt road. One of the largest trees in the world, the Bull Buck, rests in a wilderness grove of more than a hundred specimen sequoias; a 1-mile, self-guided trail runs through the grove along the banks of Nelder Creek.

Lewis Creek National Recreation Trail, 5 miles south of the southern Yosemite Gate. A 3.5-mile trail through dogwood, azalea, pines; Corlieu and Red Rock falls; fishing in Lewis Fork Creek.

Horseback riding. Yosemite Trails Pack Station, P.O. Box 100, Fish Camp, CA 93623. (800) 635–5807. Guided trips into Mariposa Grove and other parts of the park. Inquire at Marriott's Tenaya Lodge.

Golf. Wawona Golf Course. (209) 375–6572. Nine holes.

Boat rentals at Bass Lake. The Forks. (209) 642–3737.
Miller's Landing. (209) 642–3633.
The Pines Marina. (209) 642–3565.

Special Events

May. Mountain Peddlers' Fair, Oakhurst. (209) 683–7766. Some 500 antiques dealers.

June. Custom and Classic Car Show, Bass Lake. (209) 642–3676. Fifties weekend, barbecue, dance.

August. Bass Lake Arts and Crafts Festival. (209) 642–3676.

September. Sierra Mountaineer Days, Oakhurst. (209) 683–8492. Parade, carnival, dance.

December. Yosemite Pioneer Christmas. (209) 372–0265. Special programs at the Wawona Hotel, caroling, candlelight tours.

Other Recommended Restaurants and Lodgings

Oakhurst

Erna's Elderberry House Restaurant, 48688 Victoria Lane, off Highway 41. (209) 683–6800. A surprising find in this unassuming little town. European and California cuisine extraordinaire in elegant country French surroundings; lunch and dinner. Also Chateau du Sureau, Erna's out-of-this-world European-style inn, a castle with nine luxurious suites; pricey, a place for honeymoons.

Best Western Yosemite Gateway Inn, 40530 Highway 41. (209) 683–2378. Has 118 rooms in a parklike setting; mountain views; indoor and outdoor pools; some kitchens; restaurant; bar.

Accommodations in Yosemite National Park at the Awahnee Hotel, Yosemite Lodge, and Wawona Hotel and in tent cabins, cabins without baths, and campgrounds: (209) 252–4848.

Fish Camp

Narrow Gauge Inn, 48571 Highway 41. (209) 683–7720. Rooms and breakfast in a wooded setting.

Karen's Bed and Breakfast Yosemite Inn, 1144 Railroad Avene. (800) 346–1443. One mile from the park on Highway 41. Charming country-style accommodations with TLC from Karen, plus big breakfasts; very close to the park.

Bass Lake

The Pines Resort, P.O. Box 109. (800) 350–7463. Rustic condos at the lake; tennis, sauna, hot tub.

Ducey's on the Lake, P.O. Box 329. (800) 350–7463. Luxury suites on the lake; packages with meals at Ducey's restaurant are available.

Bass Lake Land Office, P.O. Box 349. (209) 642–3600. Cabins and houses to rent.

For More Information

Yosemite National Park, P.O. Box 577, Yosemite, CA 95389. General information: (209) 372–0265. Reservations (209) 252–4848. Road and weather information: (209) 372–4605.

MISTIX, campground reservations. (800) 365–2267.

Sierra National Forest Ranger District. (209) 841–3311.

Southern Yosemite Visitor's Bureau, P.O. Box 1404, Oakhurst, CA 93644. (209) 683–INFO.

Advice: Hikers and campers should keep in mind that sudden storms are not uncommon in Yosemite, any month of the year. Weather changes rapidly in the Sierras, and snow can fall as early as September.

Index